NEW MERMAIDS

General editors:
William C. Carroll, Boston University
Brian Gibbons, University of Münster
Tiffany Stern, University College, Oxford

General editor for the Bernard Shaw titles:
L. W. Conolly, Trent University

NEW MERMAIDS

NEW MERMAIDS

BERNARD SHAW

SAINT JOAN

A Chronicle Play in Six Scenes and an Epilogue

Definitive Text

Edited by Jean Chothia

Fellow of Selwyn College and Reader in Drama and Theatre,
University of Cambridge

Methuen Drama • London

New Mermaids

1 3 5 7 9 10 8 6 4 2

First published 2008

Methuen Drama
A & C Black Publishers Limited
38 Soho Square
London W1D 3HB
www.acblack.com

ISBN 978–0–7136–7996–0

Copyright 1924, 1930, George Bernard Shaw. © 1951, The Public Trustee
as Executor of the Estate of George Bernard Shaw. © 1957, The Public
Trustee as Executor of the Estate of George Bernard Shaw. Previously
unpublished Bernard Shaw text © The Trustees of the British Museum,
the Governors and Guardians of the National Gallery of Ireland, and the
Royal Academy of Dramatic Art.

Application for performing rights in Bernard Shaw's plays should be
made to the Society of Authors, 84 Drayton Gardens, London SW10 9SB,
phone: (020) 7373 6642.

A CIP catalogue record for this book is available from the British Library

This book is produced using paper made from wood grown in managed,
sustainable forests. It is natural, renewable and recyclable. The logging
and manufacturing processes conform to the environmental regulations
of the country of origin.

Typeset by RefineCatch Limited, Bungay, Suffolk
Printed in the UK by CPI Cox & Wyman, Reading, RG1 8EX

CONTENTS

ACKNOWLEDGEMENTS

For help on aspects of this edition I am grateful to Lucy Chothia; Penny Wilson; Sarah Stamford; Gareth Burgess, King's College, Cambridge; Janine Stanford, National Theatre Archive; and the staffs of the manuscript room, British Library, and the West and Rare Books Rooms, Cambridge University Library. Annette Lenton drew the map, Leonard Conolly and my fellow Shaw editors, Peter Wearing and Nicholas Grene, gave essential assistance, and Nicola Proudfoot was a meticulous copy-editor.

This edition is for Gil Bennet.

Selwyn College, Cambridge   J.K.C.
2008

BERNARD SHAW: A CHRONOLOGY

For a comprehensive and detailed chronology of Shaw's life, see A.M. Gibbs, *A Bernard Shaw Chronology* (Basingstoke, 2001). Dates of British and foreign productions of Shaw's plays are given in Raymond Mander and Joe Mitchenson, *Theatrical Companion to Shaw* (New York, 1955), and definitive bibliographical information on Shaw can be found in Dan H. Laurence, *Bernard Shaw: A Bibliography*, 2 vols. (Oxford, 1983).

1856   Born in Dublin, 26 July, to George Carr Shaw and Lucinda Elizabeth Shaw.

1871   Leaves school and takes an office job with a Dublin property agency.

1876   Moves from Dublin to London.

1879   Completes his first novel, *Immaturity* (first published 1930).

1880   Completes his second novel, *The Irrational Knot* (first published in serial form in *Our Corner*, 1885–7, and in book form 1905).

1881   Completes his third novel, *Love Among the Artists* (first published in serial form in *Our Corner*, 1887–8, and in book form 1900).

1883   Completes his fourth and fifth (his last completed) novels, *Cashel Byron's Profession* (first published in serial form in *To-Day*, 1885–6, and in book form 1886) and *An Unsocial Socialist* (first published in serial form in *To-Day*, 1884, and in book form 1887).

1884   Joins the Fabian Society.

1885   Publishes first music and drama criticism in the *Dramatic Review*. Shaw's criticism (including art and literary criticism) also appeared in periodicals such as the *Pall Mall Gazette, The World* and *The Star* before he began a three-year stint as drama critic for the *Saturday Review* (1895–8).

1891   Publishes *The Quintessence of Ibsenism*.

1892   His first play, *Widowers' Houses* (begun 1884) performed by the Independent Theatre Society, London.

1893   Completes *The Philanderer* and *Mrs Warren's Profession*.

1894   *Arms and the Man* performed at the Avenue Theatre, London, and the Herald Square Theatre, New York; completes *Candida*.

1896   Meets Charlotte Payne-Townshend, his future wife. Completes *You Never Can Tell* and *The Devil's Disciple*.

1897   *Candida* performed by the Independent Theatre Company, Aberdeen. *The Man of Destiny* performed at the Grand Theatre, Croydon. American actor Richard Mansfield produces *The Devil's Disciple* in Albany and New York.

1898   Marries Charlotte Payne-Townshend. Publishes (in two volumes) *Plays Pleasant and Unpleasant*, containing four 'pleasant' plays (*Arms and the Man, Candida, The Man of Destiny, You Never Can Tell*) and three 'unpleasant' plays (*Widowers' Houses, The Philanderer, Mrs Warren's Profession*). Completes *Caesar and Cleopatra*. *Mrs Warren's Profession* is banned by the Lord Chamberlain from public performance in England. Publishes *The Perfect Wagnerite* (on the *Ring* cycle).

1899   *You Never Can Tell* performed by the Stage Society. Writes *Captain Brassbound's Conversion*.

1901   Publishes *Three Plays for Puritans* (*The Devil's Disciple, Caesar and Cleopatra, Captain Brassbound's Conversion*). Writes *The Admirable Bashville*.

1902   *Mrs Warren's Profession* performed (a private production) by the Stage Society.

1903   Publishes *Man and Superman* (begun in 1901).

1904   Begins his partnership with Harley Granville Barker and J.E. Vedrenne at the Royal Court Theatre (until 1907). Eleven Shaw plays are produced there, including *Major Barbara* (1905).

1905   *Mrs Warren's Profession* performed (then banned) in New Haven and New York. *The Philanderer* performed by the New Stage Club, London.

1906   *Caesar and Cleopatra* performed (in German) in Berlin. Publishes *Dramatic Opinions and Essays*, and writes *The Doctor's Dilemma*.

1908   Writes *Getting Married*.

1909   *The Shewing-up of Blanco Posnet* banned in England, but performed in Dublin. *Press Cuttings* banned in England. Completes *Misalliance*.

1911   *Fanny's First Play* performed at the Little Theatre, London. Runs for 622 performances (a record for a Shaw première).

1912   Completes *Pygmalion*.

1913   *Pygmalion* performed (in German) in Vienna.

1914   *Mrs Warren's Profession* performed by the Dublin Repertory Theatre. *Pygmalion* performed at His Majesty's Theatre, London. Outbreak of World War One. Publishes *Common Sense about the War*.

1917   Visits front line sites in France. Completes *Heartbreak House*.

1918   End of World War One.

1920   *Heartbreak House* performed by the Theatre Guild, New York. Completes *Back to Methuselah*.

1922   *Back to Methuselah* performed by the Theatre Guild, New York.

1923   Completes *Saint Joan*. It is performed in New York by the Theatre Guild.

1924   First British production of *Saint Joan*, New Theatre, London. The Lord Chamberlain's ban on *Mrs Warren's Profession* is removed.

1925   First public performances in England of *Mrs Warren's Profession* (in Birmingham and London).

1926   Awarded the 1925 Nobel Prize for Literature.

1928   Publishes *The Intelligent Woman's Guide to Socialism and Capitalism*.

1929   *The Apple Cart* performed (in Polish) in Warsaw, followed by the British première at the Malvern Festival, where other British premières (*Too True to be Good, The Simpleton of the Unexpected Isles, Buoyant Billions*) and world premières (*Geneva* and *In Good King Charles's Golden Days*) of Shaw's plays were produced between 1932 and 1949.

1930   Begins publication of *The Works of Bernard Shaw*, completed (in 33 volumes) in 1938.

1931   Visits Russia; meets Gorky and Stalin.

1933   Writes *On the Rocks*.

1936   *The Millionairess* performed (in German) in Vienna.

1938   *Pygmalion* is filmed, starring Leslie Howard and Wendy Hiller.

1939   Outbreak of World War Two. Wins an Oscar for the screenplay of *Pygmalion*.

1940   *Major Barbara* is filmed, starring Rex Harrison and Wendy Hiller.

1943   Charlotte Shaw dies.

1944   Publishes *Everybody's Political What's What?*

1945   *Caesar and Cleopatra* is filmed, starring Claude Rains and Vivien Leigh. End of World War Two.

1950   Dies, 2 November, aged 94, from complications after a fall while pruning a shrub in his garden. Cremated at Golders Green Crematorium on 6 November, his ashes (mixed with his wife's) scattered at his country home in Ayot St Lawrence, Hertfordshire (now a National Trust property), on 23 November.

ABBREVIATIONS

BH	*The Bodley Head Bernard Shaw,* vol. VI, 1973
BL	British Library
corr.	letters to Shaw, 1923–4, BL Add. MS 50519, referred to by date of writing
Dukore	Bernard Dukore, ed., *The Collected Screenplays of Bernard Shaw,* 1980; for *Saint Joan,* see pp. 181–221
Enc. Brit.	*Encyclopaedia Britannica,* 1911
Evans	T.F. Evans, ed., *Shaw: The Critical Heritage,* 1976
Fr, MFr	French, Medieval French
Hill	Holly Hill, ed., *Playing Joan . . . Interviews,* 1987
L2, L3, L4	*Bernard Shaw, Collected Letters,* ed. Dan H. Laurence, vols. 2, 3 and 4, 1972, 1985, 1988
Lang	Andrew Lang, *The Maid of France,* 1908
Langner	Lawrence Langner, *GBS and the Lunatic,* 1964
Lat	Latin
LC	Licensing Copy, BL LCP 1924/9
ms file	relevant materials in BL Add. MS 50633, fos. 29–84
ms rev.	manuscript revisions to typescript, April–September, 1923, in BL Add. MS 50633, fos. 1–28
Murray	T. Douglas Murray, ed., *Jeanne d'Arc, Maid of Orleans*; references are to the revised and expanded 1907 edition
NT	Royal National Theatre, London
OED	*Oxford English Dictionary*
r.n.	Shaw's rehearsal notes, BL 50644: r.n. 1924 = notes from fos. 130–66 (New Theatre, London, 1924); r.n. 1936 = notes from fos. 299–302 (Malvern, 1936)
s.d.	stage direction
SE	Standard Edition of *Saint Joan,* 1932
SJ	Bernard Shaw, *Saint Joan,* 1924, first published edition
Taylor	Tom Taylor, *Jeanne Darc,* 1871
typescript	pages from typescript draft, BL Add. MS 50633, fos. 1–28
Tyson	B. Tyson, *The Story of Shaw's Saint Joan,* 1982; transcripts from Shaw's shorthand draft with commentary
Weintraub	Stanley Weintraub, ed., *Saint Joan Fifty Years After,* 1973

Bible references from the 1611 King James Authorised Version. Shakespeare references from the New Cambridge Shakespeare (1984–).

INTRODUCTION

About the Play

The first productions of Bernard Shaw's *Saint Joan*, under the direction of Philip Moeller and Lawrence Langner in New York and of Lewis Casson and Shaw himself in London in 1923–4,[1] made such an impact that the play, which seemed to many Shaw's greatest, was soon his best known. Near instant translations and acclaimed productions in Berlin, Paris, Vienna, Moscow, Amsterdam, Venice and Prague propelled him to the award of the Nobel Prize for 1925. Shaw had pondered over some years the meteoric rise and fall of Joan of Arc; her fervent mission to drive the English from France and her continuing iconic presence. She was claimed by both the Left and Right of French politics, according to whether read as voice from the people or ardent monarchist; she was depicted on English and American suffrage banners as an early claimant of women's rights; and she figured prominently as a military inspiration in allied propaganda during the First War.[2] To Shaw, the innumerable literary retellings[3] of the story of the girl, dead before she was twenty, seemed sentimentalising melodrama or pious hagiography, where they weren't scurrilous travesties, as the combative attention he pays to some of them in his Preface to the play makes clear. Already in 1905, he had told the actress, Eleanor Robson, that her manager should 'get a Joan of Arc play for you from some real poet' and, when a play by Edmond Rostand was proposed, asked eagerly 'Is it Joan of Arc? For this be all his sins forgiven him'.[4] In 1913, he floated the idea of writing such a play himself[5] and when, early in 1923, he finally did begin to write about 'the queerest fish among the eccentric worthies of the Middle Ages',[6]

---

1 In 1923, at the Garrick Theatre, with the Theatre Guild, New York, and in 1924 at the New Theatre, London.

2 See Timothy Wilson-Smith, *Joan of Arc: Maid, Myth and History*, 2006; Régine Pernoud and Marie-Véronique Clin, *Joan of Arc: Her Story*, translated and revised by Jeremy du Quesnay Adams, 2000.

3 Daniel C. Gerould estimated some 100 dramatisations of Jeanne in France between 1890 and 1925 ('Saint Joan in Paris', *Shaw Review* VII (January 1964), repr. A.M. Gibbs, ed., *'Man and Superman' and 'Saint Joan': A Casebook*, 1992, pp. 165–70). Quesnay Adams, op. cit., p. 238, reports seventeen versions in 1909 (the beatification year).

4 L2, pp. 550, 587.

5 Letter to Mrs Patrick Campbell, L3, pp. 201–2.

6 Shaw, quoted in Wendy and J.C. Trewin, *The Arts Theatre, London 1927–81* (London: Society for Theatre Research, 1986), p. 54, and see Preface, p. 137.

the words, he found, 'came tumbling out at such speed that my pen rushed across the paper'.[7]

On 28 February 1924, the Lord Chamberlain's Examiner of Plays, G.S. Street, reported of Shaw's *Saint Joan* that, while it was just possible that Catholics might 'take exception' if they thought the announcement of the canonisation was meant ironically, this would be unfair 'in regard to the whole spirit of the play, which is one of admiration and fairness and essential reverence'. The relief in his conclusion, 'I find nothing whatever to censor in it', is palpable.[8] The banning of Henrik Ibsen's *Ghosts*, Oscar Wilde's *Salome* and Shaw's own *Mrs Warren's Profession* in the 1890s had made Shaw an implacable enemy of censorship and a constant gad-fly of the censors. His fiercest defiance had come in 1909 with the inclusion of his extensive evidence to the select Committee on Censorship in his edition of *The Shewing-up of Blanco Posnet* which, banned in England, had been produced in Dublin. When, following the success of *Saint Joan*, a licence was granted for *Mrs Warren*, Shaw commented wryly that he now had the 'worrying odour of sanctity' about him.[9]

The Author

George Bernard Shaw was born in Dublin on 26 July 1856, into the less reputable branch of an Irish Protestant family. His father was an unsuccessful mill-owner and an alcoholic and, in 1873, his mother, an amateur singer, left with his sisters for London to follow the maverick musician, Vandaleur Lee, who had lodged with the family (and who was later the model for the mesmeric Svengali in George du Maurier's *Trilby*, 1894). Shaw's formal schooling was haphazard, but his musical education had been promoted by Lee; his visual imagination by visits to the Dublin Art Gallery; and his sense of theatre by encounters with Shakespeare and the melodramas that toured to Dublin, Taylor's among them.[10] Having left his clerking job to join his mother and sister Lucy in London in 1876, for the next decade, largely supported by them, he struggled as a freelance writer, wrote five novels of which four were serialised in socialist magazines, and fed his voracious appetite for knowledge in the British Museum Library. His tall, red-bearded, figure, as well as the range of

---

7 Langner, p. 60.

8 G.S. Street's report, 28 February 1924, BL, LCP corr. 5376.

9 Note by Shaw, included in BL, LCP corr. 5376.

10 Tom Taylor, *Jeanne Darc*, 1871, cited in Martin Meisel, *Shaw and the Nineteenth Century Theatre*, 1984, pp. 14, 368–9. Shaw also mentions seeing Percy Mackaye's *Jeanne D'Arc* in 1907 (L2, p. 689).

books he consumed, drew the attention of the critic, William Archer, who found him work reviewing and then, in 1889, a post of music critic at *The Star*. His wit and combative nature, as well as the accurate ear evident in his music reviews, and the astuteness of his theatre criticism (notably in the *Saturday Review*) made compelling reading.

He had meanwhile become, with Sidney Webb,[11] the moving spirit of the Fabian Society, his passionate socialism finding expression in lectures and policy pamphlets. Practitioner as well as proponent of radical causes, he was a vegetarian, a believer in 'rational dress' (comfortable practical clothes rather than Victorian formality and elaboration), and between 1897 and 1903 was active as a councillor for the borough of St Pancras. His political and literary interests coincided in his Fabian lecture on Ibsen, following Charles Charrington's production of *A Doll's House* in 1889, which he developed into *The Quintessence of Ibsenism*, 1891. His celebration of the 'vigilant open-mindedness' of Ibsen and his 'terrible art of sharp-shooting at the audience, trapping them, fencing with them'[12] could have been a manifesto for his own approach to playwriting.

Shaw's combative quality meant that, despite the success of his first play, *Widowers' Houses*, produced privately by J.T. Grein's Independent Theatre Society in 1892, his career as a dramatist was slow to take off. Not only was *Mrs Warren*, with its suggestions of incest and characters living off immoral earnings, banned officially but it was too strong even for Grein to contemplate. Although *Arms and the Man*, satirising romanticised youth and military heroics, ran for seventy-six performances in Florence Farr's 1894 experimental season at London's Avenue Theatre and *Candida* played out of town in 1897, Shaw's subversion of the conventions of the 'well-made play', his mocking tone and disconcertingly unresolved endings meant that there was scant attention from West End managers for the plays he continued to write throughout the 1890s. Among these were two early representations of inspirational leaders, Napoleon in *The Man of Destiny*, 1897, and Julius Caesar in *Caesar and Cleopatra*, 1899, whom he considered travestied in plays by the French dramatist Victorien Sardou (e.g. *Madame Sans-Gêne*, 1893) and by Shakespeare.

The successful publication of *Plays Pleasant and Unpleasant* in 1898, however, revealed a growing readership. This, and £200 earned from a New York production of *The Devil's Disciple* in 1897, as well as marriage to Charlotte Payne-Townshend, a wealthy Irish fellow Fabian, encouraged

11 See Preface, p. 164, n. 61.
12 *The Quintessence of Ibsenism*, 1913, p. 183.

him to abandon reviewing for drama. With the foundation of the Stage Society and its productions of *You Never Can Tell* in 1899, *Candida* in 1900, and a closed house production of the still-banned *Mrs Warren* in 1902, his conquest of the theatre began in earnest. Between 1904 and 1907, the seasons of new plays presented by Harley Granville Barker and J.E. Vedrenne at the Royal Court Theatre, London, included eleven by Shaw, among them *John Bull's Other Island*, 1904, *Major Barbara*, 1905, *Man and Superman*, 1905, and *The Doctor's Dilemma*, 1906. These demonstrated beyond doubt the stage-worthiness of his writing and the existence of an audience for his kind of dialectic. The excitement generated by his representation of evolutionary energy, his feminism evident in a succession of defiant and socially transgressive female characters, his propensity for giving the devil his due, and his subversive humour, all of which would be significant features of *Saint Joan*, underwrit, and to an extent undercut, the worthy social realism of the younger generation, Barker, John Galsworthy and St John Hankin, also featured at the Royal Court. By the end of the decade, with the 622-performance run of *Fanny's First Play*, Shaw had become the most-performed living dramatist in Britain. His conquest of the main-stream was clinched by the huge success of *Pygmalion* when produced in London in 1914 by the leading actor–manager of the day, Herbert Beerbohm Tree.

Frequent and fierce letters to the press arguing for women's suffrage, a socialised health service, cremation, Irish Home Rule, a National Theatre, and against corporal punishment, theatrical censorship, the House of Lords and British colonialism maintained Shaw's strong public profile. The tide turned somewhat with the outbreak of the war in 1914, which appalled him (although he contributed £20,000 to the British War loan) as did the terms of the Treaty of Versailles that ended it. His tract, *Common Sense about the War*, 1914, and his public defence of the Irish nationalist, Roger Casement,[13] who was tried for treason in 1916, alienated many. No major new play appeared until the première of *Heartbreak House* by the New York Theatre Guild in 1920. Although now considered one of his best, this strange, wild, condition-of-England play puzzled many and his next work, the five-play cycle, *Back to Methuselah*, which presented the evolutionary spirit from Eden to the distant future (licensed in England on the wonderfully absurd condition that Adam and Eve be 'dressed decently'), proved no more welcome. The success of *Saint Joan*, therefore, when premièred in New York, in December 1923, and London in March 1924, represented a sharp change of response.

13 See Preface, p. 159, n. 48.

While many contemporaries saw the play, as did the censor, as evidence of a newly reverent Shaw, he is as concerned here as in his earlier work not with villains but with the things 'normally innocent people' do. He is still 'sharp-shooting the audience', wanting its members to see that they too might have condemned Joan 'in the energy of their righteousness'.[14]

Although wary of honours, Shaw accepted the award of the Nobel Prize on condition that the money fund an Anglo–Swedish Foundation, whose first task would be translation of the work of August Strindberg, the Swedish dramatist who had never himself received the prize. After *Saint Joan*, Shaw turned his attention to economics, with *The Intelligent Woman's Guide to Socialism and Capitalism*, which sold out its initial print run immediately on publication in 1928. He did write fourteen more plays, however, including, in 1929, *The Apple Cart* for the inaugura-tion of Barry Jackson's Malvern Festival,[15] which became a show-case for a succession of Shaw premières and revivals. Shaw, now so much the Grand Old Man of English letters that the Prime Minister, Ramsay Macdonald had hosted his seventieth birthday celebrations, received fre-quent invitations from the BBC to speak on the new medium of radio. He agreed to the filming of *Pygmalion* and *Major Barbara*, winning an Oscar for the *Pygmalion* screenplay in 1939,[16] but, although he prepared a script of *Saint Joan*, whose Cathedral scene had been filmed by the Deforest company in 1926, negotiations first with RKO then Twentieth Century Fox foundered on the question of cuts and objections from Catholic Action.[17]

Shaw's continuing admiration for inspired individuals[18] and increasing dislike of democracy developed in the 1930s into a scarcely-critical acceptance of European totalitarianism, as embodied in Mussolini and Stalin, although he did rethink Nazism in the Second War. Devastated in 1943 by his wife's death, he continued to write and give radio talks. He died after a fall in 1950 and, assertive to the last, although St Patrick's, Dublin, and Westminster Abbey vied for his remains, his ashes were

---

14 Preface, p. 178.
15 Although written for Jackson's Malvern Festival, the play had its first performance in Warsaw. See *Bernard Shaw and Barry Jackson*, ed. L.W. Conolly, 2002, p. xxvi.
16 *Pygmalion*, dir. Anthony Asquith (UK, 1938); *Major Barbara*, dir. Gabriel Pascal, David Lean (UK, 1941).
17 See Shaw, '*Saint Joan* Banned: Film Censorship in the United States', 1936, reprinted in BH, pp. 232–41. For Shaw's film script of *Saint Joan*, see Dukore.
18 Among their number was T.E. Lawrence. Returned from Arabia, and a frequent visitor to Shaw's home in Hertfordshire at this time, he enlisted in the army under the alias 'Private Shaw'.

scattered, as directed in his will, mingled with Charlotte's in his Hertfordshire garden at the foot of his statue of Saint Joan. His fortune was shared between the Royal Academy of Dramatic Art, the British Museum, the movement for rational spelling and the National Gallery of Ireland.

History and Modernity

As so often in his earlier writing, Shaw in *Saint Joan* put his own stamp on a current dramatic mode that he found wanting. Just as *The Man of Destiny* was a bid to reclaim one of his heroes from Sardou and *Caesar and Cleopatra* another from Shakespeare, so the portrait of Joan in Shakespeare's *Henry VI, Part 1*, which had been produced, although without the most scurrilous sequences, at London's Old Vic in 1922, seemed to Shaw as much a travesty as the satirised Pucelle of Voltaire.[19] Although *Saint Joan*, as Martin Meisel points out, follows a trajectory, through Vaucouleurs, Chinon, Orleans to Rheims and the trial at Rouen, notably similar to that of Tom Taylor's *Jeanne Darc*, the Epilogue and tent scene (Scene IV) have 'no equivalent in Taylor's orthodox five act movement'.[20] Shaw also resists spectacle. He sets his scenes *before* the battle; in a side aisle *after* the coronation; and ends Scene VI in the near-empty court room with only the echoes and reflection of the off-stage burning. Where Taylor's La Hire makes plans to rescue the Joan he loves, and love for an English soldier leads Schiller's Maid to death on the battlefield and Cecil B. DeMille's to trial and the stake,[21] Shaw avoids any suggestion of the romantic liaisons that characterise historical melodrama.

In its episodic structure, resistance to romantic intrigue, and attention to documentary sources, Shaw's play is a version of the new kind of history play that emerged in Europe's *avant garde* theatres at the end of the nineteenth century.[22] In this instance, the documents, in the form of records of Jeanne D'Arc's interrogation and trial of 1431 and

---

19 Shaw's film script, however, begins with the title 'The Hundred Years War' and a quotation from Shakespeare's play: 'the cities and towns defaced / By wasting ruin of the cruel foe' (*Henry VI, Part 1*, 3.1.45–6; see Dukore). A verse translation of Voltaire's *La Pucelle* (1762) for the Lutetian Society, overseen by Ernest Dowson, had appeared in 1899.

20 Martin Meisel, *Shaw and the Nineteenth Century Theatre*, 1984, pp. 368–9.

21 Friedrich Schiller, *Die Jungfrau von Orleans*, 1801: multiple translations, including Lewis Filmore, *The maid of Orleans: A Romantic Tragedy*, 1882; *Joan, the Woman*, directed by Cecil B. DeMille (New York: Lasky Studios, 1916).

22 Among the pioneers were Leon Hennique, *The Death of the Duke of Enghein* (Théâtre Libre, Paris, 1891), and Gerhardt Hauptmann, *The Weavers* (Freie Bühne, Berlin, 1893), with, closer in date to *Saint Joan*, Büchner, *Danton's Death* (Deutsches Theater, 1916), and John Drinkwater, *Abraham Lincoln* (Birmingham Rep, 1918).

rehabilitation of 1453–6, are remarkably full and include depositions from witnesses in Domrémy, Vaucouleurs and Chinon as well as Orleans and Rouen. Translated into Court Latin from Medieval French in the fifteenth century, collected and published in modern French by Jules Quicherat between 1841 and 1849, with selections translated into English by T. Douglas Murray in 1902, these documents were already multiply-layered before Shaw's selecting and filtering imagination got to work on them. They had undergone further recent interpretation in narratives by Margaret Oliphant, Anatole France, Andrew Lang and, the one Shaw most relished, Mark Twain in a purported memoir by Jeanne's own page.[23] The conviction, drive and earthy commonsense of the Jeanne of the records, evinced as much in the reports of the hostile as in those of sympathetic witnesses, give some weight to Shaw's claim to 'owe absolutely nothing to anyone except Joan herself (to whom be the glory) and my own knack of dramatic reporting'.[24] Her answers under interrogation, many of which are incorporated into the play, were succinct and sturdy. One trial witness, describing her as 'quite wonderful in her answers', recalled that having demonstrated the error of one accuser, 'she rejoiced, saying to Boisguillaume that, if he made mistakes again, she would pull his ears'.[25]

The advent of the historical Jeanne was the turning point in the Hundred Years War between the French and English monarchies, launched by Edward III in 1337 in pursuit of hereditary claims that were reinforced by military victories from Crécy (1346) to Agincourt (1415). The Dauphin's proclaiming himself king, following the death of his father Charles VI, in 1422, challenged the settlement of the Treaty of Troyes that granted reversion of the throne to Henry V and his heir, the infant Henry VI. The English, allied with the Duke of Burgundy, had secured the whole of Northern France making Orleans strategically important for an attack on the Valois base of Bourges and thence conquest of the South (see Map, p. 2). Jeanne's total belief in her mission to drive the invaders from France had an energising impact on the demoralised Valois troops. Successive victories in the English territories, following the raising of the siege of Orleans in May 1429, enabled the symbolic gesture of Charles' coronation in Rheims Cathedral, on 29 July. Jeanne's capture in May 1430, her trial by

23 Margaret Oliphant, *Jeanne D'Arc: her life and death*, 1896; Anatole France, *La Vie de Jeanne D'Arc*, 1908; Andrew Lang, *The Maid of France*, 1908; Mark Twain, *Personal Recollections of Joan of Arc, by the Sieur Louis de Conte*, 1899.

24 L3, p. 796.

25 Murray, p. 289.

clerics loyal to the English, and death as a relapsed heretic on 30 May 1431, proved only a brief set-back for the Valois cause. Dunois and La Hire continued the fight; in 1435 peace was made with the Burgundians, and, by 1453, the English capitulation was essentially complete. Charles initiated the hearings which led, in 1456, to the nullification of Jeanne's first trial and gave further validation of his claim to the throne.

This history is absorbed into the cut and thrust of Shaw's dialogue. Much of the contextual colour and detail derives from the medieval records, which Shaw described as 'my Plutarch'.[26] Jeanne was, indeed, kept in chains as Joan complains in Scene VI, guarded by the English army (431–2); made ill by a present of carp (445–51); forbidden bleeding (457–9); repeatedly asked to submit to the Church Militant (633–5).[27] But Shaw was aware, too, of the stage limits of historical representation. Acknowledging that only by 'inevitable sacrifice of verisimilitude' could he achieve veracity, he noted in the Preface (p. 179) and the programme for the first production that invention, simplification and compression were necessary to the moulding of this material into dramatic form.[28] In Scene I, the 'miracle' of the laying hens substitutes for the complicated story of Jeanne's seeming foreknowledge of the Battle of the Herrings[29] and Jeanne's three visits to Vaucouleurs are compressed into a single occasion. Similarly, the conquest of the Dauphin in reality took days, and the interrogation and trial lasted for months. The range of historical figures is necessarily limited, too, in what remains a large cast: Warwick incorporates the role of the Duke of Bedford in overseeing the trial; D'Estivet and Courcelles, the numerous other accusers and assessors who appear in the play only as unnamed observers. The historical role of Bluebeard as Jeanne's protector and comrade-in-arms at Orleans is reduced, and her other loyal supporter, the Duke of Alençon, removed entirely, thus heightening Joan's isolation in Scene V and avoiding an overloaded Epilogue. Bluebeard's subsequent notoriety, though, is acknowledged in the Archbishop's prophecy of future disgrace (II.489).

The development of one small reference is indicative of the way Shaw absorbed hints from the record into the fabric of the play. One account of Jeanne's arrival at Chinon reads:

26 L3, p. 876. Plutarch was the major source for Shakespeare's Roman Plays.

27 Murray, e.g. pp. 8–9, 79, 124–6, 162–4, 175, 183, 191, 245.

28 The 1924 programme note, subsequently incorporated into the Preface, is reproduced in BH, pp. 212–15.

29 See Preface, p. 143, n. 12.

Just as she entered the Castle, a man, mounted on horseback, said, 'Is that The Maid?' He insulted her, and swore with horrid blasphemy. 'Oh! In God's name', she said to him, 'dost thou blaspheme God, thou who art so near thy death!' And, an hour after, this man fell into the water and was drowned.[30]

Not only does Shaw name the man, 'Foul Mouthed Frank', but he has the Dauphin's advisors gossip about the incident and uses it to inform La Hire's faith in Joan and the Archbishop's realist account of miracles.[31] Its adept integration into the texture of the play is demonstrated by contrast with Otto Preminger's 1957 film version, where Frank is lecherous rather than foul-mouthed and, instead of the fall into the well (explicable by his drunkenness), dies – undoubted miracle – immediately Joan denounces his lustful assault on her.[32]

Shaw identified in the chronicles Murray presented a Joan absolutely sure of her mission to drive the English from France and see Charles anointed with the ancestral holy oil at his coronation in Rheims Cathedral. Describing her variously as 'a sane and shrewd country girl of extraordinary strength of mind and hardihood of body', 'the spiritual mother of [the Quaker] George Fox', and a 'volcano of energy from beginning to end and never the snivelling Cinderella born to be burnt', Shaw insisted his rather than the 'namby pamby' figure of Catholic hagiography or romantic melodrama was the real Jeanne.[33] Although he notes in the Preface that Jeanne was loyal to the church to the extent of sending letters to upbraid the Hussites,[34] he gives little attention in the play to her total belief in the power of the mass, her frequent praying, insistence on daily confession and introduction of bands of priests among her armies, and he underplays her spiritual mysticism.[35] Contemporaries perceived that, as well as sharing the forthrightness and self-confidence of his feminists, from Vivie Warren to Major Barbara, his Joan had a good deal in common with the dramatist. Sybil Thorndike, who premièred the role in London, was only partly joking when she told him, 'you could play Joan better than any of us',[36] and

---

30 Murray, p. 269.
31 II.52–86, 207–27, 279–83, 330–5.
32 *Saint Joan*, dir. Otto Preminger, screenplay by Graham Greene, after Bernard Shaw (UK, 1957).
33 Respectively, Preface, p. 153, and L4, pp. 53, 723.
34 See Preface, p. 137, n. 1.
35 Murray, pp. 259, 270, 281.
36 Thorndike to Shaw, 25 April 1931 (BL 50531, Thorndike correspondence).

Pirandello declared that 'Joan at bottom, quite without knowing it, and still declaring herself a faithful daughter of the Church, is a Puritan, like Shaw himself – affirming her own life impulse, her unshakeable, her even tyrannical will to live, by accepting death itself'.[37] Shaw's Joan is pitted, as he was, against institutions of religion and state.

She is also an individual creation. Naïve, unsophisticated and startlingly young, as Shaw was not, she has none of his self-mockery to undercut her certainty of being right. He also makes a feature of her extraordinary military insight, whose brilliance and originality he described in a later radio talk as comparable with that of Leon Trotsky, architect of the Bolshevik military victory in the new Soviet Union.[38] Labelling her 'presumptuous' as well as 'original' in the opening section of the Preface, he argues that 'at eighteen Joan's pretensions were beyond those of the proudest Pope or the haughtiest emperor'. Judi Dench, who took the role in 1965, thought Joan essentially insufferable in her absolute conviction, noting 'the *arrogance* of her . . . some people who are fighting for the right are not easy to be with. I think people thought she was an arrant nuisance'.[39] The presence in the play of Stogumber, who seemed to Pirandello its most inspired invention, offers a farcical reflection of Joan's fanaticism. She has, too, a disarming literal-mindedness, evident in her earnest reassurance after Baudricourt's 'Well, I *am* damned' that, indeed, he has a place in paradise (I.237–42). But she is not gullible. She is no more impressed than the Archbishop by the miraculous nature of Foul Mouthed Frank's fall into the well (II.484–7) and is astute enough to give Dunois reasons for her military decisions (V.90–2). Her dry, commonsensical wit flairs out on occasion, as in her Scene II response to Charles' request for a miraculous turning of lead into gold: 'I can turn thee into a king, in Rheims Cathedral; and that is a miracle that will take some doing, it seems' (639–40).

To the Shaw who had long been a convert to feminism, Joan, one of the leading characters in Cicely Hamilton's feminist *Pageant of Good Women*, 1909, was a worthy successor to his independent-minded women from Vivie Warren to Major Barbara. He compared her to Sylvia Pankhurst in the Preface (p. 160, n. 51), writing that she was not sexless but 'had something else to do' (p. 142); told the suffragette, Ethel Smyth, that without her he couldn't have done Joan;[40] and in his radio talk on the

37 *New York Times*, 13 January 1924, reprinted in Evans, pp. 279–84.
38 Talk for BBC Radio, 30 May 1931 (BH, pp. 226–7).
39 Hill, p. 124.
40 L3, p. 868.

500th anniversary of her burning recalled that the suffragettes under imprisonment and physical torture likened themselves to Joan. It is hardly surprising that the matter of Jeanne's commitment to male dress, the prime charge in the Declaration of Relapse, drew the sympathy of a man whose commitment to 'rational dress', soft wool Jaeger suits instead of the stiff collars, neckties and black formal wear of his day, was total. Not only had lacing and constricting corsetry, already rejected by feminists, been generally abandoned by the early 1920s but trousers for women had gained wider currency during the First War, when they indeed emerged as rational dress for those engaged in the war work. The many young women in his audience, who had themselves tasted independence in those years, can't but have responded to Joan's rejection of expectations of domesticity when she declares, 'I do not want to be thought of as a woman. I will not dress as a woman' (III.156–7).

Shaw's insistence on the variousness of Joan's supporters and antagonists means that a raft of vivid characters accompany the central role, making this a remarkable ensemble piece. While Stogumber and D'Estivet are presented farcically, Cauchon and the Inquisitor are allowed full consciousness and the opportunity to speak truth according to their own lights. Indeed, the Shaw who gave his unredeemed brothel keeper and arms manufacturer strong self-advocating in their respective plays[41] is as much concerned here with explaining her prosecutors as he is with presenting Joan. He identified in the chronicles Murray presented a struggle not of right and wrong but between those who believe themselves to be righteous: an Hegelian clash of contrary forces that chimed with his own dramatic strategy. The clash, or, rather, series of clashes, is between orthodoxy and resistance, and between different kinds of orthodoxy and challenge to it. The tent scene is entirely given over to verbal fencing between Joan's principal opponents over how she and her dangerous ideas are to be countered. The Inquisitor's long speech about heresy in the preamble to the trial, an extraordinary example of reasoned polemic, is offered in answer to Ladvenu's alternative idea of justice and mercy (VI.305–87). Importantly, this doesn't mean that Shaw endorses their arguments. These sequences are invariably compelling in performance, despite the absence of the central character, because they stimulate perception of the ways in which the characters are victims of their limited vision; challenge the audience to sharper attention and response. As Brecht saw, 'Shaw creates a play by inventing a series of complications

41 *Mrs Warren's Profession*, 1893; *Major Barbara*, 1905.

which give his characters a chance to develop their opinions as fully as possible and to oppose them to our own'.[42]

The representation of the judges, and particularly Pierre Cauchon, and their belief that they are acting justly, is, while widely acknowledged as Shavian distortion, important to the play's dialectic. Shaw, for his part, claims in the Preface that he is countering the Rehabilitation's partisan construction of Cauchon 'as an unconscionable scoundrel, and all the questions put to her as "traps" to ensnare and destroy her' (p. 159) and, in the Epilogue, his Ladvenu tormentedly discounts such vilification (ll. 60–74). In fact, the historical Ladvenu remembered differently, stating in his deposition that, following Jeanne's relapse, 'the Bishop, coming out of the prison, met the Earl of Warwick and a great many English with him, to whom he said, laughing, in a loud and clear voice, "Farewell! Farewell! It is done; be of good cheer" '.[43] What Shaw could find, however, even in the partisan Rehabilitation record, are fleeting suggestions that Cauchon believed it was his duty 'to seek rather her salvation than her death' and that the English side accused him of proceeding too slowly with her interrogation.[44] Although evidently some recent scholars have argued, much as did Shaw, for Cauchon's sincerity,[45] when Shaw writes in his programme note that 'her excommunication was a genuine act of faith and piety',[46] we don't, in the aftermath of Soviet show trials and other twentieth-century legal abuses, necessarily accede to his view: Warwick's argument of political necessity may have a more convincing ring.

Shaw acknowledged to a friend 'I have had to magnify Cauchon, Warwick and the Inquisitor considerably to make the situation intelligible. There is no reason to believe that any of them was capable of expounding it as they do in the play. I had to wash their hands and clear their heads a bit', although he continued to insist, 'but I see no evidence that they were false to their own lights'.[47] As this suggests, Shaw was well aware that, for all his very real attention to historical documentation, dramatised history necessarily reflects the time of its writing and preoccupations of its author. Indeed, in the course of the Preface he admits that 'the writer of high tragedy and comedy, aiming at the innermost attainable truth, must needs

42 Bertold Brecht, 'Three Cheers for Shaw', 1926, in John Willett, ed., *Brecht on Theatre*, 1978 (first pub. 1957), pp. 10–13 at p. 11.

43 Murray, p. 166.

44 Murray, pp. 187, 205, 262.

45 Cited Régine Pernoud and Marie-Véronique Clin, *Joan of Arc: Her Story*, translated and revised by Jeremy du Quesnay Adams, 2000, p. 210.

46 BH, p. 214.

47 L3, p. 877.

flatter Cauchon nearly as much as the melodramatist vilifies him' (p. 179). It is this recognition that shifts the twentieth-century history play beyond a concern with documentation, episodic structure and the avoidance of melodrama. Deliberate anachronisms of language and ideas mark the presence of a modern consciousness, asking questions of history and using history to ask questions of the present.[48] This is signalled most directly in the presentation of Joan as proto-Protestant and proto-Nationalist and the very deliberate sequence in Scene IV in which Warwick and Cauchon alternately coin the terms 'Protestantism' and 'Nationalism' (IV.539, 560).

Issues of dissent and personal responsibility are key to the play. In Scene IV, Warwick's recognition, that the end of feudalism and the power of the aristocracy is at hand if each individual can have a direct line to the monarch (458–509), and Cauchon's perception, that direct communication between the individual and his or her God is a fundamental challenge to the authority of the church (384–418), are potently argued. The fifteenth century was, indeed, a period of the decline of feudalism and rise of nation states. Not for nothing did Johan Huizinger, who was one of many contemporaries to comment in detail on Shaw's play, call his classic study of the period, *The Waning of the Middle Ages*.[49] Shaw picked up fairly from the trial records the judges' emphasis on questions of authority and the challenge to the church and Jeanne's refusal to accept the church's rulings, powerfully expressed in her cry 'What other judgment can I judge by but my own?' (VI.664), a cry that expressed his own recurrent concern with individual responsibility – his fundamentally Protestant world view. The roots of Protestantism, described by Warwick as 'the protest of the individual soul against the interference of priest or peer between the private man and his God' (IV.537–9), were indeed emergent in Jeanne's day, which followed immediately on Wycliffe's and preceded Luther's. Where these proto-Protestants opposed church abuses and emphasised the struggle of the individual in the practice of faith, Jeanne's acceptance of the tenets of the church was total except where they crossed her divine inspiration. The Catholic church was, therefore, eventually able to absorb her as it was not Wycliffe, or

---

48 See Matthew H. Wikander, 'Reinventing the History Play', in *The Cambridge Companion to George Bernard Shaw*, ed. Christopher Innes, 1998, pp. 203–13 at p. 213, for a fuller discussion of Shaw's originality and an analysis of his use of anachronism.

49 A 1925 translation from the Dutch of Huizinger's review of the play in *De Gids*, 1925, is reprinted in Weintraub, pp. 54–85. *The Waning of the Middle Ages*, translated and adapted, under the author's directions, 1924 (repr. 1955).

Luther, or Galileo.[50] Shaw might acknowledge this in the Preface but doesn't engage with it, nor could he, given his concern with ideas and the play of mind.

Besides frequent teasing of the audience – particularly the English audience – with lines like Warwick's 'If we feared anything we could never govern England' (VI.170), darker areas of consciousness are addressed in the play. Shaw, in the Preface, cites wartime imprisonment of conscientious objectors and the uncontrolled behaviour of the Black and Tans in suppressing rebellion in Ireland as instances of continuing intolerance and state oppression.[51] He also twice references the trial and execution of the Irish patriot and English traitor, Roger Casement. The statement Shaw wrote for Casement's defence rehearsed Joan's claim that the court had no jurisdiction: for Joan, because she was answerable only to God; for Casement, because Ireland was a separate country, and he therefore a prisoner of war.[52] While these instances may have fuelled the writing of the play, they are buried deep but few in the post-Great War audience could have missed the resonance of Warwick's prediction of the dangers inherent in the rise of nationalism. The Irish Independence struggle is, similarly, all too present in Joan's 'God made them just like us; but He gave them their own country and their own language; and it is not His will that they should come into our country and try to speak our language' (I.486–9).

The Play

The structure of the play shapes its impact. After the upward trajectory in the first three scenes, the interpolation of the tent scene demonstrates the gathering of forces against Joan. Although she doesn't appear in person in the scene, its discussion is entirely focused on her. In Scene V, which follows, the audience encounters not the triumph of the antici-pated coronation but its aftermath and Joan's recognition of the turn in her fortunes that carries through to her cry of isolation at the end of the scene. While Shaw is evidently not much interested in delineating the spiritual quality of Joan's fervour, he creates a memorable visual image when Scene V opens on her praying alone and follows this with the aural strangeness of her sung impression for Dunois of the voices she hears on

50 See Preface, p. 161, n. 53, p. 144, n. 13, and p. 148, n. 23.

51 See Preface, pp. 170–2, and n. 79.

52 Discussed in detail by James Moran, *Staging the Easter Rising*, 2006, who sees Casement as the hidden referent in the trial scene, in terms both of his nationalism and his challenge to conventional gender roles.

the church bells. Repeatedly those who have taken the role have registered the passion they experienced as, in Barbara Jefford's words, the other characters 'gradually went away from her as they finished each rejection speech and there she was on her own. It's just a physical thing of direction and theatrical expertise which puts you in the right place and the right spirit'.[53] The movement from here onwards is to further isolation. The patterned language and action here foreground not only the moment of excommunication but the sequence in the Epilogue where each man kneels and, in echoic words which recall the *Te Deum*, praises Joan, before, again, the sonorous ritual gives way to apologetic retreat and Joan is left to speak her parting words to the audience.

As this suggests, Shaw is adept at introducing the language of ritual and parodic versions of it, and melding them into the ongoing action of the play. The excommunication itself, pronounced antiphonally by Cauchon and the Inquisitor, is made the more solemn because it interrupts the fervid rush to the stake, while Stogumber's 'Into the fire with the witch' that follows sounds even cruder by contrast with the solemnity (VI.1044). This in turn foregrounds Stogumber's broken reaction in the immediate aftermath of the burning, but also the equally intense, if quieter, response of Ladvenu who has been the most sympathetic of the clerics in Scene VI. His rebuff of Warwick (VI.1202–3) here prepares his entrance in the Epilogue and the exhibition of the deep spiritual disturbance of this character who, significantly, exits well before Joan's offer to return.

The play's inclusion of colloquialisms, however, disconcerted some in the first audience. The critic of *The Stage*, in January 1924, was not alone in complaining that 'the extraordinary mixture of archaic language, modern English and current slang ... detracts from the dignity of the play', and A.B. Walkley thought it 'a regrettable lapse into the slang of today'.[54] More perceptively, and with the benefit of the passage of time, Andrew Kennedy has argued that Shaw's 'collage of styles' in this play is an essential part of its unity which 'depends on making one dramatic mode throw ironic light on another'.[55] The variousness, that includes the stilted pomposity of the gentleman from the Vatican, the light insouciance of Dunois' Page, the earnestness of the Court Page, as well as the forensic vigour of the debates in the tent and the ecclesiastical court, is

53 Hill, p. 84.
54 Evans, pp. 278, 287.
55 A. Kennedy, *Six Dramatists in Search of a Language*, 1975, pp. 45, 73–4.

essential to the play's continuing vitality. Shaw's relish of linguistic excess flashes out in his comic insults, which set the tone in the opening scene with, for example, Baudricourt's attack on 'the worst, most incompetent, drivelling snivelling jibbering jabbering idiot of a steward in France' (I.54–5) and in Dunois' languid poeticising at the opening of Scene III. But such excess, enlivening the linguistic surface, is rarely casual. In Scene I, the Steward may be timid but he doggedly holds his ground, and Baudricourt's ebullience and bluster are powerless in the face of Joan's chirpy self-confidence. A more complex connectiveness is developed in Scene III when a link is made between Joan and the kingfisher, whose lightning appearance interrupts Dunois' lyric transports with exciting reality, before Joan's entrance when Dunois' speech quickens to brief functionality as he tests her metal.

Sian Phillips, who played Joan in 1958, gave an actor's response to the structure of Shaw's dialogue, saying, 'it is intoxicating when it is properly done . . . you think, you act on the line, in the line, through the line. *Never* between the lines. You observe the commas, the semi-colons, the full stops, and in that way it becomes very easy, in fact. And you've got to keep going fast.'[56] The cut and thrust of the Scene II sequence in which Joan wins over Charles is a case in point. Joan's continual questions and positive statements counter Charles' negatives, and her verbs of intention ('must', 'will') are repeated, until her echoing his 'Oh, if only I dare!' with the threefold conviction of 'I shall dare, dare, and dare again' makes it credible that even this Dauphin might take fire from her (II.668–70).

Even one of the trickiest sequences of the play can be effective in the theatre. Shaw repeatedly had problems in expressing deep-felt emotion and this is true of Joan's rejection of perpetual imprisonment in her 'Light your fire' speech (VI.967–95). Raymond Williams, not unfairly, labelled the evocation of 'the young lambs crying through the healthy frost' and the 'blessed blessed church bells' as 'romantic pathos'.[57] On the page, this part of the speech has a vapidity that some productions have sought to mask by introducing swelling music as background.[58] In the end, the onus is on the player to make it work but she is helped by the speech rhythms Shaw gives her. The deflation experienced by audience as well as character, when Joan, briefly losing faith in her voices, listlessly accedes to her accusers, underpins audience response to Joan's surge of renewed defiance. The reiterated

56 Hill, pp. 77, 78.

57 Raymond Williams, *Drama from Ibsen to Eliot*, 1964, p. 169.

58 An aberration in the otherwise impressive 1994 London production at the Strand Theatre, with Imogen Stubbs.

first person pronouns drive the speech on. This catches an echo of Joan's earlier long speech, her 'I am alone. France is alone' in Scene V (469–92), where the patterning is even more marked. Set against a complaint by Raymond Williams that Joan, here, speaks affirmation rather than contemplation or meditation[59] is the testimony of those who have played the role. Repeatedly, they recur to this speech as key to their performance and register awareness that it compelled audience attention.[60] Although beginning in despair, and centred on self, with the recalling of family opposition, as it moves to identify Joan's situation with country and then God the speech reconfigures her isolation as strength. The word 'France' is reiterated until, from 'Do not think you can frighten me by telling me that I am alone. France is alone; and God is alone', the words 'God', 'alone' and 'loneliness' take over. Tyson's extended quotation from the shorthand draft of the play[61] reveals that, as well as more general tightening of expression in this sequence, Shaw developed the patterned repetition of these words. The power of the speech to take hold on the minds of its hearers is registered in the memories of those who have played the role. It is probably no coincidence that repetition, particularly of the words 'lonesome' and 'alone', is a feature of Desire Under the Elms, the play Eugene O'Neill wrote in 1924, following the New York run of Shaw's play. As Ephraim Cabot concludes at the end of that play, 'God's lonesome, hain't He? God's hard and lonesome'.[62]

As this suggests, Shaw's stage sense, his awareness of the interaction of voices and spatial relationships, means that, as with all major drama, the play in performance has a compulsion different from that on the page. This is evident in the Epilogue where a cluster of stage directions call for sound signals, colour and light effects, including rustling, painted curtains, silhouetted figures, clock chimes, blackout and a gathering of light in the final moments. The Epilogue was central to Shaw's conception: thinking of a Joan play in 1913, he had proposed 'beginning with the sweeping up of the cinders and orange peel *after* her martyrdom, and going on with Joan's arrival in heaven', where she would cite the soldier's two sticks to stop God damning the common people.[63] As he explained to Lawrence Langner, 'I had to include in the play the reversal of the

59 Williams, op. cit., p. 169.
60 See, for example, Hill, pp. 50, 84, 117, 165, 175–6.
61 Tyson, pp. 44–5.
62 For discussion of O'Neill's use of repetition, see Jean Chothia, *Forging a Language*, 1979, pp. 80–1.
63 L3, p. 201.

position of the Roman Catholic Church which resulted in her being canonised in the year 1920'.[64] He had already experimented with black-out and spotlight in the 'Don Juan in Hell' scene of *Man and Superman* and engaged in a degree of absurdism in *Misalliance* which would be developed in his later 'Extravaganzas'. He told Ernest Thesiger, the 1924 Dauphin, he shouldn't 'be too tied to naturalism in the scene, which will have something of the insanity of a dream' (L3, p. 872). This insanity is emphasised by the inclusion of visions Charles could not have imagined, not just the gentleman of 1920, but the film projections of the future Winchester and Rheims, suggestive of Joan's continuing significance. This incorporation of what is now described as a character's 'afterlife', as well as its extravaganza form, is a crucial element of the play's modernity. Sian Phillips indicated one effect of the change of tone between Scene VI and the Epilogue when she wrote that people 'come out of the play feeling quite good' even having 'been through all that'.[65]

The Play on the Stage

Some reviewers of the Theatre Guild's production of the play, in December 1923, found the tone of the Epilogue disconcerting and others complained about the play's length but the reception in the theatre was enthusiastic. Shaw firmly resisted what he labelled the 'panic-stricken nonsense' of Lawrence Langner's cable, 'The play will fail unless you make textual omissions', and the public who, as Langner records, 'came flocking' seem to have agreed. The play had to transfer to a larger theatre to meet demand.[66] Among the most influential commentators, Alexander Woolcott found the play 'beautiful, engrossing and at times exciting'; Luigi Pirandello recorded the rapt attention of the audience and commended Shaw's 'half-humorous melancholy';[67] and even hostile reviewers were fired to lively discussion. News of the New York reception contributed to the anticipation in London which resulted in long queues for tickets for the 26 March opening at the New Theatre and over 2000 people turned away.[68] Desmond MacCarthy, Edmund Wilson and the medieval cultural historian Johan Huizinger were among those influential commentators who all, even while expressing

---

64 Langner, p. 81; Shaw develops his discussion of the Epilogue in the Preface, pp. 180–1.
65 Hill, p. 77.
66 Langner, pp. 67, 71.
67 Woolcott, *New York Herald*, 29 December 1923, and Pirandello, *New York Times*, 13 January 1924, both reprinted in Evans, pp. 275–6, 279–84. Other significant reviews from 1924 include *The Freeman*, 8 January; *Nation*, 23 January; *Drama*, 14 February.
68 *Daily Mirror*, quoted in Tyson, p. 94.

well-considered reservations about aspects of Shaw's argument, his presentation of medieval thought or the absence of spirituality, found it a remarkable piece of work.[69] All also declared for the Epilogue, as did the *Evening Standard* (27 March 1924), which particularly celebrated the '*Te Deum*' sequence and the 'quality of ecstasy' in the play.

The excitement is reflected in letters Shaw received through 1924: Laurence Binyon would abandon his writing of a Joan play; Henry Williamson found his 'spirit moved'; Florence Hardy found the production 'a tremendous experience' and her husband, Thomas, to whom she was reading the play, was 'greatly impressed'; and even Laurence Alma Tadema, RA and leading Victorian scene designer, despite proclaiming that he had avoided Shaw's work for years and still finding him 'a priest who puts his tongue out in the middle of mass', thought the Epilogue 'almost entirely a masterpiece'.[70] Evan Morgan, 'Private Chamberlain to the Holy Father', deeply moved by the play, wrote 'your fairness to the clerics and to the clerical court has opened and will open the eyes of a large number of people who expected you to make them ridiculous or, at best, imbecile' and asked for a pre-publication copy to send to the Vatican to counter malicious reports that might flow in.[71]

Winifred Lenihan, the New York Joan, was presented with the Gold Medal of Joan of Arc by the French Minister Plenipotentiary[72] and Sybil Thorndike, the London Joan, reprised it in seven separate productions between 1924 and 1932, since when successive leading players have continued to undertake what Joan Plowright (Chichester and NT, 1963–4) called 'a zonking great part for a woman'.[73] Thorndike, who found that by the end of rehearsals with Shaw, 'every phrase and pause had been considered', startled but also convinced audiences by playing Joan as rough and boyish, infuriating as well as inspirational.[74] This was Shaw's conception

---

69 Respectively, *New Statesman*, 12 April 1924, *New Republic*, 27 August 1924, and *De Gids*, 1925 (reprinted in Weintraub, pp. 31–8, 39–43, 54–85).

70 Letters to Shaw (corr., 30 April, 18 June, 24 June, 3 July, 19 August 1924).

71 Letter to Shaw (corr., 26 April 1924).

72 L3, p. 869.

73 Hill, p. 113. Distinguished performers in the role include Wendy Hiller, Constance Cumming, Siobhan McKenna, Judy Dench, Lynn Redgrave, Eileen Atkins, Frances de la Tour, Imogen Stubbs and, in 2007, Anne Marie Duff (NT) and Tara Rosling (Canadian Shaw Festival). Thorndike also played Joan on BBC radio in 1967 and Cumming on both radio and TV (1941; 1947 and 1951), while other TV Joans include Ann Casson (1946) and Janet Suzman (1968). Sian Phillips (Coventry, 1958), describing the demanding centrality of the role, commented 'there are very few women's parts that you have to be that fit to play', Hill, p. 78.

74 Thorndike in R. Mander and J. Mitchenson, *Theatrical Companion to Shaw*, 1954, p. 18.

of the role and he continually excoriated those who played against the text to make Joan sweet or intensely pious.

While Shaw insisted on interviewing all potential English Joans and kept a watching brief on productions, such control was impossible in the foreign productions which followed immediately on the English pre-mières. He was furious to learn that colloquialisms like Joan's 'Blethers' (II.563) and 'I call that muck' (II.630) were cut in Max Reinhardt's October 1924 production at the Deutsches Theater, Berlin, and feared that Elisabeth Bergner was playing up Joan's piety.[75] The production by Georges Pitoëff, at the Théâtre des Arts in Paris in 1925 with Ludmilla Pitoëff as Joan, was a notorious example of playing against what Shaw took to be the spirit of his text. Frequently revived over the next ten years, it was Shaw's first – and greatest – French success owing not a little to the tremendous emotional force of Ludmilla's acting. Reviewers, quick to find contemporary implications about the need for national unity in post-War France, responded to Shaw's presentation of an impassioned, strategic Joan and recognised that what they saw as his satirisation of the other characters made her shine out all the more.[76] According to the report in *Figaro*, the audience were '*bouleversés*' (completely overcome) while the *Petit Journal* critic described them as spellbound throughout by the play, '*une chose splendide, unique, féroce, terrible et savoureuse*'.[77] Initially delighted by reports of its success, once he had seen the produc-tion in 1930 Shaw declared that 'Ludmilla Pitoëff missed it completely, and revived the snivelling womanly heroine of the old sentimental melo-dramas with appalling intensity'. In the trial scene Pitoëff's positioning of Joan facing the audience with the court massed behind her emphasised the pathos of her situation, her frailty rather than her resilience. To Pitoëff's argument that any great role is open to interpretation, Shaw insisted 'No there is only one right way', and told his French translator, 'it was to destroy that sort of Saint Joan that I wrote the play'.[78]

Another influential European director, Alexander Tairov, was quick to seize on the play and create a very different emphasis. Taking a lead from

75 Variously mentioned, including L4, p. 508, and Samuel A. Weiss, ed., *Bernard Shaw's Letters to Siegfried Trebitsch*, 1986, pp. 257–8.

76 Daniel C. Gerould, op. cit., repr. A.M. Gibbs, ed., '*Man and Superman' and 'Saint Joan': A Casebook*, 1992, pp. 166 ff.

77 *Figaro*, 11 May 1925; *Petit Journal*, quoted in L3, p. 911. François Mauriac was among those praising the play, and, more particularly, Ludmilla's interpretation, *Nouvelle revue française XXIV*, 1 June 1925.

78 Respectively: Shaw, *The Era*, 10 January 1934 (repr. BH, pp. 229–31 at p. 231); Hill, p. 39; L4, p. 174.

the Epilogue, his production for the Moscow Kamerny stressed political modernity, with a multi-levelled, 'Gothic Constructivist' set that, according to a contemporary witness, was 'predominantly red' with a 'background of vertical spears to suggest the military motive and collapsible church benches the ecclesiastical one'.[79] Elements of caricature and pantomime in the play were exaggerated although, except for cuts of anything suggesting the miraculous, the text was hardly altered. Warwick, in a recurrent Soviet imaging of the English aristocracy, sported a notable monocle, while the Dauphin wore the costume and painted face of a clown, except that his over-large shoes had curling medieval toes and his throne was dressed with ermine.[80]

When the play re-emerged in war-time Europe, the representation of embattled nationalism drew responses from very different audiences. German scholars in the Third Reich read the play as a celebration of the charismatic nationalist leader and a demonstration of the perfidy of French and English political expediency. A production at the Deutsches Theater in Berlin had run successfully from 1934–6; another was included in a Berlin Shaw season that made him the most performed English dramatist in Germany in 1938–9; and in 1941 the play was chosen to mark the eighth anniversary of Hitler's taking office.[81] In Paris in 1940, the occupying German authorities, considering that the play demonised the English and the traitorous Free French who were their allies, permitted its performance. The play was taken instead as a call for resistance, its central character identified not with Hitler but with De Gaulle who had already begun to identify himself with Jeanne, taking the cross of Lorraine as his symbol and evoking her spirit in his speeches.[82] Back in England, Joan's single-minded confidence in eventual success seemed to endorse the war effort, first in the 1942 BBC radio production and then when toured through towns and villages by Basil Langton's Travelling Repertory Theatre,[83] with Sybil Thorndike's daughter, Ann Casson, in the title role. Revived in 1945, with Lewis Casson as advisor and occasional performer, the production played in Holland, France, Belgium and Germany. Ann Casson recalled an audience of 2–3000

79 Huntly Carter, *The New Spirit in Russian Theatre*, 1929, p. 235; Nikolai Gorchakov, *The Theatre in Soviet Russia*, 1957, p. 233.

80 Illustration in a file of cuttings (BL 50590, fo. 36).

81 Glen R. Cuomo, ' "Saint Joan Before the Cannibals": George Bernard Shaw and the Third Reich', *German Studies Review* 16 (1993), 435–61 at 445 and 450.

82 Timothy Wilson-Smith, *Joan of Arc: Maid, Myth and History*, 2006, p. 208. See, too, Harold Hobson, *The French Theatre of Today*, 1953.

83 Shaw to the radio producer Douglas Allen, 6 February 1942 (L4, p. 626).

allied troops rising as one in a Hamburg theatre to applaud Joan's 'your council is of the devil, and . . . mine is of God' and the 'electrifying' atmosphere of a performance to a boat-load of returning troops, with the cast in uniform and searchlights as stage lighting, in the immediate aftermath of news of the dropping of the atomic bomb.[84]

Shaw's preference was for simple setting, solid but also sparse, as on the Elizabethan stage. He feared the Theatre Guild's 'drift to the conventional', suggesting for their 1923 production 'a single pillar of the Gordon Craig type will make the cathedral. All the Loire needs is a horizon and a few of Simonson's lanterns'.[85] He declared at the London dress rehearsal (1924) that 'scenery and costumes have ruined my play' and longed for 'plain clothes as at rehearsal'.[86] The sheer visual pleasure of Charles Ricketts' universally admired sets and costumes, however, evidently won him over since he told his German translator, Trebitsch, that these could not 'be improved on by any artist in Europe'.[87] Evoking, rather than reproducing, the medieval past, Ricketts incorporated colour and light with quasi-Gothic tapestries and stained glass windows modelled on those of King's College Chapel. The medieval costumes were described by A.B. Walkley as 'a separate ecstasy'.[88] Huizinger, comparing the London and the much more abstract Amsterdam staging, which probably came closer to Shaw's specifications, wrote that he had 'never seen more convincing historical staging' than Ricketts' whose '*Heures de Chantilly* come to life' lingered in his memory.[89]

Shaw's notes to the Theatre Guild, for instance that Poulengey and Baudricourt were insufficiently military or that 'Joan's gesture with her hand in the air tearing the recantation' was 'the last word in operatic artificiality', demonstrate his alertness to questions of staging and details of dress and manner. What he wanted was detailed observation – for example, that an angry woman tears paper downwards and throws it on the floor.[90] Shaw's extant rehearsal notes for the 1924 London production are mainly concerned with correcting verbal slips or suggesting tone. He found Baudricourt's 'Oh, come, Polly' (I.313), for instance, 'too good

84 Hill, pp. 34–5.
85 L3, p. 863; Langner, p. 58.
86 A. Russell Thorndike, *Sybil Thorndike*, 1929, p. 293.
87 Letter from Shaw, 12 June 1924, in Samuel A. Weiss, ed., *Bernard Shaw's Letters to Siegfried Trebitsch*, 1986, p. 246.
88 Evans, p. 287.
89 Weintraub, p. 60; BL 50590, fos. 40–2.
90 L3, p. 863.

humored'; told the Archbishop in Scene II to 'keep it cool and superior'; and, in the trial scene, instructed Thorndike to play 'more heartily' Joan's 'Thou art a rare noodle' (VI.564).[91] Casson's endeavour was to increase the tempo, slowed by Shaw's meticulous attention to accurate delivery.

More recently, productions have demonstrated how readily Shaw's stage directions adapt to black box and 'plain clothes' presentations. Representation of place, status and purpose come mainly, as on the Elizabethan stage, through costume, dialogue and a few suggestive furnishings (e.g. a throne, a pennon, a table, in the early scenes; benches for the trial scene; a bed for the Epilogue). Essential properties (e.g. basket of eggs, crown, Book of Hours, Ladvenu's cross) can be carried on. In 2007, the Canadian Shaw Festival production used a bare stage, Appia-style steps and an eclectic mix of First War military costumes with medieval fabrics and colour for courtiers and ecclesiastics. In the 2007 NT production, breastplates, clerical robes and touches of quasi-medieval decoration worn over basic dark trousers and unstructured jackets or tee-shirts served for the costumes, while palace, battlefield, cathedral and fire were created with wooden chairs and a stage that could be pivoted upward to enable Joan and her standard to seem to mount the walls of Orleans.

Directors have responded variously to the Epilogue. Of the three productions at the Canadian Shaw Festival, the director in 1981, Christopher Newton, included it only under protest on the insistence of the Shaw estate. He staged the scene, following a long break after Scene VI, with the actors out of costume, reading from lecterns. A decade later, in 1993, presented as an integral part of the play, it met no audience resistance and, in 2007, it was used as a framing device, with part played as a prologue. In London, in the same year, it was included in shortened form, without Charles' bed or the distinctive costume of the gentleman from 1920, and with parts of the Preface spoken as commentary.

Shaw's Joan quickly became, and remains, the pre-eminent dramatic version of Jeanne. She has entered the public imaginary as thoroughly as has Shakespeare's Richard III, bearing out Alexander Woolcott's prediction, in his 1923 review, that other images of Joan 'will give way insensibly to this brisk, friendly, boyish lass'.[92] Where George Kaiser's *Joanne and Gilles*, 1923, and Maxwell Anderson's *Joan of Lorraine*, 1946, have faded, Shaw's play has survived and helped shape subsequent dramatisation not just of Jeanne's story but of history more generally. Carl Dreyer's film, *La Passion de Jeanne d'Arc*, 1928, uses images, telling

91 r.n. 1924, fos. 143, 141, 161.
92 Evans, p. 276.

camera angles and the play of light on clean white surfaces rather than words to convey feeling, but his Jeanne, a simple girl prey to the court, is, like Shaw's, a Protestant, her judges men of their time. Shaw's Epilogue had a shaping influence on Noel Coward's *Post Mortem*, 1930, in which John Craven, a ghost from the First War, visits the future and is defeated by its very heroising of him. In Germany, Brecht, who had encountered Shaw's play when an assistant on Reinhardt's 1924 production, developed the dialectical mode in his twentieth-century version *Saint Joan of the Stockyards*, 1931, and, later, *Galileo*, 1939, providing a further model for Robert Bolt's *A Man for All Seasons*, 1960, and John Osborne's *Luther*, 1961. Even T.S. Eliot, who had been hostile to what he perceived as the play's travesty of history and religion, when he in turn came to present an historical life in *Murder in the Cathedral* acknowledged Shaw's influence on the self-explaining of Thomas à Beckett's murderers,[93] and it was after translating Shaw's play that Jean Anouilh wrote his own version, *L'Alouette* (*The Lark*, 1953).

As well as the strong central role, the dialectical texture is a major factor in the play's seeming contemporaneity. Reverberations of the recent First War devastations, of feminism, of Roger Casement's trial, were present in Shaw's own day; contemporary French critics identified political reasons for the play's success; and the work struck an immediate chord in the 1940s in occupied Paris and war-torn Europe. In the early twenty-first century, it is, perhaps, the religious drive of the central character and the disruption she creates which startle freshly, as the links made between Joan and Islamic terrorism in the 2007 NT programme suggest. In his review of that production, Michael Billington wrote, 'What amazes me is that we have managed to live without this potent political masterpiece for so long'. His comment endorses the response of the Trewins to Michael Langham's 1954 production: 'After thirty years the play was still what some of the prescient had said it was on a spring night in 1924, an unflinching modern classic.'[94]

A Note on the Text

The text used here is the authorised edition (Bodley Head, 1973) made from Shaw's 'final corrected copy' (Standard Edition, 1932), which incorporates minor corrections Shaw made subsequent to the first English

93 'Poetry and Drama', 1950, in *Selected Prose*, 1963, p. 74.

94 Billington, *Guardian*, 12 July 2007; Wendy and J.C. Trewin, *The Arts Theatre, London 1927–81*, 1986, p. 54. Langham's production opened at the Arts Theatre, London, in 1954 and then transferred to St. Martin's Theatre.

edition (Constable, June 1924). Starting on 29 April 1923, Shaw composed the play from the beginning to the Epilogue, which he finished on 24 August. After Shaw had finished his shorthand draft[95] of each scene, his secretary typed it up. Manuscript revisions were made to the resulting typescript pages during the period of composition (i.e. April–August) and continuing until 28 September 1923. Most of the typescript was destroyed by Shaw in 1926, except twenty-eight pages with his significant manuscript changes, which are preserved in the British Library. A version of Shaw's text, incorporating in essence these manuscript revisions, became the Licensing Copy approved by the Lord Chamberlain (also held in the British Library), which was used for the 1924 London première. Further changes, including the alteration of the Licensing Copy's traditional five acts to the six scenes and an Epilogue, of what Shaw labelled 'A Chronicle Play' were incorporated into the 1924 edition, along with the newly completed Preface.

Shaw's concern with the detail of his text is evinced in his correspondence with directors and translators. On 3 December 1923 he wrote to Lawrence Langner at the Theatre Guild, 'when I heard that you were actually rehearsing from a copy which you knew to be an unrevised proof, I tore my hair . . . I did tell you very expressly that what you had was not the play in its final form' and, in May 1924, he wrote to Trebitsch, his German translator, to whom he had given a copy in 1923, 'for Heaven's sake do not let Saint Joan get into print until you have the final corrected copy to work from'.[96]

Although Shaw's successive changes are rarely large, they demonstrate his attention to historical accuracy and performance qualities. Alteration of the initial shorthand draft (see Tyson) sharpened historical information and rhetorical texture. The manuscript revision of the typescript attended particularly to the endings of scenes and, with each version up to June 1924, the expressive particularity of the stage directions was developed. So, the Steward '*squats on his knees*' (I.119) rather than '*sits*' (LC), Joan is described as '*plumping down on the stool again, like an obedient schoolgirl*' (I.576) for LC's '*rising and standing to attention*', and Warwick as '*hardening*' in response to Stogumber's hysteria (VI.1142) for LC's '*understanding*'. The 1924 edition includes action developed in or for performance. The end of Scene II adds to LC's '*all kneel*', '*except the Archbishop, who gives his benediction with a sign, and La Trémouille, who*

---

95   The shorthand draft is referred to in detail in Tyson, passim.
96   L3, p. 856; Weiss, op. cit., p. 245.

collapses, cursing' (II.706–7), and positions on stage are refigured in the trial scene and responses written in for the Assessors. A more colloquial note is sounded when, for example, 'folks' (II.503) replaces 'people' (LC) and interjections increasing the cut and thrust or punctuating lengthy speeches are added, although, significantly, there are no interruptions when ideas fundamental to the play are expounded, as with Cauchon on Nationalism (IV.551 ff.) or the Inquisitor on heresy (VI.310 ff.). Significant changes are recorded in the notes on the play.

The text in this edition retains most of Shaw's idiosyncratic punctuation and spelling practices. For example, he preferred to use the apostrophe only when absolutely necessary (believing it to be redundant in most cases, and always typographically ugly), so eliminated it whenever he could, e.g. *Ive, isnt, havnt.* He had to retain it, however, in instances where its omission might cause confusion, e.g. *It's, he'll.* He also retained a few archaic spellings (e.g. *shew* for *show*) and dropped the 'u' in 'our' spellings (e.g. *armor*).

Shaw's practice of using spacing between letters to indicate emphasis (e.g. d i d), reserving the use of italics for stage directions, has caused considerable confusion over the years, since variable spacing between letters in a word has not always been immediately apparent to editors, typesetters and proofreaders. Thus, different editions of any particular Shaw play provide different readings, sometimes indicating emphasis of a word, sometimes not. In order to avoid prolonging the confusion, and to restore and confirm Shaw's intentions for emphasising words (as reflected in manuscript versions and in editions prepared under Shaw's supervision), this edition of *Saint Joan* uses italics in the conventional way for dramatic texts, i.e. both for stage directions and to indicate emphasis of specific words or phrases in the dialogue.

In addition, the Preface, written in 1924 for inclusion in the published version of the play, usually appears before the play text, but here is placed after it, followed by a note about the historical models for the characters.

FURTHER READING

Bibliography and Texts

Dan H. Laurence, *Bernard Shaw: A Bibliography*, 2 vols., 1983.

The British Library Catalogue of Shaw Papers, 2005.

Bernard Shaw, *Saint Joan*, June 1924.

Bernard Shaw, *Saint Joan*, with 12 colour plates and 4 b/w illustrations, October 1924.

Bernard Shaw, *The Bodley Head Bernard Shaw, Collected Plays with their Prefaces*, vol. VI, 1973.

Bernard Shaw, *The Collected Screenplays of Bernard Shaw*, ed. Bernard Dukore, 1980.

Brian Tyson, *The Story of Shaw's Saint Joan*, 1982.

Biography

A.M. Gibbs, *Bernard Shaw: A Life*, 2005.

Michael Holroyd, *Bernard Shaw*, Vol. 3: *1918–1950: the Lure of Fantasy*, 1991.

Correspondence

Bernard Shaw, *Bernard Shaw, Collected Letters*, ed. Dan H. Laurence, vols. 2, 3 and 4, 1972, 1985, 1988.

British Library Add. MS 50519: correspondence 1923–4 (mainly letters to Shaw).

Lawrence Langner, *GBS and the Lunatic*, 1964.

Contextual / Historical

Encyclopaedia Britannica, 1911.

T. Douglas Murray, ed., *Jeanne d'Arc, Maid of Orleans, Deliverer of France; Being the Story of Her Life, Her Achievements, and Her Death, as Attested on Oath and Set Forth in the Original Documents*, 1902; rev. edn 1907. Translation and selection from Jules Quicherat, *Le Procès de Jeanne d'Arc*, 1841–9.

Régine Pernoud and Marie-Véronique Clin, *Joan of Arc: Her Story*, translated and revised by Jeremy du Quesnay Adams, 2000.

Timothy Wilson-Smith, *Joan of Arc: Maid, Myth and History*, 2006.

Website

http://www.joan-of-arc-studies.org/

Collections of Criticism

T.F. Evans, ed., *George Bernard Shaw: The Critical Heritage*, 1976.

A.M. Gibbs, ed., '*Man and Superman*' *and* '*Saint Joan*': *A Casebook*, 1992, pp. 165–70.

Holly Hill, ed., *Playing Joan: Actresses on the Challenge of Shaw's Saint Joan, Twenty Six Interviews*, 1987.

Christopher Innes, ed., *The Cambridge Companion to George Bernard Shaw*, 1998.

Stanley Weintraub, ed., *Saint Joan Fifty Years After*, 1973.

Criticism

Eric Bentley, *Bernard Shaw*, 4th edn 1957.

Jean Chothia, *English Drama of the Early Modern Period, 1890–1940*, 1996.

Nicholas Grene, *Bernard Shaw: A Critical View*, 1984.

Andrew Kennedy, *Six Dramatists in Search of a Language*, 1975.

Declan Kiberd, *Inventing Ireland*, 1996.

Desmond MacCarthy, *Shaw*, 1951.

R. Mander and J. Mitchenson, *Theatrical Companion to Shaw*, 1954.

Martin Meisel, *Shaw and the Nineteenth Century Theatre*, 1984.

BERNARD SHAW

SAINT JOAN

A Chronicle Play in Six Scenes
and an Epilogue

A Map of France in 1429

THE PERSONS OF THE PLAY

[The Theatre Guild, Garrick Theatre, New York,
28 December 1923]

[The New Theatre, London, 26 March 1924]

	New York	London
ROBERT DE BAUDRICOURT	*Ernest Cossart*	*Shayle Gardner*
STEWARD	*William M. Griffith*	*Francis Hope*
JOAN	*Winifred Lenihan*	*Sybil Thorndike*
BERTRAND DE POULENGEY	*Frank Tweed*	*Victor Lewisohn*
LA TRÉMOUILLE (Constable of France)	*Herbert Ashton*	*Bruce Winston*
THE ARCHBISHOP OF RHEIMS	*Albert Bruning*	*Robert Cunningham*
COURT PAGE	*Jo Mielziner*	*Sam Pickles*
BLUEBEARD (GILLES DE RAIS)	*Walton Butterfield*	*Milton Rosmer*
CAPTAIN LA HIRE	*Morris Carnovsky*	*Raymond Massey*
THE DAUPHIN (later CHARLES VII)	*Philip Leigh*	*Ernest Thesiger*
THE DUCHESS DE LA TRÉMOUILLE	*Elizabeth Pearré*	*Beatrice Smith*
DUNOIS	*Maurice Colbourne*	*Robert Horton*
DUNOIS' PAGE	*James Norris*	*Jack Hawkins*
EARL OF WARWICK	*A. H. Van Buren*	*E. Lyall Swete*
DE STOGUMBER	*Henry Travers*	*Lewis Casson*
WARWICK'S PAGE	*Seth Baldwin*	*Sidney Bromley*
PETER CAUCHON	*Ian Maclaren*	*Eugene Leahy*
THE INQUISITOR	*Joseph Macaulay*	*O. B. Clarence*
JOHN D'ESTIVET	*Albert Perry*	*Raymond Massey*
THOMAS DE COURCELLES	*Walton Butterfield*	*Francis Hope*
BROTHER MARTIN LADVENU	*Morris Carnovsky*	*Laurence Anderson*
THE EXECUTIONER	*Herbert Ashton*	*Victor Lewisohn*

AN ENGLISH SOLDIER	*Frank Tweed*	*Kenneth Kent*
A CLERICAL GENTLEMAN	*Ernest Cossart*	*Matthew Forsyth*

Also Courtiers, Monks, Soldiers etc.

For information on the historical equivalents of the characters of the play, see Appendix. Throughout, 'Joan' is used to describe the character, 'Jeanne' the historical figure.

THE SCENES OF THE PLAY

Period – The Fifteenth Century, during the Hundred Years War. In France

For places named, see the Map, p. 2.

SCENE I

A fine spring morning on the river Meuse, between Lorraine and Champagne, in the year 1429 AD, in the castle of Vaucouleurs.

CAPTAIN ROBERT DE BAUDRICOURT, *a military squire, handsome and physically energetic, but with no will of his own, is disguising that defect in his usual fashion by storming terribly at his* STEWARD, *a trodden worm, scanty of flesh, scanty of hair, who might be any age from 18 to 55, being the sort of man whom age cannot wither because he has never bloomed.*   5

The two are in a sunny stone chamber on the first floor of the castle. At a plain strong oak table, seated in chair to match, THE CAP-   10
TAIN *presents his left profile.* THE STEWARD *stands facing him at the other side of the table, if so deprecatory a stance as his can be called standing. The mullioned thirteenth-century window is open behind him. Near it in the corner is a turret with a narrow arched doorway leading to a winding stair which descends to the courtyard. There is a*   15
stout fourlegged stool under the table, and a wooden chest under the window.

ROBERT

No eggs! No eggs!! Thousand thunders, man, what do you
mean by no eggs?   20

STEWARD

Sir: it is not my fault. It is the act of God.

---

0   *Scene I* SJ (Act I LC)
1–2 s.d. *A . . . 1429* SJ (*13 May 1428* typescript; *February 23 1429* ms rev.). After rejecting
     specific dates of Jeanne's visits to Baudricourt, Shaw acknowledges the compression with
     Baudricourt's 'here still?' (ll. 100–1), and '*at last*' (l. 164).
3   s.d. BAUDRICOURT Shaw saw him as '*a youngish gentleman with more energy than he
     can work off in the routine of his military command*' (LC); 'smart, a *beau sabreur* a little
     the worse for wear, but still a dashing fellow' (L3, p. 856).
5   s.d. STEWARD He was, Shaw instructed the Theatre Guild (New York, 1923), 'not a zany, but
     a respectable elderly man whom nobody nowadays would dream of assaulting' (L3, p. 862),
     but he described him to the producer of the 1942 BBC radio production as 'a weak old
     sniveller' (L4, p. 626).
7   s.d. *age cannot wither* Shaw, teasingly, quotes Enobarbus' praise of Cleopatra, 'Age cannot
     wither her, nor custom stale / Her infinite variety' (*Antony and Cleopatra*, 2.2.241–2).
13   s.d. *mullioned* ms rev. (*unglazed* typescript); divided by a vertical stone bar. Other small
     changes to the typescript stage directions emphasised the plain solidity of the furnishings.

ROBERT

Blasphemy. You tell me there are no eggs; and you blame your
Maker for it.   25

STEWARD

Sir: what can I do? I cannot lay eggs.

ROBERT [*sarcastic*]

Ha! You jest about it.

STEWARD   30

No, sir, God knows. We all have to go without eggs just as you
have, sir. The hens will not lay.

ROBERT

Indeed! [*Rising*] Now listen to me, you.

STEWARD [*humbly*]   35

Yes, sir.

ROBERT

What am I?

STEWARD

What are you, sir?   40

ROBERT [*coming at him*]

Yes: what am I? Am I Robert, squire of Baudricourt and captain
of this castle of Vaucouleurs; or am I a cowboy?

STEWARD

Oh, sir, you know you are a greater man here than the king   45
himself.

ROBERT

Precisely. And now, do you know what you are?

STEWARD

I am nobody, sir, except that I have the honor to be your   50
steward.

ROBERT [*driving him to the wall, adjective by adjective*]

You have not only the honor of being my steward, but the privilege of being the worst, most incompetent, drivelling snivelling
jibbering jabbering idiot of a steward in France. [*He strides back* 55
to the table]

STEWARD [*cowering on the chest*]

Yes, sir: to a great man like you I must seem like that.

ROBERT [*turning*]

My fault, I suppose. Eh?   60

24–5   *your Maker* ms rev. (God typescript)
   32   *hens will not lay* a traditional omen of things awry

6

STEWARD [*coming to him deprecatingly*]

Oh, sir: you always give my most innocent words such a turn!

ROBERT

I will give your neck a turn if you dare tell me, when I ask you
how many eggs there are, that you cannot lay any.   65

STEWARD [*protesting*]

Oh sir, oh sir –

ROBERT

No: not oh sir, oh sir, but no sir, no sir. My three Barbary hens
and the black are the best layers in Champagne. And you come   70
and tell me that there are no eggs! Who stole them? Tell me that,
before I kick you out through the castle gate for a liar and a
seller of my goods to thieves. The milk was short yesterday, too:
do not forget that.

STEWARD [*desperate*]   75

I know, sir. I know only too well. There is no milk: there are no
eggs: tomorrow there will be nothing.

ROBERT

Nothing! You will steal the lot: eh?

STEWARD   80

No, sir: nobody will steal anything. But there is a spell on us: we
are bewitched.

ROBERT

That story is not good enough for me. Robert de Baudricourt
burns witches and hangs thieves. Go. Bring me four dozen eggs   85
and two gallons of milk here in this room before noon, or
Heaven have mercy on your bones! I will teach you to make a
fool of me. [*He resumes his seat with an air of finality*]

STEWARD

Sir: I tell you there are no eggs. There will be none – not if you 90
were to kill me for it – as long as The Maid is at the door.

ROBERT

The Maid! What maid? What are you talking about?

STEWARD

The girl from Lorraine, sir. From Domrémy.   95

---

69   *Barbary hens* deriving from the North African coastal region
78–81 ROBERT ... *But* SJ
88   s.d. SJ
90   *eggs* SJ (eggs. There is no milk worth mentioning LC)

7

ROBERT [*rising in fearful wrath*]

Thirty thousand thunders! Fifty thousand devils! Do you mean
to say that that girl, who had the impudence to ask to see me
two days ago, and whom I told you to send back to her father
with my orders that he was to give her a good hiding, is here   100
still?

STEWARD

I have told her to go, sir. She wont.

ROBERT

I did not tell you to tell her to go: I told you to throw her out.   105
You have fifty men-at-arms and a dozen lumps of able-bodied
servants to carry out my orders. Are they afraid of her?

STEWARD

She is so positive, sir.

ROBERT [*seizing him by the scruff of the neck*]   110

Positive! Now see here. I am going to throw you downstairs.

STEWARD

No, sir. Please.

ROBERT

Well, stop me by being positive. It's quite easy: any slut of a girl   115
can do it.

STEWARD [*hanging limp in his hands*]

Sir, sir: you cannot get rid of *her* by throwing *me* out. [ROBERT
*has to let him drop. He squats on his knees on the floor, contemplat-
ing his master resignedly*] You see, sir, you are much more positive   120
than I am. But so is she.

ROBERT

I am stronger than you are, you fool.

STEWARD

No, sir: it isnt that: it's your strong character, sir. She is weaker   125
than we are: she is only a slip of a girl; but we cannot make her go.

ROBERT

You parcel of curs: you are afraid of her.

STEWARD [*rising cautiously*]

No sir: we are afraid of you; but she puts courage into us. She   130
really doesnt seem to be afraid of anything. Perhaps you could
frighten her, sir.

119   s.d. *squats on his knees* SJ (*sits* LC)
128   *curs* low-bred dogs

ROBERT [*grimly*]

Perhaps. Where is she now?

STEWARD   135

Down in the courtyard, sir, talking to the soldiers as usual. She
is always talking to the soldiers except when she is praying.

ROBERT

Praying! Ha! You believe she prays, you idiot. I know the sort of
girl that is always talking to soldiers. She shall talk to me a bit.   140
[*He goes to the window and shouts fiercely through it*] Hallo, you
there!

A GIRL'S VOICE [*bright, strong, and rough*]

Is it me, sir?

ROBERT   145

Yes, you.

THE VOICE

Be you captain?

ROBERT

Yes, damn your impudence, I be captain. Come up here. [*To the*   150
soldiers in the yard] Shew her the way, you. And shove her along
quick. [*He leaves the window, and returns to his place at the*
table, where he sits magisterially]

STEWARD [*whispering*]

She wants to go and be a soldier herself. She wants you to give   155
her soldier's clothes. Armor, sir! And a sword! Actually! [*He*
steals behind ROBERT]

JOAN *appears in the turret doorway. She is an able-bodied*
country girl of 17 or 18, respectably dressed in red, with an uncom-
mon face; eyes very wide apart and bulging as they often do in very   160
imaginative people, a long well-shaped nose with wide nostrils, a
short upper lip, resolute but full-lipped mouth, and handsome
fighting chin. She comes eagerly to the table, delighted at having
penetrated to BAUDRICOURT'*s presence at last, and full of hope as*
to the result. His scowl does not check or frighten her in the least.   165

148 *Be you captain?* 'Are you the captain?' The colloquial syntax, reinforced in Baudricourt's
     irate response, establishes Joan as an uneducated country-girl and signals that the actress
     should use a rural accent. Joan's speech hereafter is only lightly marked syntactically, but
     cf. III.71 'Be you Bastard?'

156-7 s.d. *He . . .* ROBERT SJ

159 s.d. *dressed in red* a detail which provides a flash of vivid colour against the grey stone.
     Cf. Lang, p. 80, 'Jeanne changed her poor girl's dress of red cloth for the tunic etc. of a page.'
     J.M. Synge's Irish peasant women in *Riders to the Sea*, 1904, also wear red flannel.

Her voice is normally a hearty coaxing voice, very confident, very appealing, very hard to resist.

JOAN [*bobbing a curtsey*]

Good morning, captain squire. Captain: you are to give me a horse and armor and some soldiers, and send me to the 170 Dauphin. Those are your orders from my Lord.

ROBERT [*outraged*]

Orders from *your* lord! And who the devil may your lord be? Go back to him, and tell him that I am neither duke nor peer at his orders: I am squire of Baudricourt; and I take no orders 175 except from the king.

JOAN [*reassuringly*]

Yes, squire: that is all right. My Lord is the King of Heaven.

ROBERT

Why, the girl's mad. [*To* THE STEWARD] Why didnt you tell me 180 so, you blockhead?

STEWARD

Sir: do not anger her: give her what she wants.

JOAN [*impatient, but friendly*]

They all say I am mad until I talk to them, squire. But you see 185 that it is the will of God that you are to do what He has put into my mind.

ROBERT

It is the will of God that I shall send you back to your father with orders to put you under lock and key and thrash the 190 madness out of you. What have you to say to that?

JOAN

You think you will, squire; but you will find it all coming quite different. You said you would not see me; but here I am.

STEWARD [*appealing*] 195

Yes, sir. You see, sir.

ROBERT

Hold your tongue, you.

STEWARD [*abjectly*]

Yes, sir. 200

ROBERT [*to* JOAN, *with a sour loss of confidence*]

So you are presuming on my seeing you, are you?

178 *My . . . Heaven*' "But who is this Lord of whom you speak?" asked Robert of her. "The King of Heaven," she replied' (Poulengey's deposition in Murray, p. 225).

JOAN [*sweetly*]

Yes, squire.

ROBERT [*feeling that he has lost ground, brings down his two fists*   205
squarely on the table, and inflates his chest imposingly to cure the
unwelcome and only too familiar sensation]

Now listen to me. I am going to assert myself.

JOAN [*busily*]

Please do, squire. The horse will cost sixteen francs. It is a good   210
deal of money: but I can save it on the armor. I can find a soldier's armor that will fit me well enough: I am very hardy; and I
do not need beautiful armor made to my measure like you
wear. I shall not want many soldiers: the Dauphin will give me
all I need to raise the siege of Orleans.   215

ROBERT [*flabbergasted*]

To raise the siege of Orleans!

JOAN [*simply*]

Yes, squire: that is what God is sending me to do. Three men will be
enough for you to send with me if they are good men and gentle to   220
me. They have promised to come with me. Polly and Jack and –

ROBERT

Polly!! You impudent baggage, do you dare call squire Bertrand
de Poulengey Polly to my face?

JOAN   225

His friends call him so, squire: I did not know he had any other
name. Jack –

ROBERT

That is Monsieur John of Metz, I suppose?

JOAN   230

Yes, squire. Jack will come willingly: he is a very kind gentleman, and gives me money to give to the poor. I think John
Godsave will come, and Dick the Archer, and their servants

210   *The horse* SJ (A horse for me LC)
215   *siege of Orleans* Orleans, chief town of the Loire, essential to communications between the
       Loire basin and Paris and key to the occupation of southern France, had been besieged by
       the English since October 1428.
216   s.d. *flabbergasted* astonished
219   *Three men* Joan proceeds to list six, the actual number that accompanied Jeanne from
       Vaucouleurs to Chinon.
227–31   *Jack . . . willingly* SJ (Jack – that is Monsieur John of Metz – will come willingly LC)
232–3   *John Godsave* The group that accompanied Jeanne from Vaucouleurs to Chinon were those
        named, except that the second member was not 'John Godsave' but the royal courier, Colet
        de Vienne. Tyson (p. 21) notes that he was listed in Shaw's shorthand ms.

John of Honecourt and Julian. There will be no trouble for you,
squire: I have arranged it all: you have only to give the order.   235

ROBERT [*contemplating her in a stupor of amazement*]

Well, I *am* damned!

JOAN [*with unruffled sweetness*]

No, squire: God is very merciful; and the blessed saints Catherine
and Margaret, who speak to me every day [*he gapes*], will inter-   240
cede for you. You will go to paradise; and your name will be
remembered for ever as my first helper.

ROBERT [*to* THE STEWARD, *still much bothered, but changing his
tone as he pursues a new clue*]

Is this true about Monsieur de Poulengey?   245

STEWARD [*eagerly*]

Yes, sir, and about Monsieur de Metz too. They both want to go
with her.

ROBERT [*thoughtful*]

Mf! [*He goes to the window, and shouts into the courtyard*]   250
Hallo! You there: send Monsieur de Poulengey to me, will you?
[*He turns to* JOAN] Get out; and wait in the yard.

JOAN [*smiling brightly at him*]

Right, squire. [*She goes out*]

ROBERT [*to* THE STEWARD]   255

Go with her, you, you dithering imbecile. Stay within call; and
keep your eye on her. I shall have her up here again.

STEWARD

Do so in God's name, sir. Think of those hens, the best layers in
Champagne; and –   260

ROBERT

Think of my boot; and take your backside out of reach of it.

THE STEWARD *retreats hastily and finds himself confronted in
the doorway by* BERTRAND DE POULENGEY, *a lymphatic French
gentleman-at-arms, aged 36 or thereabout, employed in the depart-*   265
*ment of the provost-marshal, dreamily absent-minded, seldom
speaking unless spoken to, and then slow and obstinate in reply;
altogether in contrast to the self-assertive, loud-mouthed,*

239–41   *No . . . you* the first of many instances of Joan taking figurative language literally. Where
Baudricourt mocked the Steward's literalness (ll. 23–5), Joan's taking his casual oath
seriously here turns the joke against him.

264   s.d. *lymphatic* pale, sluggish appearance ascribed to malfunction of the lymph glands

superficially energetic, fundamentally will-less ROBERT. THE
STEWARD *makes way for him, and vanishes.*   270
    POULENGEY *salutes, and stands awaiting orders.*
ROBERT [*genially*]
    It isnt service, Polly. A friendly talk. Sit down. [*He hooks the
    stool from under the table with his instep*]
        POULENGEY, *relaxing, comes into the room; places the stool*   275
    between the table and the window; and sits down ruminatively.
    ROBERT, *half sitting on the end of the table, begins the friendly
    talk.*
ROBERT
    Now listen to me, Polly. I must talk to you like a father.   280
        POULENGEY *looks up at him gravely for a moment, but says
    nothing.*
ROBERT
    It's about this girl you are interested in. Now, I have seen her. I
    have talked to her. First, she's mad. That doesnt matter. Second,   285
    she's not a farm wench. She's a bourgeoise. That matters a good
    deal. I know her class exactly. Her father came here last year to
    represent his village in a lawsuit: he is one of their notables. A
    farmer. Not a gentleman farmer: he makes money by it, and
    lives by it. Still, not a laborer. Not a mechanic. He might have a   290
    cousin a lawyer, or in the Church. People of this sort may be of
    no account socially; but they can give a lot of bother to the
    authorities. That is to say, to *me*. Now no doubt it seems to you
    a very simple thing to take this girl away, humbugging her into
    the belief that you are taking her to the Dauphin. But if you get   295
    her into trouble, you may get *me* into no end of a mess, as I am
    her father's lord, and responsible for her protection. So friends
    or no friends, Polly, hands off her.
POULENGEY [*with deliberate impressiveness*]
    I should as soon think of the Blessed Virgin herself in that way,   300
    as of this girl.
ROBERT [*coming off the table*]
    But she says you and Jack and Dick have offered to go with her.
    What for? You are not going to tell me that you take her crazy
    notion of going to the Dauphin seriously, are you?   305

---

286   *a bourgeoise* a deliberate anachronism, but Jacques D'Arc, Jeanne's father, was a peasant
     proprietor, so Baudricourt's gloss is a fair indication of his social standing. At her trial,
     Jeanne objected to being called a shepherd girl.

POULENGEY [*slowly*]

There is something about her. They are pretty foulmouthed
and foulminded down there in the guardroom, some of them.
But there hasnt been a word that has anything to do with her
being a woman. They have stopped swearing before her. There   310
is something. Something. It may be worth trying.

ROBERT

Oh, come, Polly! pull yourself together. Commonsense was
never your strong point; but this is a little too much. [*He
retreats disgustedly*]   315

POULENGEY [*unmoved*]

What is the good of commonsense? If we had any commonsense we should join the Duke of Burgundy and the English
king. They hold half the country, right down to the Loire. They
have Paris. They have this castle: you know very well that we had   320
to surrender it to the Duke of Bedford, and that you are only
holding it on parole. The Dauphin is in Chinon, like a rat in a
corner, except that he wont fight. We dont even know that he *is*
the Dauphin: his mother says he isnt; and she ought to know.
Think of that! the queen denying the legitimacy of her own son!   325

ROBERT

Well, she married her daughter to the English king. Can you
blame the woman?

POULENGEY

I blame nobody. But thanks to her, the Dauphin is down and   330
out; and we may as well face it. The English will take Orleans:
the Bastard will not be able to stop them.

ROBERT

He beat the English the year before last at Montargis. I was with
him.   335

318–19   *Duke . . . king* Philip of Burgundy's alliance with the English had enabled the extension of
        the rule of English Henry VI across the whole of France north of the Loire by 1429 (see Map,
        p. 2).

321   *Duke of Bedford* John, Regent of France, Henry VI's uncle

322   *parole* captive's pledge not to engage in hostile activity

325–30   *son! . . . Dauphin* SJ (son! And the old king was mad. Can you expect soldiers to fight for
        such a Dauphin when he has never been crowned king. The Dauphin LC)

327   *English king* The king here is Henry V, victor of Agincourt (1415). By the Treaty of Troyes
        (1420), he married Catherine of France and gained reversion of the French throne on the
        death of Charles VI. His infant son, Henry VI, was proclaimed king of France in 1422, with
        the approval of his grandmother, the newly widowed Queen Isabeau.

332   *the Bastard* Jean, Count of Dunois

POULENGEY

No matter: his men are cowed now; and he cant work miracles. And I tell you that nothing can save our side now but a miracle.

ROBERT

Miracles are all right, Polly. The only difficulty about them is 340 that they dont happen nowadays.

POULENGEY

I used to think so. I am not so sure now. [*Rising and moving ruminatively towards the window*] At all events this is not a time to leave any stone unturned. There is something about the girl. 345

ROBERT

Oh! You think the girl can work miracles, do you?

POULENGEY

I think the girl herself is a bit of a miracle. Anyhow, she is the last card left in our hand. Better play her than throw up the 350 game. [*He wanders to the turret*]

ROBERT [*wavering*]

You really think that?

POULENGEY [*turning*]

Is there anything else left for us to think? 355

ROBERT [*going to him*]

Look here, Polly. If you were in my place would you let a girl like that do you out of sixteen francs for a horse?

POULENGEY

I will pay for the horse. 360

ROBERT

You will!

POULENGEY

Yes: I will back my opinion.

ROBERT 365

You will really gamble on a forlorn hope to the tune of sixteen francs?

POULENGEY

It is not a gamble.

ROBERT 370

What else is it?

POULENGEY

It is a certainty. Her words and her ardent faith in God have put fire into me.

ROBERT [*giving him up*] 375

Whew! You are as mad as she is.

POULENGEY [*obstinately*]

We want a few mad people now. See where the sane ones have landed us!

ROBERT [*his irresoluteness now openly swamping his affected*   380
decisiveness]

I shall feel like a precious fool. Still, if you feel sure –?

POULENGEY

I feel sure enough to take her to Chinon – unless you stop me.

ROBERT   385

This is not fair. You are putting the responsibility on me.

POULENGEY

It is on you whichever way you decide.

ROBERT

Yes: thats just it. Which way am I to decide? You dont see how   390
awkward this is for me. [*Snatching at a dilatory step with an
unconscious hope that* JOAN *will make up his mind for him*] Do
you think I ought to have another talk to her?

POULENGEY [*rising*]

Yes. [*He goes to the window and calls*] Joan!   395

JOAN'S VOICE

Will he let us go, Polly?

POULENGEY

Come up. Come in. [*Turning to* ROBERT] Shall I leave you with
her?   400

ROBERT

No: stay here; and back me up.

    POULENGEY *sits down on the chest.* ROBERT *goes back to his
magisterial chair, but remains standing to inflate himself more
imposingly.* JOAN *comes in, full of good news.*   405

JOAN

Jack will go halves for the horse.

ROBERT

Well!! [*He sits, deflated*]

POULENGEY [*gravely*]   410

Sit down, Joan.

JOAN [*checked a little, and looking to* ROBERT]

May I?

402–5 *No . . . imposingly* SJ (Well – er – No: I think not LC)
408–9 ROBERT *. . . deflated]* SJ

ROBERT

Do what you are told. 415

JOAN *curtsies and sits down on the stool between them.*
ROBERT *outfaces his perplexity with his most peremptory air.*

ROBERT

What is your name?

JOAN [*chattily*] 420

They always call me Jenny in Lorraine. Here in France I am
Joan. The soldiers call me The Maid.

ROBERT

What is your surname?

JOAN 425

Surname? What is that? My father sometimes calls himself
d'Arc; but I know nothing about it. You met my father. He –

ROBERT

Yes, yes; I remember. You come from Domrémy in Lorraine, I
think. 430

JOAN

Yes; but what does it matter? we all speak French.

ROBERT

Dont ask questions: answer them. How old are you?

JOAN 435

Seventeen: so they tell me. It might be nineteen. I dont remember.

ROBERT

What did you mean when you said that St Catherine and
St Margaret talked to you every day? 440

JOAN

They do.

ROBERT

What are they like?

JOAN [*suddenly obstinate*] 445

I will tell you nothing about that: they have not given me leave.

---

421 *Jenny in Lorraine* The depositions from Domrémy frequently use the diminutive
'Jeannette' (Murray, pp. 210–26).

432 *we all speak French* Domrémy, although French speaking, was not strictly French territory
in the early fifteenth century. This expression of Joan's nationalism was of particular significance in the aftermath of the First War when Lorraine, which with Alsace had been under
German occupation from 1870–1918, was returned to France.

ROBERT

But you actually see them; and they talk to you just as I am talking to you?

JOAN 450

No: it is quite different. I cannot tell you: you must not talk to me about my voices.

ROBERT

How do you mean? voices?

JOAN 455

I hear voices telling me what to do. They come from God.

ROBERT

They come from your imagination.

JOAN

Of course. That is how the messages of God come to us. 460

POULENGEY

Checkmate.

ROBERT

No fear! [*To* JOAN] So God says you are to raise the siege of Orleans? 465

JOAN

And to crown the Dauphin in Rheims Cathedral.

ROBERT [*gasping*]

Crown the D——! Gosh!

JOAN 470

And to make the English leave France.

ROBERT [*sarcastic*]

Anything else?

JOAN [*charming*]

Not just at present, thank you, squire. 475

ROBERT

I suppose you think raising a siege is as easy as chasing a cow out of a meadow. You think soldiering is anybody's job?

JOAN

I do not think it can be very difficult if God is on your side, and 480 you are willing to put your life in His hand. But many soldiers are very simple.

ROBERT [*grimly*]

Simple! Did you ever see English soldiers fighting?

462   *Checkmate* winning move in chess
464   *No fear!* SJ (Gammon! LC)

18

JOAN   485

They are only men. God made them just like us; but He gave
them their own country and their own language; and it is not
His will that they should come into our country and try to
speak our language.

ROBERT   490

Who has been putting such nonsense into your head? Dont you
know that soldiers are subject to their feudal lord, and that it is
nothing to them or to you whether he is the duke of Burgundy
or the king of England or the king of France? What has their
language to do with it?   495

JOAN

I do not understand that a bit. We are all subject to the King of
Heaven; and He gave us our countries and our languages, and
meant us to keep to them. If it were not so it would be murder
to kill an Englishman in battle; and you, squire, would be in   500
great danger of hell fire. You must not think about your duty to
your feudal lord, but about your duty to God.

POULENGEY

It's no use, Robert: she can choke you like that every time.

ROBERT   505

Can she, by Saint Dennis! We shall see. [To JOAN] We are not
talking about God: we are talking about practical affairs. I ask
you again, girl, have you ever seen English soldiers fighting?
Have you ever seen them plundering, burning, turning the
countryside into a desert? Have you heard no tales of their   510
Black Prince who was blacker than the devil himself, or of the
English king's father?

JOAN

You must not be afraid, Robert –

ROBERT   515

Damn you, I am not afraid. And who gave you leave to call me
Robert?

JOAN

You were called so in church in the name of our Lord. All the
other names are your father's or your brother's or anybody's.   520

506 *Saint Dennis* the patron saint of France
511 *Black Prince* Edward, eldest son of Edward III, victor at Poitiers in 1356 and captor of the
     French king, died before he could succeed. The throne passed to his son, Richard II.

ROBERT

Tcha!

JOAN

Listen to me, squire. At Domrémy we had to fly to the next village to escape from the English soldiers. Three of them were   525
left behind, wounded. I came to know these three poor goddams quite well. They had not half my strength.

ROBERT

Do you know why they are called goddams?

JOAN   530

No. Everyone calls them goddams.

ROBERT

It is because they are always calling on their God to condemn
their souls to perdition. That is what goddam means in their
language. How do you like it?   535

JOAN

God will be merciful to them; and they will act like His good
children when they go back to the country He made for them,
and made them for. I have heard the tales of the Black Prince.
The moment he touched the soil of our country the devil   540
entered into him, and made him a black fiend. But at home, in
the place made for him by God, he was good. It is always so. If I
went into England against the will of God to conquer England,
and tried to live there and speak its language, the devil would
enter into me; and when I was old I should shudder to remem-   545
ber the wickednesses I did.

ROBERT

Perhaps. But the more devil you were the better you might
fight. That is why the goddams will take Orleans. And you
cannot stop them, nor ten thousand like you.   550

JOAN

One thousand like me can stop them. Ten like me can stop
them with God on our side. [*She rises impetuously, and goes at
him, unable to sit quiet any longer*] You do not understand,

521–2   ROBERT *Tcha!* SJ, no interruption in LC
526–7   *goddams* Englishmen. This medieval slang, from the supposedly habitual oath 'God damn',
        appears as 'goddons' in Murray, p. 280.
552–3   *Ten . . . side* Cf. 'If I had to do it again, I'd do it with 10 or 15 of absolute faith. It does not
        matter how small you are if you have faith or a plan of action', Fidel Castro, on his Cuban
        Revolution (much quoted, including in *Observer*, 26 August 2007).
553–4   s.d. SJ

20

squire. Our soldiers are always beaten because they are fighting   555
only to save their skins; and the shortest way to save your skin
is to run away. Our knights are thinking only of the money they
will make in ransoms: it is not kill or be killed with them, but
pay or be paid. But I will teach them all to fight that the will of
God may be done in France; and then they will drive the poor   560
goddams before them like sheep. You and Polly will live to see
the day when there will not be an English soldier on the soil of
France; and there will be but one king there: not the feudal
English king, but God's French one.

ROBERT [*to* POULENGEY]   565
This may be all rot, Polly; but the troops might swallow it,
though nothing that we can say seems able to put any fight into
them. Even the Dauphin might swallow it. And if she can put
fight into him, she can put it into anybody.

POULENGEY   570
I can see no harm in trying. Can you? And there is something
about the girl –

ROBERT [*turning to* JOAN]
Now listen you to me; and [*desperately*] dont cut in before I
have time to think.   575

JOAN [*plumping down on the stool again, like an obedient schoolgirl*]
Yes, squire.

ROBERT
Your orders are, that you are to go to Chinon under the escort
of this gentleman and three of his friends.   580

JOAN [*radiant, clasping her hands*]
Oh, squire! Your head is all circled with light, like a saint's.

POULENGEY
How is she to get into the royal presence?

ROBERT [*who has looked up for his halo rather apprehensively*]   585
I dont know: how did she get into *my* presence? If the Dauphin
can keep her out he is a better man than I take him for. [*Rising*]
I will send her to Chinon; and she can say I sent her. Then let
come what may: I can do no more.

JOAN   590
And the dress? I may have a soldier's dress, maynt I, squire?

ROBERT
Have what you please. I wash my hands of it.

576   s.d. SJ (*rising and standing to attention* LC)

21

JOAN [*wildly excited by her success*]

Come, Polly. [*She dashes out*] 595

ROBERT [*shaking* POULENGEY's *hand*]

Goodbye, old man, I am taking a big chance. Few other men would have done it. But as you say, there is something about her.

POULENGEY 600

Yes: there is something about her. Goodbye. [*He goes out*]

ROBERT, *still very doubtful whether he has not been made a fool of by a crazy female, and a social inferior to boot, scratches his head and slowly comes back from the door.*

THE STEWARD *runs in with a basket.* 605

STEWARD

Sir, sir –

ROBERT

What now?

STEWARD 610

The hens are laying like mad, sir. Five dozen eggs!

ROBERT [*stiffens convulsively: crosses himself: and forms with his pale lips the words*]

Christ in heaven! [*Aloud but breathless*] She *did* come from God.

597–8   *Few . . . it* SJ (But we are in for it anyhow LC)
   603   s.d. *to boot* also
610–14 Like Taylor, Shaw ends his first scene with an invented domestic miracle, as he acknowledged in his 1924 programme note, BH, p. 213.
   614   *She did come from God* In his proposed film script, Shaw inserted between Scenes I and II a sequence of horsemen riding 'practically in silhouette' against a setting sun as 'church bells sound' (see Dukore). Such an insertion is one of the most striking sequences of Otto Preminger's 1957 film.

SCENE II

Chinon, in Touraine. An end of the throne room in the castle, curtained off to make an antechamber. THE ARCHBISHOP OF RHEIMS, *close on 50, a full-fed prelate with nothing of the ecclesiastic about him except his imposing bearing, and* THE LORD CHAMBERLAIN, MONSEIGNEUR DE LA TRÉMOUILLE, *a monstrous arrogant wineskin of a man, are waiting for* THE DAUPHIN. *There is a door in the wall to the right of the two men. It is late in the afternoon on the 8th of March, 1429.* THE ARCHBISHOP *stands with dignity whilst* THE CHAMBERLAIN, *on his left, fumes about in the worst of tempers.*

LA TRÉMOUILLE

What the devil does the Dauphin mean by keeping us waiting like this? I dont know how you have the patience to stand there like a stone idol.

THE ARCHBISHOP

You see, I am an archbishop; and an archbishop is a sort of idol. At any rate he has to learn to keep still and suffer fools patiently. Besides, my dear Lord Chamberlain, it is the Dauphin's royal privilege to keep you waiting, is it not?

LA TRÉMOUILLE

Dauphin be damned! saving your reverence. Do you know how much money he owes me?

THE ARCHBISHOP

Much more than he owes me, I have no doubt, because you are a much richer man. But I take it he owes you all you could afford to lend him. That is what he owes me.

LA TRÉMOUILLE

Twenty-seven thousand: that was his last haul. A cool twenty-seven thousand!

---

0   *Scene II* SJ (Act II, sc i. LC)
1–392 Scene II, like Scenes I and III, begins with discussion before Joan's entrance which sets the scene but, here, also functions as a 'separation scene', allowing time for Joan's costume change from the dress of Scene I to armour and cropped hair. Barbara Jefford, the Old Vic's Joan (London, 1960), noted that Shaw 'gives her the rests at the right times, so that you've got time to settle down before you attack the big scenes' (Hill, p. 84).
1–2 s.d. *curtained ... antechamber* a 'carpenter's scene' common in nineteenth-century illusionist theatre, which allowed an elaborate scene to be set on the full stage while a brief exchange happened on the forestage

THE ARCHBISHOP

What becomes of it all? He never has a suit of clothes that I   30
would throw to a curate.

LA TRÉMOUILLE

He dines on a chicken or a scrap of mutton. He borrows my
last penny; and there is nothing to shew for it. [A PAGE *appears
in the doorway*] At last!   35

THE PAGE

No, my lord: it is not His Majesty. Monsieur de Rais is
approaching.

LA TRÉMOUILLE

Young Bluebeard! Why announce *him*?   40

THE PAGE

Captain La Hire is with him. Something has happened, I think.

GILLES DE RAIS, *a young man of 25, very smart and self-
possessed, and sporting the extravagance of a little curled beard
dyed blue at a clean-shaven court, comes in. He is determined to   45
make himself agreeable, but lacks natural joyousness, and is not
really pleasant. In fact when he defies the Church some eleven
years later he is accused of trying to extract pleasure from horrible
cruelties, and hanged. So far, however, there is no shadow of the
gallows on him. He advances gaily to* THE ARCHBISHOP. THE   50
PAGE *withdraws*.

BLUEBEARD

Your faithful lamb, Archbishop. Good day, my lord. Do you
know what has happened to La Hire?

LA TRÉMOUILLE   55

He has sworn himself into a fit, perhaps.

BLUEBEARD

No: just the opposite. Foul Mouthed Frank, the only man in
Touraine who could beat him at swearing, was told by a soldier
that he shouldnt use such language when he was at the point of   60
death.

THE ARCHBISHOP

Nor at any other point. But *was* Foul Mouthed Frank on the
point of death?

---

34   s.d. A PAGE The three page roles, initially played by three different actors, among them
Jo Mielziner in New York and Jack Hawkins in London, have in subsequent productions
more usually been taken by the same actor. Shaw instructed the BBC (radio production,
1942), 'dont give the part to a woman . . . He must be a real boy' (L4, p. 626).

34–5   s.d. *appears in the doorway* SJ (*enters* LC)

BLUEBEARD   65

Yes: he has just fallen into a well and been drowned. La Hire is
frightened out of his wits.

CAPTAIN LA HIRE *comes in: a war dog with no court man-*
ners and pronounced camp ones.

BLUEBEARD   70

I have just been telling the Chamberlain and the Archbishop.
The Archbishop says you are a lost man.

LA HIRE [*striding past* BLUEBEARD, *and planting himself between*
THE ARCHBISHOP *and* LA TRÉMOUILLE]

This is nothing to joke about. It is worse than we thought. It   75
was not a soldier, but an angel dressed as a soldier.

THE ARCHBISHOP ⎫
THE CHAMBERLAIN ⎬ [*exclaiming all together*] An angel!
BLUEBEARD ⎭

LA HIRE   80

Yes, an angel. She has made her way from Champagne with half
a dozen men through the thick of everything: Burgundians,
Goddams, deserters, robbers, and Lord knows who; and they
never met a soul except the country folk. I know one of them:
de Poulengey. He says she's an angel. If ever I utter an oath   85
again may my soul be blasted to eternal damnation!

THE ARCHBISHOP

A very pious beginning, Captain.

BLUEBEARD *and* LA TRÉMOUILLE *laugh at him.* THE PAGE
returns.   90

THE PAGE

His Majesty.

They stand perfunctorily at court attention. THE DAUPHIN,
aged 26, really KING CHARLES THE SEVENTH *since the death of*
his father, but as yet uncrowned, comes in through the curtains   95
with a paper in his hands. He is a poor creature physically; and

93   s.d. DAUPHIN Shaw, who thought Ernest Thesiger perfect in the role (London, 1924, and
     Malvern, 1936), advised the Theatre Guild (for New York production, 1923) it needed 'a
     comedian who can be at the same time a credible zany and a credible scion of the House of
     Valois' (L3, p. 586). Others who have taken the role with distinction include Georges Pitoëff
     (Paris, 1925); Max Adrian (BBC TV, 1951); and, in London, Alex McCowen (Old Vic, 1960)
     and Paul Ready (NT, 2007).

the current fashion of shaving closely, and hiding every scrap of
hair under the headcovering or headdress, both by women and
men, makes the worst of his appearance. He has little narrow eyes,
near together, a long pendulous nose that droops over his thick   100
short upper lip, and the expression of a young dog accustomed to
be kicked, yet incorrigible and irrepressible. But he is neither
vulgar nor stupid; and he has a cheeky humor which enables him
to hold his own in conversation. Just at present he is excited, like a
child with a new toy. He comes to THE ARCHBISHOP's *left hand.*   105

   BLUEBEARD *and* LA HIRE *retire towards the curtains.*

CHARLES

   Oh, Archbishop, do you know what Robert de Baudricourt is
   sending me from Vaucouleurs?

THE ARCHBISHOP [*contemptuously*]   110

   I am not interested in the newest toys.

CHARLES [*indignantly*]

   It isnt a toy. [*Sulkily*] However, I can get on very well without
   your interest.

THE ARCHBISHOP   115

   Your Highness is taking offence very unnecessarily.

CHARLES

   Thank you. You are always ready with a lecture, arnt you?

LA TRÉMOUILLE [*roughly*]

   Enough grumbling. What have you got there?   120

CHARLES

   What is that to you?

LA TRÉMOUILLE

   It is my business to know what is passing between you and the
   garrison at Vaucouleurs. [*He snatches the paper from* THE   125
   DAUPHIN's *hand, and begins reading it with some difficulty, fol-*
   lowing the words with his finger and spelling them out syllable by
   syllable]

97–9   s.d. *current . . . appearance* 'his portrait allows that his hair was completely concealed by
       the fashion of the time, giving him a curiously starved and bald appearance' (L3, p. 863). In
       1923, too, younger men tended to be clean-shaven, although Shaw, like many of his genera-
       tion, maintained a notable beard.

102   s.d. *irrepressible* SJ (*irrepressible. His small rickety figure and spindle shanks make it*
       impossible for him to achieve the dignity of bearing proper to his exalted position LC)

126–8 s.d. *following . . . by syllable* It was not uncommon for medieval aristocracy to be illiterate.
       Clerks were employed to read and write for them.

CHARLES [*mortified*]

You all think you can treat me as you please because I owe you   130
money, and because I am no good at fighting. But I have the
blood royal in my veins.

THE ARCHBISHOP

Even that has been questioned, your Highness. One hardly rec-
ognizes in you the grandson of Charles the Wise.   135

CHARLES

I want to hear no more of my grandfather. He was so wise that
he used up the whole family stock of wisdom for five genera-
tions, and left me the poor fool I am, bullied and insulted by all
of you.   140

THE ARCHBISHOP

Control yourself, sir. These outbursts of petulance are not
seemly.

CHARLES

Another lecture! Thank you. What a pity it is that though you   145
are an archbishop saints and angels dont come to see *you*!

THE ARCHBISHOP

What do you mean?

CHARLES

Aha! Ask that bully there [*pointing to* LA TRÉMOUILLE].   150

LA TRÉMOUILLE [*furious*]

Hold your tongue. Do you hear?

CHARLES

Oh, I hear. You neednt shout. The whole castle can hear. Why
dont you go and shout at the English, and beat them for me?   155

LA TRÉMOUILLE [*raising his fist*]

You young –

CHARLES [*running behind* THE ARCHBISHOP]

Dont you raise your hand to me. It's high treason.

LA HIRE   160

Steady, Duke! Steady!

THE ARCHBISHOP [*resolutely*]

Come, come! this will not do. My Lord Chamberlain: please! please!
we must keep some sort of order. [*To* THE DAUPHIN] And you,
sir: if you cannot rule your kingdom, at least try to rule yourself.   165

135   *Charles the Wise* one of the more successful Valois kings. As Charles V (1364–80), he fortified towns, gradually reconquering land and cities lost to the English; established a strong
navy; collected a huge and valuable library, and instituted building works, including extensive renovation of his palace, the Louvre.

CHARLES

Another lecture! Thank you.

LA TRÉMOUILLE [*handing over the paper to* THE ARCHBISHOP]

Here: read the accursed thing for me. He has sent the blood
boiling into my head: I cant distinguish the letters. 170

CHARLES [*coming back and peering round* LA TRÉMOUILLE'*s left
shoulder*]

I will read it for you if you like. I *can* read, you know.

LA TRÉMOUILLE [*with intense contempt, not at all stung by the taunt*]

Yes: reading is about all you are fit for. Can you make it out, 175
Archbishop?

THE ARCHBISHOP

I should have expected more commonsense from De Baudricourt.
He is sending some cracked country lass here –

CHARLES [*interrupting*] 180

No: he is sending a saint: an angel. And she is coming to me: to
me, the king, and not to you, Archbishop, holy as you are. She
knows the blood royal if you dont. [*He struts up to the curtains
between* BLUEBEARD *and* LA HIRE]

THE ARCHBISHOP 185

You cannot be allowed to see this crazy wench.

CHARLES [*turning*]

But I am the king; and I will.

LA TRÉMOUILLE [*brutally*]

Then she cannot be allowed to see *you.* Now! 190

CHARLES

I tell you I will. I am going to put my foot down –

BLUEBEARD [*laughing at him*]

Naughty! What would your wise grandfather say?

CHARLES 195

That just shews your ignorance, Bluebeard. My grandfather had
a saint who used to float in the air when she was praying, and
told him everything he wanted to know. My poor father had two
saints, Marie de Maillé and the Gasque of Avignon. It is in our
family; and I dont care what you say: I will have my saint too. 200

175   *reading . . . for* The implication is that Charles is no better than a clerk, whose literacy
would be employed by the higher orders as a service.

198–9   *My . . . Avignon* Charles VI was intermittently insane in the latter part of his reign. His
'saints' were both contemporary. Jeanne-Marie de Maillé was revered for her chastity and
selling her goods to ransom her husband. In widowhood, her humility and holiness
attracted pilgrims to Tours. Marie Robine, the Gasque of Avignon, a visionary rather than a
saint, prophesied that France would be restored by an armed virgin from Lorraine.

THE ARCHBISHOP

This creature is not a saint. She is not even a respectable
woman. She does not wear women's clothes. She is dressed like
a soldier, and rides round the country with soldiers. Do you
suppose such a person can be admitted to your Highness's   205
court?

LA HIRE

Stop. [*Going to* THE ARCHBISHOP] Did you say a girl in armor,
like a soldier?

THE ARCHBISHOP   210

So De Baudricourt describes her.

LA HIRE

But by all the devils in hell – Oh, God forgive me, what am I
saying? – by Our Lady and all the saints, this must be the angel
that struck Foul Mouthed Frank dead for swearing.   215

CHARLES [*triumphant*]

You see! A miracle!

LA HIRE

She may strike the lot of us dead if we cross her. For Heaven's
sake, Archbishop, be careful what you are doing.   220

THE ARCHBISHOP [*severely*]

Rubbish! Nobody has been struck dead. A drunken blackguard
who has been rebuked a hundred times for swearing has fallen
into a well, and been drowned. A mere coincidence.

LA HIRE   225

I do not know what a coincidence is. I do know that the man is
dead, and that she told him he was going to die.

THE ARCHBISHOP

We are all going to die, Captain.

LA HIRE [*crossing himself*]   230

I hope not. [*He backs out of the conversation*]

BLUEBEARD

We can easily find out whether she is an angel or not. Let us
arrange when she comes that I shall be the Dauphin, and see
whether she will find me out.   235

CHARLES

Yes: I agree to that. If she cannot find the blood royal I will have
nothing to do with her.

233   *We . . . not* SJ (Give the saint a chance LC)

29

THE ARCHBISHOP

It is for the Church to make saints: let De Baudricourt mind his   240
own business, and not dare usurp the function of his priest. I
say the girl shall not be admitted.

BLUEBEARD

But, Archbishop –

THE ARCHBISHOP [*sternly*]   245

I speak in the Church's name. [*To* THE DAUPHIN] Do you dare
say she shall?

CHARLES [*intimidated but sulky*]

Oh, if you make it an excommunication matter, I have nothing
more to say, of course. But you havnt read the end of the letter.   250
De Baudricourt says she will raise the siege of Orleans, and beat
the English for us.

LA TRÉMOUILLE

Rot!

CHARLES   255

Well, will *you* save Orleans for us, with all your bullying?

LA TRÉMOUILLE [*savagely*]

Do not throw that in my face again: do you hear? I have done
more fighting than you ever did or ever will. But I cannot be
everywhere.   260

THE DAUPHIN

Well, thats something.

BLUEBEARD [*coming between* THE ARCHBISHOP *and* CHARLES]

You have Jack Dunois at the head of your troops in Orleans: the
brave Dunois, the handsome Dunois, the wonderful invincible   265
Dunois, the darling of all the ladies, the beautiful bastard. Is it
likely that the country lass can do what he cannot do?

CHARLES

Why doesnt he raise the siege, then?

LA HIRE   270

The wind is against him.

BLUEBEARD

How can the wind hurt him at Orleans? It is not on the Channel.

243–5   BLUEBEARD . . . *sternly* SJ
246–9   *I . . . matter* The medieval church, representing God on earth, claimed authority over
        terrestrial rulers, who could be excommunicated for disobedience (excluded from the
        church, and hence the prospect of salvation).
273   *the Channel* the sea between England and France, where a contrary wind would prevent a
        fleet's crossing

LA HIRE

It is on the river Loire; and the English hold the bridgehead. He   275
must ship his men across the river and upstream, if he is to take
them in the rear. Well, he cannot, because there is a devil of a
wind blowing the other way. He is tired of paying the priests to
pray for a west wind. What he needs is a miracle. You tell me
that what the girl did to Foul Mouthed Frank was no miracle.   280
No matter: it finished Frank. If she changes the wind for
Dunois, that may not be a miracle either; but it may finish the
English. What harm is there in trying?

THE ARCHBISHOP [*who has read the end of the letter and become
more thoughtful*]   285

It is true that De Baudricourt seems extraordinarily impressed.

LA HIRE

De Baudricourt is a blazing ass; but he is a soldier; and if he
thinks she can beat the English, all the rest of the army will
think so too.   290

LA TRÉMOUILLE [*to* THE ARCHBISHOP, *who is hesitating*]

Oh, let them have their way. Dunois' men will give up the town
in spite of him if somebody does not put some fresh spunk into
them.

THE ARCHBISHOP   295

The Church must examine the girl before anything decisive is
done about her. However, since his Highness desires it, let her
attend the Court.

LA HIRE

I will find her and tell her. [*He goes out*]   300

CHARLES

Come with me, Bluebeard; and let us arrange so that she will
not know who I am. You will pretend to be me. [*He goes out
through the curtains*]

BLUEBEARD   305

Pretend to be that thing! Holy Michael! [*He follows* THE
DAUPHIN]

LA TRÉMOUILLE

I wonder will she pick him out!

---

293   *spunk* courage
296   *The Church must examine* The medieval church claimed jurisdiction over men's souls
      and, therefore, the right to judge them. Jeanne was subjected to lengthy examination before
      being admitted to Charles' presence.

THE ARCHBISHOP 310

Of course she will.

LA TRÉMOUILLE

Why? How is she to know?

THE ARCHBISHOP

She will know what everybody in Chinon knows: that the 315
Dauphin is the meanest-looking and worst-dressed figure in
the Court, and that the man with the blue beard is Gilles de
Rais.

LA TRÉMOUILLE

I never thought of that. 320

THE ARCHBISHOP

You are not so accustomed to miracles as I am. It is part of my
profession.

LA TRÉMOUILLE [puzzled and a little scandalized]

But that would not be a miracle at all. 325

THE ARCHBISHOP [calmly]

Why not?

LA TRÉMOUILLE

Well, come! what is a miracle?

THE ARCHBISHOP 330

A miracle, my friend, is an event which creates faith. That is the
purpose and nature of miracles. They may seem very wonderful to the people who witness them, and very simple to those
who perform them. That does not matter: if they confirm or
create faith they are true miracles. 335

LA TRÉMOUILLE

Even when they are frauds, do you mean?

THE ARCHBISHOP

Frauds deceive. An event which creates faith does not deceive:
therefore it is not a fraud, but a miracle. 340

LA TRÉMOUILLE [scratching his neck in his perplexity]

Well, I suppose as you are an archbishop you must be right. It
seems a bit fishy to me. But I am no churchman, and dont
understand these matters.

THE ARCHBISHOP 345

You are not a churchman; but you are a diplomatist and a soldier. Could you make our citizens pay war taxes, or our soldiers
sacrifice their lives, if they knew what is really happening
instead of what seems to them to be happening?

LA TRÉMOUILLE   350

No, by Saint Dennis: the fat would be in the fire before sundown.

THE ARCHBISHOP

Would it not be quite easy to tell them the truth?

LA TRÉMOUILLE

Man alive, they wouldnt believe it.   355

THE ARCHBISHOP

Just so. Well, the Church has to rule men for the good of their
souls as you have to rule them for the good of their bodies. To do
that, the Church must do as you do: nourish their faith by poetry.

LA TRÉMOUILLE   360

Poetry! I should call it humbug.

THE ARCHBISHOP

You would be wrong, my friend. Parables are not lies because
they describe events that have never happened. Miracles are not
frauds because they are often – I do not say always – very simple   365
and innocent contrivances by which the priest fortifies the faith
of his flock. When this girl picks out the Dauphin among his
courtiers, it will not be a miracle for me, because I shall know
how it has been done, and my faith will not be increased. But as
for the others, if they feel the thrill of the supernatural, and   370
forget their sinful clay in a sudden sense of the glory of God, it
will be a miracle and a blessed one. And you will find that the
girl herself will be more affected than anyone else. She will
forget how she really picked him out. So, perhaps, will you.

LA TRÉMOUILLE   375

Well, I wish I were clever enough to know how much of you is
God's archbishop and how much the most artful fox in
Touraine. Come on, or we shall be late for the fun; and I want
to see it, miracle or no miracle.

THE ARCHBISHOP [*detaining him a moment*]   380

Do not think that I am a lover of crooked ways. There is a new
spirit rising in men: we are at the dawning of a wider epoch. If I
were a simple monk, and had not to rule men, I should seek
peace for my spirit with Aristotle and Pythagoras rather than
with the saints and their miracles.   385

---

371   *clay* the physical body
381–5 *new . . . miracles* With a proleptic reference to the coming Reformation, the Archbishop
       acknowledges the power over a meditative mind of the rationalism of such Ancient Greek
       philosophers as Aristotle and Pythagoras.

LA TRÉMOUILLE

And who the deuce was Pythagoras?

THE ARCHBISHOP

A sage who held that the earth is round, and that it moves round the sun.   390

LA TRÉMOUILLE

What an utter fool! Couldnt he use his eyes?

They go out together through the curtains, which are presently withdrawn, revealing the full depth of the throne room with THE COURT *assembled. On the right are two Chairs of State on a dais.*   395 BLUEBEARD *is standing theatrically on the dais, playing the king, and, like* THE COURTIERS, *enjoying the joke rather obviously. There is a curtained arch in the wall behind the dais; but the main door, guarded by men-at-arms, is at the other side of the room; and a clear path across is kept and lined by* THE COURTIERS.   400 CHARLES *is in this path in the middle of the room.* LA HIRE *is on his right.* THE ARCHBISHOP, *on his left, has taken his place by the dais:* LA TRÉMOUILLE *at the other side of it.* THE DUCHESS DE LA TRÉMOUILLE, *pretending to be the Queen, sits in the Consort's chair, with a group of* LADIES IN WAITING *close by,*   405 *behind* THE ARCHBISHOP.

The chatter of THE COURTIERS *makes such a noise that nobody notices the appearance of* THE PAGE *at the door.*

THE PAGE

The Duke of – [*Nobody listens*] The Duke of – [*The chatter con-*   410 *tinues. Indignant at his failure to command a hearing, he snatches the halberd of the nearest man-at-arms, and thumps the floor with it. The chatter ceases; and everybody looks at him in silence*] Attention! [*He restores the halberd to the man-at-arms*] The Duke of Vendôme presents Joan the Maid to his Majesty.   415

CHARLES [*putting his finger on his lip*]

Ssh! [*He hides behind the nearest* COURTIER, *peering out to see what happens*]

394–5   s.d. THE COURT *assembled* The curtain opens on a carefully-blocked scene in full progress. On the proscenium arch stage, the curtain must remain closed long enough to enable the actors who have just exited to assemble in position. On a revolving stage (e.g. NT, 1983), the Archbishop and La Trémouille walk into place as the Chinon set comes into view, demonstrating Shaw's comment that a revolve 'would have come in very handy for Joan' (L3, p. 862). On more open stages, regal banners have been let down and courtiers entered talking while attendants carried on the throne.

395   s.d. *dais* raised platform

403   s.d. DUCHESS Recent productions (Canadian Shaw Festival and NT, 2007) have cut this role.

412   s.d. *halberd* a weapon, combining spear and axe-shaped head, also used ceremonially, as here

BLUEBEARD [*majestically*]

Let her approach the throne.   420

    JOAN, *dressed as a soldier, with her hair bobbed and hanging thickly round her face, is led in by a bashful and speechless* NOBLEMAN, *from whom she detaches herself to stop and look around eagerly for* THE DAUPHIN.

THE DUCHESS [*to the nearest* LADY IN WAITING]   425

My dear! Her hair!

    ALL THE LADIES *explode in uncontrollable laughter.*

BLUEBEARD [*trying not to laugh, and waving his hand in deprecation of their merriment*]

Ssh—ssh! Ladies! Ladies!!   430

JOAN [*not at all embarrassed*]

I wear it like this because I am a soldier. Where be Dauphin?

    A titter runs through THE COURT *as she walks to the dais.*

BLUEBEARD [*condescendingly*]

You are in the presence of the Dauphin.   435

    JOAN *looks at him sceptically for a moment, scanning him hard up and down to make sure. Dead silence, all watching her. Fun dawns in her face.*

JOAN

Coom, Bluebeard! Thou canst not fool me. Where be Dauphin?   440

    A roar of laughter breaks out as GILLES, *with a gesture of surrender, joins in the laugh, and jumps down from the dais beside* LA TRÉMOUILLE. JOAN, *also on the broad grin, turns back, searching along the row of* COURTIERS, *and presently makes a dive, and drags out* CHARLES *by the arm.*   445

JOAN [*releasing him and bobbing him a little curtsey*]

Gentle little Dauphin, I am sent to you to drive the English away from Orleans and from France, and to crown you king in the cathedral at Rheims, where all true kings of France are crowned.

---

421   s.d. *her hair bobbed* Jeanne famously cut off her hair. By specifying a 'bob' and the shocked reaction of the Duchess and her ladies to it, Shaw mocks the hair style newly fashionable among advanced young women ('flappers') of 1923. Scott Fitzgerald's story 'Bernice Bobs Her Hair' had been published in 1922.

422–4 s.d. *is . . .* DAUPHIN SJ (*enters. She stops to take in the scene and find the Dauphin* LC)

447–9 *Gentle . . . crowned* ' "Gentle Dauphin", she replied, "I am called Jeanne the Maid; and the King of Heaven sends you word by me that you will be consecrated and crowned at Rheims, and that you will be the lieutenant of the King of Heaven, who is King of France" ' (Murray, pp. 269–70).

CHARLES [*triumphant, to* THE COURT]   450
    You see, all of you: she knew the blood royal. Who dare say now
    that I am not my father's son? [*To* JOAN] But if you want me to
    be crowned at Rheims you must talk to the Archbishop, not to
    me. There he is [*he is standing behind her*]!

JOAN [*turning quickly, overwhelmed with emotion*]   455
    Oh, my lord! [*She falls on both knees before him, with bowed
    head, not daring to look up*] My lord: I am only a poor country
    girl; and you are filled with the blessedness and glory of God
    Himself; but you will touch me with your hands, and give me
    your blessing, wont you?   460

BLUEBEARD [*whispering to* LA TRÉMOUILLE]
    The old fox blushes.

LA TRÉMOUILLE
    Another miracle!

THE ARCHBISHOP [*touched, putting his hand on her head*]   465
    Child: you are in love with religion.

JOAN [*startled: looking up at him*]
    Am I? I never thought of that. Is there any harm in it?

THE ARCHBISHOP
    There is no harm in it, my child. But there is danger.   470

JOAN [*rising, with a sunflush of reckless happiness irradiating her face*]
    There is always danger, except in heaven. Oh, my lord, you have
    given me such strength, such courage. It must be a most won-
    derful thing to be Archbishop.

    THE COURT *smiles broadly: even titters a little.*   475

THE ARCHBISHOP [*drawing himself up sensitively*]
    Gentlemen: your levity is rebuked by this maid's faith. I am,
    God help me, all unworthy; but your mirth is a deadly sin.
    Their faces fall. Dead silence.

BLUEBEARD   480
    My lord: we were laughing at her, not at you.

THE ARCHBISHOP
    What? Not at my unworthiness but at her faith! Gilles de Rais:
    this maid prophesied that the blasphemer should be drowned
    in his sin –   485

JOAN [*distressed*]
    No!

THE ARCHBISHOP [*silencing her by a gesture*]
    I prophesy now that you will be hanged in yours if you do not
    learn when to laugh and when to pray.   490

36

BLUEBEARD

My lord: I stand rebuked. I am sorry: I can say no more. But if
you prophesy that I shall be hanged, I shall never be able to
resist temptation, because I shall always be telling myself that I
may as well be hanged for a sheep as a lamb.   495

THE COURTIERS *take heart at this. There is more tittering.*

JOAN [*scandalized*]

You are an idle fellow, Bluebeard; and you have great impudence to answer the Archbishop.

LA HIRE [*with a huge chuckle*]   500

Well said, lass! Well said!

JOAN [*impatiently to* THE ARCHBISHOP]

Oh, my lord, will you send all these silly folks away so that I
may speak to the Dauphin alone?

LA HIRE [*goodhumoredly*]   505

I can take a hint. [*He salutes; turns on his heel; and goes out*]

THE ARCHBISHOP

Come, gentlemen. The Maid comes with God's blessing, and
must be obeyed.

THE COURTIERS *withdraw, some through the arch, others at*   510
the opposite side. THE ARCHBISHOP *marches across to the door,*
followed by THE DUCHESS *and* LA TRÉMOUILLE. *As* THE
ARCHBISHOP *passes* JOAN, *she falls on her knees, and kisses the*
hem of his robe fervently. He shakes his head in instinctive remon-
strance; gathers the robe from her; and goes out. She is left   515
kneeling directly in THE DUCHESS*'s way.*

THE DUCHESS [*coldly*]

Will you allow me to pass, please?

JOAN [*hastily rising, and standing back*]

Beg pardon, maam, I am sure.   520

THE DUCHESS *passes on.* JOAN *stares after her; then whispers*
to THE DAUPHIN.

JOAN

Be that Queen?

CHARLES   525

No. She thinks she is.

494–5   *I may . . . lamb* since the penalty is the same, I may as well commit the more serious crime
         (proverbial): a nod to Bluebeard's future crimes and reputation
503   *folks* SJ (people LC)

JOAN [*again staring after* THE DUCHESS]

    Oo-oo-ooh! [*Her awestruck amazement at the figure cut by the magnificently dressed lady is not wholly complimentary*]

LA TRÉMOUILLE [*very surly*]   530

    I'll trouble your Highness not to gibe at my wife. [*He goes out. The others have already gone*]

JOAN [*to* THE DAUPHIN]

    Who be old Gruff-and-Grum?

CHARLES   535

    He is the Duke de la Trémouille.

JOAN

    What be his job?

CHARLES

    He pretends to command the army. And whenever I find a   540
friend I can care for, he kills him.

JOAN

    Why dost let him?

CHARLES [*petulantly moving to the throne side of the room to escape from her magnetic field*]   545

    How can I prevent him? He bullies me. They all bully me.

JOAN

    Art afraid?

CHARLES

    Yes: I am afraid. It's no use preaching to me about it. It's all very   550
well for these big men with their armor that is too heavy for
me, and their swords that I can hardly lift, and their muscle and
their shouting and their bad tempers. They like fighting: most
of them are making fools of themselves all the time they are not
fighting; but I am quiet and sensible; and I dont want to kill   555
people: I only want to be left alone to enjoy myself in my own
way. I never asked to be a king: it was pushed on me. So if you
are going to say 'Son of St Louis: gird on the sword of your
ancestors, and lead us to victory' you may spare your breath to

540   *pretends to command* SJ (commands LC)
552   *swords . . . lift* Charles' feebleness foregrounds Joan's easy wielding of the sword at the end
      of the scene (ll. 698–9).
555   *I am quiet and sensible; and* ms rev.
557   *I . . . me* ms rev.
558   *St Louis* Louis IX, ruled 1226–70. Both a spiritual and a temporal leader, he imposed order
      on his own nobles and oversaw the introduction of the Inquisition into France. He died of
      plague while on his second crusade and was canonised in 1297.
559–60 *spare . . . porridge* keep quiet (idiomatic)

cool your porridge; for I cannot do it. I am not built that way; 560
and there is an end of it.

JOAN [*trenchant and masterful*]

Blethers! We are all like that to begin with. I shall put courage
into thee.

CHARLES 565

But I dont want to have courage put into me. I want to sleep in
a comfortable bed, and not live in continual terror of being
killed or wounded. Put courage into the others, and let them
have their bellyful of fighting; but let me alone.

JOAN 570

It's no use, Charlie: thou must face what God puts on thee. If
thou fail to make thyself king, thoult be a beggar: what else art
fit for? Come! Let me see thee sitting on the throne. I have
looked forward to that.

CHARLES 575

What is the good of sitting on the throne when the other fellows give all the orders? However! [*he sits enthroned, a piteous
figure*] here is the king for you! Look your fill at the poor devil.

JOAN

Thourt not king yet, lad: thourt but Dauphin. Be not led away 580
by them around thee. Dressing up dont fill empty noddle. I
know the people: the real people that make thy bread for thee;
and I tell thee they count no man king of France until the holy
oil has been poured on his hair, and himself consecrated and
crowned in Rheims Cathedral. And thou needs new clothes, 585
Charlie. Why does not Queen look after thee properly?

CHARLES

We're too poor. She wants all the money we can spare to put on
her own back. Besides, I like to see her beautifully dressed; and
I dont care what I wear myself: I should look ugly anyhow. 590

JOAN

There is some good in thee, Charlie; but it is not yet a king's good.

---

563   *Blethers* Nonsense (a stronger oath would have been censored in 1924)
571–85   *It's . . . Cathedral* ms rev., September, 1923
581   *noddle* head
583–5   *holy . . . Cathedral* Anointing was believed to confer God's authority. The 'Sacred Ampoule'
used in Rheims for French coronations reputedly contained oil brought by a dove from
heaven for the coronation of Clovis in 496. Cf. 'RICHARD: Not all the water in the rough
rude sea / Can wash the balm from an anointed king' (*Richard II*, 3.2.54–5). Anointing is
still part of the British coronation ceremony.

CHARLES

We shall see. I am not such a fool as I look. I have my eyes
open; and I can tell you that one good treaty is worth ten good   595
fights. These fighting fellows lose all on the treaties that they
gain on the fights. If we can only have a treaty, the English are
sure to have the worst of it, because they are better at fighting
than at thinking.

JOAN   600

If the English win, it is they that will make the treaty; and then
God help poor France! Thou must fight, Charlie, whether thou
will or no. I will go first to hearten thee. We must take our
courage in both hands: aye, and pray for it with both hands too.

CHARLES [*descending from his throne and again crossing the room*   605
to escape from her dominating urgency]

Oh do stop talking about God and praying. I cant bear people
who are always praying. Isnt it bad enough to have to do it at
the proper times?

JOAN [*pitying him*]   610

Thou poor child, thou hast never prayed in thy life. I must
teach thee from the beginning.

CHARLES

I am not a child: I am a grown man and a father; and I will not
be taught any more.   615

JOAN

Aye, you have a little son. He that will be Louis the Eleventh
when you die. Would you not fight for him?

CHARLES

No: a horrid boy. He hates me. He hates everybody, selfish little   620
beast! I dont want to be bothered with children. I dont want to
be a father; and I dont want to be a son: especially a son of
St Louis. I dont want to be any of these fine things you all have
your heads full of: I want to be just what I am. Why cant you
mind your own business, and let me mind mine?   625

595–7   *one . . . fights* These words, written so soon after the disasters of the Great War, of which
Shaw had been a notorious opponent, and the ill-founded Treaty of Versailles, of which he
was a critic, may have had particular resonance for his audience.

605–6   s.d. *and . . . urgency* SJ

617–21 *Louis . . . beast!* Louis did quarrel with his father. He allied himself with the Duke of
Burgundy and he spent the last five years of Charles' reign in voluntary exile following his
unauthorised marriage to Charlotte of Savoy.

JOAN [*again contemptuous*]

Minding your own business is like minding your own body: it's the shortest way to make yourself sick. What is my business? Helping mother at home. What is thine? Petting lapdogs and sucking sugar-sticks. I call that muck. I tell thee it is God's busi-   630
ness we are here to do: not our own. I have a message to thee from God; and thou must listen to it, though thy heart break with the terror of it.

CHARLES

I dont want a message; but can you tell me any secrets? Can you   635
do any cures? Can you turn lead into gold, or anything of that sort?

JOAN

I can turn thee into a king, in Rheims Cathedral; and that is a miracle that will take some doing, it seems.   640

CHARLES

If we go to Rheims, and have a coronation, Anne will want new dresses. We cant afford them. I am all right as I am.

JOAN

As you are! And what is that? Less than my father's poorest   645
shepherd. Thourt not lawful owner of thy own land of France till thou be consecrated.

CHARLES

But I shall not be lawful owner of my own land anyhow. Will the consecration pay off my mortgages? I have pledged my last   650
acre to the Archbishop and that fat bully. I owe money even to Bluebeard.

JOAN [*earnestly*]

Charlie: I come from the land, and have gotten my strength working on the land; and I tell thee that the land is thine to rule   655
righteously and keep God's peace in, and not to pledge at the pawnshop as a drunken woman pledges her children's clothes. And I come from God to tell thee to kneel in the cathedral and solemnly give thy kingdom to Him for ever and ever, and

636 *turn lead into gold* a prime goal of medieval alchemy
639–40 *that . . . seems* ms rev. (God only knows how I can do it typescript)
642 *Anne* one of Shaw's few factual errors. Charles' Queen was Marie d'Anjou, who was one of Jeanne's advocates.
645–6 *Less . . . shepherd* ms rev.
653–707 ms rev.; this extensive ms addition, pasted onto the typescript and dated September 1923, reintroduces the Court. According to Tyson (pp. 29–30), the initial draft closed less optimistically with Joan predicting that after she had had him crowned Charles would betray her.

41

become the greatest king in the world as His steward and His   660
bailiff, His soldier and His servant. The very clay of France will
become holy: her soldiers will be the soldiers of God: the rebel
dukes will be rebels against God: the English will fall on their
knees and beg thee let them return to their lawful homes in
peace. Wilt be a poor little Judas, and betray me and Him that   665
sent me?

CHARLES [tempted at last]

Oh, if I only dare!

JOAN

I shall dare, dare, and dare again, in God's name! Art for or   670
against me?

CHARLES [excited]

I'll risk it, I warn you I shant be able to keep it up; but I'll risk
it. You shall see. [Running to the main door and shouting] Hallo!
Come back, everybody. [To JOAN, as he runs back to the arch   675
opposite] Mind you stand by and dont let me be bullied.
[Through the arch] Come along, will you: the whole Court. [He
sits down in the royal chair as they all hurry in to their former
places, chattering and wondering] Now I'm in for it; but no
matter: here goes! [To THE PAGE] Call for silence, you little   680
beast, will you?

THE PAGE [snatching a halberd as before and thumping with it
repeatedly]

Silence for His Majesty the King. The King speaks. [Peremptorily]
Will you be silent there? [Silence]   685

CHARLES [rising]

I have given the command of the army to The Maid. The Maid
is to do as she likes with it. [He descends from the dais]

   General amazement. LA HIRE, delighted, slaps his steel thigh-
piece with his gauntlet.   690

LA TRÉMOUILLE [turning threateningly towards CHARLES]

What is this? I command the army.

   JOAN quickly puts her hand on CHARLES's shoulder as
he instinctively recoils. CHARLES, with a grotesque effort culminating in an extravagant gesture, snaps his fingers in THE   695
CHAMBERLAIN's face.

---

665   Judas the disciple who betrayed Christ
693–4   s.d. JOAN ... recoils SJ

42

JOAN

Thou't answered, old Gruff-and-Grum. [*Suddenly flashing out her sword as she divines that her moment has come*] Who is for God and His Maid? Who is for Orleans with me?   700

LA HIRE [*carried away, drawing also*]

For God and His Maid! To Orleans!

ALL THE KNIGHTS [*following his lead with enthusiasm*]

To Orleans!

JOAN, *radiant, falls on her knees in thanksgiving to God. They*   705
all kneel, except THE ARCHBISHOP, *who gives his benediction*
with a sign, and LA TRÉMOUILLE, *who collapses, cursing.*

699 s.d. *her moment has come* Shaw told the Theatre Guild Joan should be 'in command of the stage in the good old fashioned way from the point of view of the audience, and not beautifully composed in the middle of the picture with all the other people turning their backs' (Langner, p. 75).

699–704 *Who . . . Orleans!* echoes Act II of Taylor, which, following Joan's cry, 'Who follows me to rescue Orleans and ransom France?', ends: 'LA HIRE: I do for one! [*The crowd draw their swords and press forward with a general shout*]: And I!' (cited Martin Meisel, *Shaw and the Nineteenth Century Theatre*, 1984, p. 368).

706–7 s.d. *except . . . cursing* SJ

SCENE III

Orleans, 29th April 1429. DUNOIS, *aged 26, is pacing up and down a patch of ground on the south bank of the silver Loire, commanding a long view of the river in both directions. He has had his lance stuck up with a pennon, which streams in a strong east wind. His shield with its bend sinister lies beside it. He has his commander's baton in his hand. He is well built, carrying his armor easily. His broad brow and pointed chin give him an equilaterally triangular face, already marked by active service and responsibility, with the expression of a goodnatured and capable man who has no affectations and no foolish illusions. His* PAGE *is sitting on the ground, elbows on knees, cheeks on fists, idly watching the water. It is evening; and both man and boy are affected by the loveliness of the Loire.*

DUNOIS [*halting for a moment to glance up at the streaming pennon and shake his head wearily before he resumes his pacing*]
   West wind, west wind, west wind. Strumpet: steadfast when you should be wanton, wanton when you should be steadfast. West wind on the silver Loire: what rhymes to Loire? [*He looks again at the pennon, and shakes his fist at it*] Change, curse you, change, English harlot of a wind, change. West, west, I tell you. [*With a growl he resumes his march in silence, but soon begins again*] West wind, wanton wind, wilful wind, womanish wind, false wind from over the water, will you never blow again?
THE PAGE [*bounding to his feet*]
   See! There! There she goes!

   0   *Scene III* SJ (Act II, sc. ii. LC)
   1   s.d. *29th April* SE (*May 29* LC)
        DUNOIS Described by Shaw as 'the beauty man', his voice 'a tenor' (L4, p. 626), this role also
        incorporates that of the historical Duke of Alençon, commander of the Loire army and also
        a friend to Jeanne (see Preface, pp. 176–7).
   4   s.d. *pennon* a narrow, triangular flag
   5   s.d. *bend sinister* SJ (*bar sinister* LC); corrected 1924, before the London production
        (L3, p. 867). In heraldry, the strip running from the left top to right base indicates an
        acknowledged, illegitimate son of monarchy or nobility.
   13–14 s.d. SJ (*to himself as he paces* LC)
   15–22 *West . . . again* Dunois' elaboration of the conceit of the west wind as wild and whorish and
        his evident delight in alliteration are indications of his poetic tendency.
   16   *wanton* wild, ungovernable
   17   *silver Loire* Shaw instructed Dunois: 'look at River for a moment' (r.n. 1924, fo. 145).
   19   *harlot* whore

DUNOIS [*startled from his reverie: eagerly*]   25
Where? Who? The Maid?

THE PAGE
No: the kingfisher. Like blue lightning. She went into that bush.

DUNOIS [*furiously disappointed*]
Is that all? You infernal young idiot: I have a mind to pitch you   30
into the river.

THE PAGE [*not afraid, knowing his man*]
It looked frightfully jolly, that flash of blue. Look! There goes
the other!

DUNOIS [*running eagerly to the river brim*]   35
Where? Where?

THE PAGE [*pointing*]
Passing the reeds.

DUNOIS [*delighted*]
I see.   40

They follow the flight till the bird takes cover.

THE PAGE
You blew me up because you were not in time to see them
yesterday.

DUNOIS   45
You knew I was expecting The Maid when you set up your
yelping. I will give you something to yelp for next time.

THE PAGE
Arnt they lovely? I wish I could catch them.

DUNOIS   50
Let me catch you trying to trap them, and I will put you in the
iron cage for a month to teach you what a cage feels like. You
are an abominable boy.

THE PAGE *laughs, and squats down as before.*

DUNOIS [*pacing*]   55
Blue bird, blue bird, since I am friend to thee, change thou the
wind for me. No: it does not rhyme. He who has sinned for thee:
thats better. No sense in it, though. [*He finds himself close to* THE
PAGE] You abominable boy! [*He turns away from him*] Mary in
the blue snood, kingfisher color: will you grudge me a west wind?   60

---

30   *Is that all?* Shaw noted Robert Horton's delivery of these words as 'too quick' (r.n. 1924,
       fo. 154).

60   *snood* a hood or wide band over the hair, worn traditionally by unmarried women. The
       Virgin Mary is usually depicted wearing a blue-coloured snood.

A SENTRY'S VOICE WESTWARD

Halt! Who goes there?

JOAN'S VOICE

The Maid.

DUNOIS 65

Let her pass. Hither, Maid! To me!

JOAN, in splendid armor, rushes in in a blazing rage. The wind drops; and the pennon flaps idly down the lance; but DUNOIS *is too much occupied with* JOAN *to notice it.*

JOAN [*bluntly*] 70

Be you Bastard of Orleans?

DUNOIS [*cool and stern, pointing to his shield*]

You see the bend sinister. Are you Joan the Maid?

JOAN

Sure. 75

DUNOIS

Where are your troops?

JOAN

Miles behind. They have cheated me. They have brought me to the wrong side of the river. 80

DUNOIS

I told them to.

JOAN

Why did you? The English are on the other side!

DUNOIS 85

The English are on both sides.

JOAN

But Orleans is on the other side. We must fight the English there. How can we cross the river?

DUNOIS [*grimly*] 90

There is a bridge.

JOAN

In God's name, then, let us cross the bridge, and fall on them.

---

66 *Hither* come here (archaic)

67 s.d. *rushes in in a blazing rage* SJ (*comes quickly in from the westward. She looks displeased* LC)

71–84 *Be . . . side!* 'Then Jeanne said to me: "Are you the Bastard of Orleans?" . . . "Was it you who said I was to pass on this side, and that I should not go direct to the side on which are Talbot and the English?" ' (Dunois' testimony in Murray, p. 228).

DUNOIS

    It seems simple; but it cannot be done.   95

JOAN

    Who says so?

DUNOIS

    I say so; and older and wiser heads than mine are of the same
    opinion.   100

JOAN [*roundly*]

    Then your older and wiser heads are fat-heads: they have made
    a fool of you; and now they want to make a fool of me too,
    bringing me to the wrong side of the river. Do you not know
    that I bring you better help than ever came to any general or   105
    any town?

DUNOIS [*smiling patiently*]

    Your own?

JOAN

    No: the help and counsel of the King of Heaven. Which is the   110
    way to the bridge?

DUNOIS

    You are impatient, Maid.

JOAN

    Is this a time for patience? Our enemy is at our gates; and here   115
    we stand doing nothing. Oh, why are you not fighting? Listen
    to me: I will deliver you from fear. I –

DUNOIS [*laughing heartily, and waving her off*]

    No, no, my girl: if you delivered me from fear I should be a
    good knight for a story book, but a very bad commander of the   120
    army. Come! let me begin to make a soldier of you. [*He takes
    her to the water's edge*] Do you see those two forts at this end of
    the bridge? the big ones?

JOAN

    Yes. Are they ours or the goddams'?   125

DUNOIS

    Be quiet, and listen to me. If I were in either of those forts with
    only ten men I could hold it against an army. The English have
    more than ten times ten goddams in those forts to hold them
    against us.   130

120   *of* SE (for LC)
121–2   s.d. SJ

JOAN

They cannot hold them against God. God did not give them the land under those forts: they stole it from Him. He gave it to us. I will take those forts.

DUNOIS 135

Single-handed?

JOAN

Our men will take them. I will lead them.

DUNOIS

Not a man will follow you. 140

JOAN

I will not look back to see whether anyone is following me.

DUNOIS [*recognizing her mettle, and clapping her heartily on the shoulder*]

Good. You have the makings of a soldier in you. You are in love 145
with war.

JOAN [*startled*]

Oh! And the Archbishop said I was in love with religion.

DUNOIS

I, God forgive me, am a little in love with war myself, the ugly 150
devil! I am like a man with two wives. Do you want to be like a
woman with two husbands?

JOAN [*matter-of-fact*]

I will never take a husband. A man in Toul took an action
against me for breach of promise; but I never promised him. I 155
am a soldier: I do not want to be thought of as a woman. I will
not dress as a woman. I do not care for the things women care
for. They dream of lovers, and of money. I dream of leading a
charge, and of placing the big guns. You soldiers do not know
how to use the big guns: you think you can win battles with a 160
great noise and smoke.

DUNOIS [*with a shrug*]

True. Half the time the artillery is more trouble than it is
worth.

JOAN 165

Aye, lad; but you cannot fight stone walls with horses: you must
have guns, and much bigger guns too.

143–4 s.d. SJ
143 s.d. *mettle* courage, spirit
155 *breach of promise* a legal term for default on a promise to marry

DUNOIS [*grinning at her familiarity, and echoing it*]

    Aye, lass; but a good heart and a stout ladder will get over the
    stoniest wall.   170

JOAN

    I will be first up the ladder when we reach the fort, Bastard. I
    dare you to follow me.

DUNOIS

    You must not dare a staff officer, Joan: only company officers   175
    are allowed to indulge in displays of personal courage. Besides,
    you must know that I welcome you as a saint, not as a soldier. I
    have daredevils enough at my call, if they could help me.

JOAN

    I am not a daredevil: I am a servant of God. My sword   180
    is sacred: I found it behind the altar in the church of
    St Catherine, where God hid it for me; and I may not strike a
    blow with it. My heart is full of courage, not of anger. I will
    lead; and your men will follow: that is all I can do. But I must
    do it: you shall not stop me.   185

DUNOIS

    All in good time. Our men cannot take those forts by a sally
    across the bridge. They must come by water, and take the
    English in the rear on this side.

JOAN [*her military sense asserting itself*]   190

    Then make rafts and put big guns on them; and let your men
    cross to us.

DUNOIS

    The rafts are ready; and the men are embarked. But they must
    wait for God.   195

JOAN

    What do you mean? God is waiting for them.

DUNOIS

    Let Him send us a wind then. My boats are downstream: they
    cannot come up against both wind and current. We must wait   200

168–9   *and . . . but* SJ

180–2   *My . . . Catherine* The sword Jeanne carried was said to have been that with which Charles
      Martel had vanquished the Saracens, hidden until her voices directed her, when she was en
      route to Chinon, to its hiding place under the altar at the Church of St Catherine, Fierbois.

187   *in good time* Shaw here made an ms cut from the typescript of some fourteen lines
      concerned with military strategy.

190   s.d. SJ

until God changes the wind. Come: let me take you to the church.

JOAN

No. I love church; but the English will not yield to prayers: they understand nothing but hard knocks and slashes. I will not go 205 to church until we have beaten them.

DUNOIS

You must: I have business for you there.

JOAN

What business? 210

DUNOIS

To pray for a west wind. I have prayed; and I have given two silver candlesticks; but my prayers are not answered. Yours may be: you are young and innocent.

JOAN 215

Oh yes: you are right. I will pray: I will tell St Catherine: she will make God give me a west wind. Quick: shew me the way to the church.

THE PAGE [*sneezes violently*]

At-cha!!! 220

JOAN

God bless you, child! Coom, Bastard.

They go out. THE PAGE *rises to follow. He picks up the shield, and is taking the spear as well when he notices the pennon, which is now streaming eastward.* 225

THE PAGE [*dropping the shield and calling excitedly after them*]

Seigneur! Seigneur! Mademoiselle!

DUNOIS [*running back*]

What is it? The kingfisher? [*He looks eagerly for it up the river*]

JOAN [*joining them*] 230

Oh, a kingfisher! Where?

THE PAGE

No: the wind, the wind, the wind [*pointing to the pennon*]: that is what made me sneeze.

212–13   *and I . . . candlesticks* As part of the medieval context, Shaw's generals, like his churchmen, are shown to share in contemporary superstitions.

222   *Coom* Come; Sybil Thorndike played Joan with a North Country accent.

DUNOIS [*looking at the pennon*]   235
    The wind has changed. [*He crosses himself*] God has spoken.
    [*Kneeling and handing his baton to* JOAN] You command the
    king's army. I am your soldier.
THE PAGE [*looking down the river*]
    The boats have put off. They are ripping upstream like anything.   240
DUNOIS [*rising*]
    Now for the forts. You dared me to follow. Dare you lead?
JOAN [*bursting into tears and flinging her arms round* DUNOIS,
    kissing him on both cheeks]
    Dunois, dear comrade in arms, help me. My eyes are blinded   245
    with tears. Set my foot on the ladder, and say 'Up, Joan'.
DUNOIS [*dragging her out*]
    Never mind the tears: make for the flash of the guns.
JOAN [*in a blaze of courage*]
    Ah!   250
DUNOIS [*dragging her along with him*]
    For God and Saint Dennis!
THE PAGE [*shrilly*]
    The Maid! The Maid! God and The Maid! Hurray-ay-ay! [*He
    snatches up the shield and lance, and capers out after them, mad   255
    with excitement*]

236   *The wind has changed* 'At that moment, the wind being contrary, and thereby preventing
        the boats going up river and reaching Orleans, turned all at once and became favorable'
        (Dunois' testimony in Murray, p. 299). This significant stage effect has been managed
        variously with wires or a wind machine.
        s.d. *crosses himself* makes sign of cross with right hand across own chest and head
236–8 *God . . . soldier* This sequence is Shaw's invention, although Dunois did declare he believed
        Jeanne came from God (Dunois' testimony in Murray, pp. 229, 230).
240   *They . . . anything* ms rev.
241–2 DUNOIS *. . . lead* ms rev.
246   *'Up, Joan'* LC ('Go forward' typescript)
247–54 DUNOIS *. . . The Maid! The Maid!* ms rev., except Joan's exclamation at 249–50, which
        was added in SJ
256   s.d. Later productions have often added a battle scene here. Shaw in the Preface (p. 180)
        derides the coronations, battles and burnings of nineteenth-century spectacular melodrama
        but his film script includes some three pages of instructions for the battle for Orleans
        (see Dukore).

SCENE IV

A tent in the English camp. A bullnecked English CHAPLAIN *of 50 is
sitting on a stool at a table, hard at work writing. At the other side of
the table an imposing* NOBLEMAN, *aged 46, is seated in a handsome
chair turning over the leaves of an illuminated Book of Hours.* THE
NOBLEMAN *is enjoying himself:* THE CHAPLAIN *is struggling with*   5
suppressed wrath. There is an unoccupied leather stool on THE
NOBLEMAN's *left. The table is on his right.*

THE NOBLEMAN

Now this is what I call workmanship. There is nothing on earth
more exquisite than a bonny book, with well-placed columns of   10
rich black writing in beautiful borders, and illuminated pictures
cunningly inset. But nowadays, instead of looking at books,
people read them. A book might as well be one of those orders
for bacon and bran that you are scribbling.

THE CHAPLAIN   15

I must say, my lord, you take our situation very coolly. Very
coolly indeed.

THE NOBLEMAN [*supercilious*]

What is the matter?

THE CHAPLAIN   20

The matter, my lord, is that we English have been defeated.

THE NOBLEMAN

That happens, you know. It is only in history books and ballads
that the enemy is always defeated.

THE CHAPLAIN   25

But we are being defeated over and over again. First, Orleans –

0 *Scene IV* SJ (Act III, sc. i. LC)

1 s.d. *CHAPLAIN* Shaw said the role, described by Pirandello as 'the truly admirable creation in
   this drama' (*New York Times*, 13 January 1924), needed 'a powerful emotional man' (L3, p. 855).

3 s.d. *NOBLEMAN* Shaw, teasing audience and readers, frequently held back names until they
   emerge in formal introductions later in the scene (see ll. 117–19). From Lyall Swete, who
   seemed 'the materialistic fox of the middle ages come to life' (*Sunday Times*, 30 March
   1924), to Angus Wright (at NT, 2007), who 'silkily insinuate[d]' (*Observer*, 15 July 2007),
   many actors, including Casson on tour in Europe in 1945, have relished the role. See p. xxxi.

4 s.d. *illuminated Book of Hours* medieval manuscript prayer book, embellished with exquisite illustration in colour and, often, gold leaf. The 'Bedford Hours', commissioned for Henry
   VI's uncle, the French Regent, is held by the British Library.

10 *bonny* fine (colloquial) from French '*bon*' (good). The *OED* records its first usage as 1529.

THE NOBLEMAN [*poohpoohing*]

Oh, Orleans!

THE CHAPLAIN

I know what you are going to say, my lord: that was a clear case   30
of witchcraft and sorcery. But we are still being defeated.
Jargeau, Meung, Beaugency, just like Orleans. And now we have
been butchered at Patay, and Sir John Talbot taken prisoner.
[*He throws down his pen, almost in tears*] I feel it, my lord: I feel
it very deeply. I cannot bear to see my countrymen defeated by   35
a parcel of foreigners.

THE NOBLEMAN

Oh! you are an Englishman, are you?

THE CHAPLAIN

Certainly not, my lord: I am a gentleman. Still, like your lord-   40
ship, I was born in England; and it makes a difference.

THE NOBLEMAN

You are attached to the soil, eh?

THE CHAPLAIN

It pleases your lordship to be satirical at my expense: your   45
greatness privileges you to be so with impunity. But your lordship knows very well that I am not attached to the soil in a
vulgar manner, like a serf. Still, I have a feeling about it; [*with
growing agitation*] and I am not ashamed of it; and [*rising
wildly*] by God, if this goes on any longer I will fling my cassock   50
to the devil, and take arms myself, and strangle the accursed
witch with my own hands.

THE NOBLEMAN [*laughing at him goodnaturedly*]

So you shall, chaplain: so you shall, if we can do nothing better.
But not yet, not quite yet.   55

27   s.d. *poohpoohing* dismissing
32–3   *Jargeau ... Patay* towns attacked and taken by the French in June 1429, culminating in the
        convincing defeat of the English at Patay on the 18th. Charles' coronation followed on 17 July.
33   *Sir John Talbot* a figure familiar from Shakespeare's *Henry VI, Part 1*. He had served in
        Henry IV's Welsh wars and been governor of Ireland before going to France in 1427.
        Captured at Patay, he remained in prison for four years. See 231n.
40   *Certainly ... gentleman* Shaw makes the point that the court and aristocracy in England
        since the Norman Conquest of 1066 were, unlike the Anglo-Saxon populace of feudal
        England, of French descent, as the Chaplain's name *de* Stogumber indicates.
48   *serf* a peasant confined to the land of his feudal lord, hence rather literally 'attached to
        the soil'
50   *cassock* priest's robe

53

THE CHAPLAIN *resumes his seat very sulkily.*

THE NOBLEMAN [*airily*]

I should not care very much about the witch – you see, I have
made my pilgrimage to the Holy Land; and the Heavenly Powers,
for their own credit, can hardly allow me to be worsted by a   60
village sorceress – but the Bastard of Orleans is a harder nut to
crack; and as he has been to the Holy Land too, honors are easy
between us as far as that goes.

THE CHAPLAIN

He is only a Frenchman, my lord.   65

THE NOBLEMAN

A Frenchman! Where did you pick up that expression? Are these
Burgundians and Bretons and Picards and Gascons beginning to
call themselves Frenchmen, just as our fellows are beginning to
call themselves Englishmen? They actually talk of France and   70
England as their countries. *Theirs*, if you please! What is to
become of me and you if that way of thinking comes into fashion?

THE CHAPLAIN

Why, my lord? Can it hurt us?

THE NOBLEMAN   75

Men cannot serve two masters. If this cant of serving their
country once takes hold of them, goodbye to the authority of
their feudal lords, and goodbye to the authority of the Church.
That is, goodbye to you and me.

THE CHAPLAIN   80

I hope I am a faithful servant of the Church; and there are only
six cousins between me and the barony of Stogumber, which
was created by the Conqueror. But is that any reason why I
should stand by and see Englishmen beaten by a French bastard
and a witch from Lousy Champagne?   85

THE NOBLEMAN

Easy, man, easy: we shall burn the witch and beat the bastard all
in good time. Indeed I am waiting at present for the Bishop of

---

59   *pilgrimage to the Holy Land* Leaving England in 1407, Beauchamp made the pilgrimage
     via Paris, Rome, Venice and Jaffa, to Jerusalem, the goal of devout Christians, and set up his
     arms in the temple.

68   *Burgundians . . . Gascons* inhabitants of the medieval provinces in what is now France

82–3 *barony . . . Conqueror* title granted by William of Normandy following his conquest of the
     Anglo-Saxons at the Battle of Hastings in 1066. Shaw, through Stogumber, mocks contem-
     porary social snobbery and claims to ancient lineage.

Beauvais, to arrange the burning with him. He has been turned
out of his diocese by her faction.   90

THE CHAPLAIN

You have first to catch her, my lord.

THE NOBLEMAN

Or buy her. I will offer a king's ransom.

THE CHAPLAIN   95

A king's ransom! For that slut!

THE NOBLEMAN

One has to leave a margin. Some of Charles's people will sell
her to the Burgundians; the Burgundians will sell her to us; and
there will probably be three or four middlemen who will expect   100
their little commissions.

THE CHAPLAIN

Monstrous. It is all those scoundrels of Jews: they get in every
time money changes hands. I would not leave a Jew alive in
Christendom if I had my way.   105

THE NOBLEMAN

Why not? The Jews generally give value. They make you pay;
but they deliver the goods. In my experience the men who want
something for nothing are invariably Christians.

    A PAGE *appears.*   110

THE PAGE

The Right Reverend the Bishop of Beauvais: Monseigneur
Cauchon.

    CAUCHON, *aged about 60, comes in.* THE PAGE *withdraws.*
    The two Englishmen rise.   115

THE NOBLEMAN [*with effusive courtesy*]

My dear Bishop, how good of you to come! Allow me to
introduce myself: Richard de Beauchamp, Earl of Warwick, at
your service.

---

90 *diocese* religious jurisdiction
94 *a king's ransom* colloquially, a vast sum of money but here meant literally. When the
    monarch led his troops into battle it was common to agree financial payment to ransom him
    in the event of capture. Such a ransom was paid for Richard I, whereas Shakespeare's Henry
    V scornfully refused to compound for a ransom before Agincourt (*Henry V*, 4.3.90–124).
104 *not leave a Jew alive* Making Stogumber not only a snob and rabid nationalist but also an
    anti-Semite enables further mockery of prejudices of Shaw's own day.
114 s.d. CAUCHON Shaw wrote that the part needed 'a heavy man of great authority and force';
    'rather stern' (L3, pp. 856, 863).

CAUCHON   120
    Your lordship's fame is well known to me.
WARWICK
    This reverend cleric is Master John de Stogumber.
THE CHAPLAIN [glibly]
    John Bowyer Spenser Neville de Stogumber, at your service, my   125
    lord: Bachelor of Theology, and Keeper of the Private Seal to
    His Eminence the Cardinal of Winchester.
WARWICK [to CAUCHON]
    You call him the Cardinal of England, I believe. Our king's uncle.
CAUCHON   130
    Messire John de Stogumber: I am always the very good friend
    of His Eminence. [He extends his hand to THE CHAPLAIN who
    kisses his ring]
WARWICK
    Do me the honor to be seated. [He gives CAUCHON his chair,   135
    placing it at the head of the table]
        CAUCHON accepts the place of honor with a grave inclination.
    WARWICK fetches the leather stool carelessly, and sits in his
    former place. THE CHAPLAIN goes back to his chair.
        Though WARWICK has taken second place in calculated   140
    deference to THE BISHOP, he assumes the lead in opening the
    proceedings as a matter of course. He is still cordial and expan-
    sive; but there is a new note in his voice which means that he is
    coming to business.
WARWICK   145
    Well, my Lord Bishop, you find us in one of our unlucky
    moments. Charles is to be crowned at Rheims, practically by
    the young woman from Lorraine; and – I must not deceive you,
    nor flatter your hopes – we cannot prevent it. I suppose it will
    make a great difference to Charles's position.   150
CAUCHON
    Undoubtedly. It is a masterstroke of The Maid's.
THE CHAPLAIN [again agitated]
    We were not fairly beaten, my lord. No Englishman is ever
    fairly beaten.   155

---

127 *Cardinal of Winchester* Henry Beaufort, half-brother of Henry V
136–45 s.d. *placing ...* WARWICK SJ (*who acknowledges this civility, and takes the stool for
    himself* LC)

56

CAUCHON *raises his eyebrow slightly, then quickly composes his face.*

WARWICK

Our friend here takes the view that the young woman is a sorceress. It would, I presume, be the duty of your reverend lordship to   160
denounce her to the Inquisition, and have her burnt for that
offence.

CAUCHON

If she were captured in my diocese: yes.

WARWICK [*feeling that they are getting on capitally*]   165
Just so. Now I suppose there can be no reasonable doubt that
she is a sorceress.

THE CHAPLAIN

Not the least. An arrant witch.

WARWICK [*gently reproving their interruption*]   170
We are asking for the Bishop's opinion, Messire John.

CAUCHON

We shall have to consider not merely our own opinions here,
but the opinions – the prejudices, if you like – of a French court.

WARWICK [*correcting*]   175
A Catholic court, my lord.

CAUCHON

Catholic courts are composed of mortal men, like other courts,
however sacred their function and inspiration may be. And if
the men are Frenchmen, as the modern fashion calls them, I am   180
afraid the bare fact that an English army has been defeated by a
French one will not convince them that there is any sorcery in
the matter.

THE CHAPLAIN

What! Not when the famous Sir John Talbot himself has been   185
defeated and actually taken prisoner by a drab from the ditches
of Lorraine!

CAUCHON

Sir John Talbot, we all know, is a fierce and formidable soldier,
Messire; but I have yet to learn that he is an able general. And   190

161 *the Inquisition* ecclesiastical tribunal (known as the Holy Office) initiated by Pope Innocent
III in the thirteenth century for the suppression of heresy
176 *Catholic court* i.e. an *Inter*national court, under the aegis of the Catholic church
190 *I . . . general* The English defeat at Patay, in June 1429, is generally acknowledged as owing as
much to Talbot's rashness and obstinacy as to effective French generalship.

57

though it pleases you to say that he has been defeated by this girl, some of us may be disposed to give a little of the credit to Dunois.

THE CHAPLAIN [*contemptuously*]

The Bastard of Orleans!   195

CAUCHON

Let me remind –

WARWICK [*interposing*]

I know what you are going to say, my lord. Dunois defeated *me* at Montargis.   200

CAUCHON [*bowing*]

I take that as evidence that the Seigneur Dunois is a very able commander indeed.

WARWICK

Your lordship is the flower of courtesy. I admit, on our side,   205 that Talbot is a mere fighting animal, and that it probably served him right to be taken at Patay.

THE CHAPLAIN [*chafing*]

My lord: at Orleans this woman had her throat pierced by an English arrow, and was seen to cry like a child from the pain of   210 it. It was a death wound; yet she fought all day; and when our men had repulsed all her attacks like true Englishmen, she walked alone to the wall of our fort with a white banner in her hand; and our men were paralyzed, and could neither shoot nor strike whilst the French fell on them and drove them on to   215 the bridge, which immediately burst into flames and crumbled under them, letting them down into the river, where they were drowned in heaps. Was this your bastard's generalship? or were those flames the flames of hell, conjured up by witchcraft?

WARWICK   220

You will forgive Messire John's vehemence, my lord; but he has put our case. Dunois is a great captain, we admit; but why could he do nothing until the witch came?

---

200 *Montargis* The rout of the English at Montargis in 1427 had announced the arrival of Dunois, then aged twenty-four, as a brilliant commander.

205 *the flower of courtesy* a perfect example of knightly virtues, from the title of John Lydgate's early-fifteenth-century poem *The Flower of Courtesy*. Cf. 'NURSE: [Romeo] is not the flower of courtesy, but, I'll warrant him, as gentle as a lamb' (*Romeo and Juliet*, 2.5.42–3). See also 544 s.d.

CAUCHON

I do not say that there were no supernatural powers on her side. 225
But the names on that white banner were not the names of Satan
and Beelzebub, but the blessed names of our Lord and His holy
mother. And your commander who was drowned – Clahz-da I
think you call him –

WARWICK 230

Glasdale. Sir William Glasdale.

CAUCHON

Glass-dell, thank you. He was no saint; and many of our people
think that he was drowned for his blasphemies against The
Maid. 235

WARWICK [*beginning to look very dubious*]

Well, what are we to infer from all this, my lord? Has The Maid
converted you?

CAUCHON

If she had, my lord, I should have known better than to have 240
trusted myself here within your grasp.

WARWICK [*blandly deprecating*]

Oh! oh! My lord!

CAUCHON

If the devil is making use of this girl – and I believe he is – 245

WARWICK [*reassured*]

Ah! You hear, Messire John? I knew your lordship would not
fail us. Pardon my interruption. Proceed.

CAUCHON

If it be so, the devil has longer views than you give him credit for. 250

WARWICK

Indeed? In what way? Listen to this, Messire John.

CAUCHON

If the devil wanted to damn a country girl, do you think so easy
a task would cost him the winning of half a dozen battles? No, 255
my lord: any trumpery imp could do that much if the girl
could be damned at all. The Prince of Darkness does not con-
descend to such cheap drudgery. When he strikes, he strikes at

227 *Beelzebub* among the chief of Satan's fallen angels
231 *Sir William Glasdale* The commander of the besieging English force, Glasdale was killed
     following his rebuttal of Jeanne's demand at the bridge fortress of Les Tourelles that he
     abandon the siege of Orleans. Shaw initially planned to include Talbot and Glasdale in this
     scene (Tyson, p. 34).

the Catholic Church, whose realm is the whole spiritual world. When he damns, he damns the souls of the entire human race. 260 Against that dreadful design The Church stands ever on guard. And it is as one of the instruments of that design that I see this girl. She is inspired, but diabolically inspired.

THE CHAPLAIN

I told you she was a witch. 265

CAUCHON [*fiercely*]

She is not a witch. She is a heretic.

THE CHAPLAIN

What difference does that make?

CAUCHON 270

You, a priest, ask me that! You English are strangely blunt in the mind. All these things that you call witchcraft are capable of a natural explanation. The woman's miracles would not impose on a rabbit: she does not claim them as miracles herself. What do her victories prove but that she has a better head on her 275 shoulders than your swearing Glass-dells and mad bull Talbots, and that the courage of faith, even though it be a false faith, will always outstay the courage of wrath?

THE CHAPLAIN [*hardly able to believe his ears*]

Does your lordship compare Sir John Talbot, three times 280 Governor of Ireland, to a mad bull?!!!

WARWICK

It would not be seemly for you to do so, Messire John, as you are still six removes from a barony. But as I am an earl, and Talbot is only a knight, I may make bold to accept the compari- 285 son. [*To* THE BISHOP] My lord: I wipe the slate as far as the witchcraft goes. None the less, we must burn the woman.

CAUCHON

I cannot burn her. The Church cannot take life. And my first duty is to seek this girl's salvation. 290

---

261 *The Church* In this scene alone, 'Church' takes a capitalised definite article (except at ll. 516 and 591–2) in Cauchon's, Stogumber's and Warwick's speeches (introduced in SJ but more consistently in SE).

267 *heretic* holder of theological opinion conflicting with orthodox teaching. From the twelfth century onwards the church introduced formal measures to detect and punish heretical thinking and teaching and to destroy heretical writings.

285 *only a knight* Warwick superciliously pulls rank on the Chaplain. The historical Talbot was, in fact, Warwick's son-in-law through marriage to his eldest daughter Margaret.

WARWICK

No doubt. But you do burn people occasionally.

CAUCHON

No. When The Church cuts off an obstinate heretic as a dead
branch from the tree of life, the heretic is handed over to the   295
secular arm. The Church has no part in what the secular arm
may see fit to do.

WARWICK

Precisely. And I shall be the secular arm in this case. Well, my
lord, hand over your dead branch; and I will see that the fire is   300
ready for it. If you will answer for The Church's part, I will
answer for the secular part.

CAUCHON [with smouldering anger]

I can answer for nothing. You great lords are too prone to treat
The Church as a mere political convenience.   305

WARWICK [smiling and propitiatory]

Not in England, I assure you.

CAUCHON

In England more than anywhere else. No, my lord: the soul of
this village girl is of equal value with yours or your king's   310
before the throne of God; and my first duty is to save it. I will
not suffer your lordship to smile at me as if I were repeating a
meaningless form of words, and it were well understood
between us that I should betray the girl to you. I am no mere
political bishop: my faith is to me what your honor is to you;   315
and if there be a loophole through which this baptized child of
God can creep to her salvation, I shall guide her to it.

THE CHAPLAIN [rising in a fury]

You are a traitor.

CAUCHON [springing up]   320

You lie, priest. [Trembling with rage] If you dare do what this
woman has done – set your country above the holy Catholic
Church – you shall go to the fire with her.

296 *secular arm* the state power. The Inquisition used torture but did not kill. Its handing to the sec-
      ular powers, despite formal recommendations to mercy, was understood as a sentence of death
      by burning which, if not carried out, would result in excommunication of the secular authorities.

309 *In ... else* While teasing his own audience, Shaw has Cauchon make a fair point, for the
      Inquisition never took hold in England which, with its own ecclesiastical courts, rarely
      sought judgments from Rome.

321 *You lie, priest* When 'a certain English Doctor' told Cauchon he was wrong to admit
      Jeanne's recantation, 'the Bishop, irritated, told this person that he lied: for, as a judge, in the
      cause of faith, he must seek rather her salvation than her death' (Murray, pp. 205, 206).

THE CHAPLAIN

My lord: I — I went too far. I — [*he sits down with a submissive*   325
gesture].

WARWICK [*who has risen apprehensively*]

My lord: I apologize to you for the word used by Messire John de
Stogumber. It does not mean in England what it does in France.
In your language traitor means betrayer: one who is perfidious,   330
treacherous, unfaithful, disloyal. In our country it means simply
one who is not wholly devoted to our English interests.

CAUCHON

I am sorry: I did not understand. [*He subsides into his chair
with dignity*]   335

WARWICK [*resuming his seat, much relieved*]

I must apologize on my own account if I have seemed to take the
burning of this poor girl too lightly. When one has seen whole
countrysides burnt over and over again as mere items in military
routine, one has to grow a very thick skin. Otherwise one might   340
go mad: at all events, I should. May I venture to assume that your
lordship also, having to see so many heretics burned from time
to time, is compelled to take – shall I say a professional view of
what would otherwise be a very horrible incident?

CAUCHON   345

Yes: it is a painful duty: even, as you say, a horrible one. But in
comparison with the horror of heresy it is less than nothing. I
am not thinking of this girl's body, which will suffer for a few
moments only, and which must in any event die in some more
or less painful manner, but of her soul, which may suffer to all   350
eternity.

WARWICK

Just so; and God grant that her soul may be saved! But the
practical problem would seem to be how to save her soul without saving her body. For we must face it, my lord: if this cult of   355
The Maid goes on, our cause is lost.

THE CHAPLAIN [*his voice broken like that of a man who has been
crying*]

May I speak, my lord?

331–2   *In . . . interests* an ironic reference to the recent trial for treason of Roger Casement (see
Preface, p. 159, n. 48)

338–40   *When . . . skin* The terrible slaughter of the War of 1914–18 shadows Warwick's statements
about war.

WARWICK   360

Really, Messire John, I had rather you did not, unless you can
keep your temper.

THE CHAPLAIN

It is only this. I speak under correction; but The Maid is full of
deceit: she pretends to be devout. Her prayers and confessions   365
are endless. How can she be accused of heresy when she neg-
lects no observance of a faithful daughter of The Church?

CAUCHON [*flaming up*]

A faithful daughter of The Church! The Pope himself at his
proudest dare not presume as this woman presumes. She acts   370
as if she herself were The Church. She brings the message of
God to Charles; and The Church must stand aside. She will
crown him in the cathedral of Rheims: *she,* not The Church!
She sends letters to the king of England giving him God's command through *her* to return to his island on pain of God's   375
vengeance, which *she* will execute. Let me tell you that the writing of such letters was the practice of the accursed Mahomet,
the anti-Christ. Has she ever in all her utterances said one word
of The Church? Never. It is always God and herself.

WARWICK   380

What can you expect? A beggar on horseback! Her head is
turned.

CAUCHON

Who has turned it? The devil. And for a mighty purpose. He is
spreading this heresy everywhere. The man Hus, burnt only thir-   385
teen years ago at Constance, infected all Bohemia with it. A man
named WcLeef, himself an anointed priest, spread the pestilence
in England; and to your shame you let him die in his bed. We
have such people here in France too: I know the breed. It is

---

374   *sends ... England* Jeanne sent the first of her letters to Henry VI on 22 March 1429
        (Murray, pp. 39–40, 96).

381   *beggar on horseback* proverbial saying, that concludes 'will ride to Hell', suggesting a
        person, originally poor, made arrogant by the acquisition of wealth. George Kaufman's play
        Beggar on Horseback opened in New York, February 1924, suggesting that the phrase had
        common currency in this period.

385–6 *Hus ... it* John Huss, condemned as a heretic by the church authorities at the Council of
        Constance, became a popular hero in his native Bohemia. See Preface, p. 137, n. 1.
        thirteen years ago ms rev.

387–8 *WcLeef ... bed* John Wycliffe preached the individual relationship of each Christian with God.
        Though Wycliffe had died a natural death by 1428, the decree of the Council of Constance that
        his bones be dug up and burned had been carried out (see Preface, p. 161, n. 53).

63

cancerous: if it be not cut out, stamped out, burnt out, it will not   390
stop until it has brought the whole body of human society into
sin and corruption, into waste and ruin. By it an Arab camel
driver drove Christ and His Church out of Jerusalem, and rav-
aged his way west like a wild beast until at last there stood only
the Pyrenees and God's mercy between France and damnation.   395
Yet what did the camel driver do at the beginning more than this
shepherd girl is doing? He had his voices from the angel Gabriel:
she has her voices from St Catherine and St Margaret and the
Blessed Michael. He declared himself the messenger of God, and
wrote in God's name to the kings of the earth. Her letters to   400
them are going forth daily. It is not the Mother of God now to
whom we must look for intercession, but to Joan the Maid. What
will the world be like when The Church's accumulated wisdom
and knowledge and experience, its councils of learned, venerable
pious men, are thrust into the kennel by every ignorant laborer   405
or dairymaid whom the devil can puff up with the monstrous
self-conceit of being directly inspired from heaven? It will be a
world of blood, of fury, of devastation, of each man striving for
his own hand: in the end a world wrecked back into barbarism.
For now you have only Mahomet and his dupes, and the Maid   410
and her dupes; but what will it be when every girl thinks herself a
Joan and every man a Mahomet? I shudder to the very marrow
of my bones when I think of it. I have fought it all my life; and I
will fight it to the end. Let all this woman's sins be forgiven her
except only this sin; for it is the sin against the Holy Ghost; and if   415
she does not recant in the dust before the world, and submit herself to the last inch of her soul to her Church, to the fire she shall
go if she once falls into my hand.

WARWICK [*unimpressed*]

You feel strongly about it, naturally.   420

392–3   *Arab camel driver* Mohammed
   393   *Jerusalem* SJ (Byzantium LC). Thanking S.K. Ratcliffe for alerting him to the error, Shaw
         wrote 'Byzantium was a pure howler: I have substituted Jerusalem' (L3, p. 866).
   395   *Pyrenees ... damnation* The Muslim conquest of Spain from 711 threatened southern
         France, until rebuffed at Poitiers in 732. Moorish rule of Spain ended, following extended
         wars of reconquest, in the thirteenth century.
         damnation LC (his cruel crescent typescript)

CAUCHON

Do not you?

WARWICK

I am a soldier, not a churchman. As a pilgrim I saw something
of the Mahometans. They were not so ill-bred as I had been led   425
to believe. In some respects their conduct compared favorably
with ours.

CAUCHON [*displeased*]

I have noticed this before. Men go to the East to convert the infidels. And the infidels pervert them. The Crusader comes back   430
more than half a Saracen. Not to mention that all Englishmen
are born heretics.

THE CHAPLAIN

Englishmen heretics!!! [*Appealing to* WARWICK] My lord:
must we endure this? His lordship is beside himself. How can   435
what an Englishman believes be heresy? It is a contradiction in
terms.

CAUCHON

I absolve you, Messire de Stogumber, on the ground of invincible ignorance. The thick air of your country does not breed   440
theologians.

WARWICK

You would not say so if you heard us quarrelling about religion,
my lord! I am sorry you think I must be either a heretic or a
blockhead because, as a travelled man, I know that the follow-   445
ers of Mahomet profess great respect for our Lord, and are
more ready to forgive St Peter for being a fisherman than your
lordship is to forgive Mahomet for being a camel driver. But at
least we can proceed in this matter without bigotry.

CAUCHON   450

When men call the zeal of the Christian Church bigotry I know
what to think.

WARWICK

They are only east and west views of the same thing.

CAUCHON [*bitterly ironical*]   455

Only east and west! Only!!

430–1 *Crusader ... Saracen* T.E. Lawrence's commitment to the Arab independence struggle
against the Turks is alluded to here.
431   *Saracen* a catch-all name for Muslim enemies of the crusaders

WARWICK

Oh, my Lord Bishop, I am not gainsaying you. You will carry
The Church with you; but you have to carry the nobles also.
To my mind there is a stronger case against The Maid than the   460
one you have so forcibly put. Frankly, I am not afraid of this
girl becoming another Mahomet, and superseding The Church
by a great heresy. I think you exaggerate that risk. But have
you noticed that in these letters of hers, she proposes to all the
kings of Europe, as she has already pressed on Charles, a trans-   465
action which would wreck the whole social structure of
Christendom?

CAUCHON

Wreck The Church. I tell you so.

WARWICK [*whose patience is wearing out*]   470

My lord: pray get The Church out of your head for a moment;
and remember that there are temporal institutions in the world as
well as spiritual ones. I and my peers represent the feudal aristocracy as you represent The Church. We are the temporal power.
Well, do you not see how this girl's idea strikes at us?   475

CAUCHON

How does her idea strike you, except as it strikes at all of us,
through The Church?

WARWICK

Her idea is that the kings should give their realms to God, and   480
then reign as God's bailiffs.

CAUCHON [*not interested*]

Quite sound theologically, my lord. But the king will hardly
care, provided he reign. It is an abstract idea: a mere form of
words.   485

WARWICK

By no means. It is a cunning device to supersede the aristocracy, and make the king sole and absolute autocrat. Instead of
the king being merely the first among his peers, he becomes
their master. That we cannot suffer: we call no man master.   490
Nominally we hold our lands and dignities from the king,
because there must be a keystone to the arch of human society;
but we hold our lands in our own hands, and defend them with
our own swords and those of our own tenants. Now by The
Maid's doctrine the king will take our lands – *our* lands! – and   495
make them a present to God; and God will then vest them
wholly in the king. ▸

CAUCHON

　　Need you fear that? You are the makers of kings after all. York
　　or Lancaster in England, Lancaster or Valois in France: they　　500
　　reign according to your pleasure.

WARWICK

　　Yes; but only as long as the people follow their feudal lords, and
　　know the king only as a travelling show, owning nothing but
　　the highway that belongs to everybody. If the people's thoughts　　505
　　and hearts were turned to the king, and their lords became only
　　the king's servants in their eyes, the king could break us across
　　his knee one by one; and then what should we be but liveried
　　courtiers in his halls?

CAUCHON　　510

　　Still you need not fear, my lord. Some men are born kings; and
　　some are born statesmen. The two are seldom the same. Where
　　would the king find counsellors to plan and carry out such a
　　policy for him?

WARWICK [with a not too friendly smile]　　515

　　Perhaps in the Church, my lord.

　　　CAUCHON, with an equally sour smile, shrugs his shoulders,
　　and does not contradict him.

WARWICK

　　Strike down the barons; and the cardinals will have it all their　　520
　　own way.

CAUCHON [conciliatory, dropping his polemical tone]

　　My lord: we shall not defeat The Maid if we strive against one
　　another. I know well that there is a Will to Power in the world. I
　　know that while it lasts there will be a struggle between the　　525
　　Emperor and the Pope, between the dukes and the political car-
　　dinals, between the barons and the kings. The devil divides us
　　and governs. I see you are no friend to The Church: you are an
　　earl first and last, as I am a churchman first and last. But can we
　　not sink our differences in the face of a common enemy? I see　　530
　　now that what is in your mind is not that this girl has never
　　once mentioned The Church, and thinks only of God and

499　*makers of kings* The aristocracy, through its ability to raise armies, underwrit the power of
　　medieval monarchy. Its force was famously demonstrated in support of the usurpation of
　　Richard II by Henry Bolingbroke in 1399. It was Beauchamp's successor in the earldom,
　　Richard Neville, who gained the soubriquet 'the King-maker', for his politicking during the
　　Wars of the Roses, as Shaw notes in a letter of February 1924 (L3, p. 876).

herself, but that she has never once mentioned the peerage, and
thinks only of the king and herself.

WARWICK   535

Quite so. These two ideas of hers are the same idea at bottom.
It goes deep, my lord. It is the protest of the individual soul
against the interference of priest or peer between the private
man and his God. I should call it Protestantism if I had to find
a name for it.   540

CAUCHON [*looking hard at him*]

You understand it wonderfully well, my lord. Scratch an
Englishman, and find a Protestant.

WARWICK [*playing the pink of courtesy*]

I think you are not entirely void of sympathy with The Maid's   545
secular heresy, my lord. I leave you to find a name for it.

CAUCHON

You mistake me, my lord. I have no sympathy with her political
presumptions. But as a priest I have gained a knowledge of the
minds of the common people; and there you will find yet another   550
most dangerous idea. I can express it only by such phrases as
France for the French, England for the English, Italy for the
Italians, Spain for the Spanish, and so forth. It is sometimes so
narrow and bitter in country folk that it surprises me that this
country girl can rise above the idea of her village for its villagers.   555
But she can. She does. When she threatens to drive the English
from the soil of France she is undoubtedly thinking of the whole
extent of country in which French is spoken. To her the French-
speaking people are what the Holy Scriptures describe as a nation.
Call this side of her heresy Nationalism if you will: I can find you   560
no better name for it. I can only tell you that it is essentially anti-
Catholic and anti-Christian; for the Catholic Church knows only
one realm, and that is the realm of Christ's kingdom. Divide that
kingdom into nations, and you dethrone Christ. Dethrone Christ,
and who will stand between our throats and the sword? The   565
world will perish in a welter of war.

WARWICK

Well, if you will burn the Protestant, I will burn the Nationalist,
though perhaps I shall not carry Messire John with me there.
England for the English will appeal to him.   570

544   s.d. See 205n.
550–1   *there ... idea* SJ (I can tell you that you will find yet another idea which you have not
        mentioned LC)

68

THE CHAPLAIN

Certainly England for the English goes without saying: it is the
simple law of nature. But this woman denies to England her
legitimate conquests, given her by God because of her peculiar
fitness to rule over less civilized races for their own good. I do   575
not understand what your lordships mean by Protestant and
Nationalist: you are too learned and subtle for a poor clerk like
myself. But I know as a matter of plain commonsense that the
woman is a rebel; and that is enough for me. She rebels against
Nature by wearing man's clothes, and fighting. She rebels   580
against The Church by usurping the divine authority of the
Pope. She rebels against God by her damnable league with
Satan and his evil spirits against our army. And all these rebel-
lions are only excuses for her great rebellion against England.
That is not to be endured. Let her perish. Let her burn. Let her   585
not infect the whole flock. It is expedient that one woman die
for the people.

WARWICK [rising]

My lord: we seem to be agreed.

CAUCHON [rising also, but in protest]   590

I will not imperil my soul. I will uphold the justice of the
Church. I will strive to the utmost for this woman's salvation.

WARWICK

I am sorry for the poor girl. I hate these severities. I will spare
her if I can.   595

THE CHAPLAIN [implacably]

I would burn her with my own hands.

CAUCHON [blessing him]

Sancta simplicitas!

---

575   *fitness . . . good* In the 1920s, the claim of Empire had already been dismissed in Ireland and
strong stirrings were beginning in post-War India.

599   *Sancta simplicitas!* ms rev.; Lat = Holy simplicity! Cauchon's own politic speaking is
acknowledged in his blessing the Chaplain's lack of it.

SCENE V

The ambulatory in the cathedral of Rheims, near the door of the vestry. A pillar bears one of the stations of the cross. The organ is playing the people out of the nave after the coronation. JOAN *is kneeling in prayer before the station. She is beautifully dressed, but still in male attire. The organ ceases as* DUNOIS, *also splendidly arrayed, comes into the ambulatory from the vestry.*   5

DUNOIS

Come, Joan! you have had enough praying. After that fit of crying you will catch a chill if you stay here any longer. It is all over: the cathedral is empty; and the streets are full. They are   10
calling for The Maid. We have told them you are staying here alone to pray; but they want to see you again.

JOAN

No: let the king have all the glory.

DUNOIS   15

He only spoils the show, poor devil. No, Joan: you have crowned him; and you must go through with it.

  JOAN *shakes her head reluctantly.*

DUNOIS [*raising her*]

Come come! it will be over in a couple of hours. It's better than   20
the bridge at Orleans: eh?

JOAN

Oh, dear Dunois, how I wish it were the bridge at Orleans again! We *lived* at that bridge.

DUNOIS   25

Yes, faith, and died too: some of us.

---

  0   *Scene V* SJ (Act III, sc. ii. LC)
  1   s.d. *ambulatory* cloister. Although Jeanne stood beside Charles at his coronation, Shaw
        chooses to stage not the triumph but its quiet aftermath; not the nave of the Cathedral but a
        side cloister. His film script, in contrast, like Taylor's play, includes directions for a splendid
        coronation sequence (see Dukore). Charles was crowned on 17 July 1429.
  2   s.d. *stations of the cross* images, usually fourteen, showing events in the last hours of
        Christ's life
  8–9 *After that fit of crying* ms rev., drawing on Dunois' deposition in Murray, p. 230

JOAN

Isnt it strange, Jack? I am such a coward: I am frightened
beyond words before a battle; but it is so dull afterwards when
there is no danger: oh, so dull! dull! dull!   30

DUNOIS

You must learn to be abstemious in war, just as you are in your
food and drink, my little saint.

JOAN

Dear Jack: I think you like me as a soldier likes his comrade.   35

DUNOIS

You need it, poor innocent child of God. You have not many
friends at court.

JOAN

Why do all these courtiers and knights and churchmen hate me?   40
What have I done to them? I have asked nothing for myself
except that my village shall not be taxed; for we cannot afford war
taxes. I have brought them luck and victory: I have set them right
when they were doing all sorts of stupid things: I have crowned
Charles and made him a real king; and all the honors he is hand-   45
ing out have gone to them. Then why do they not love me?

DUNOIS [rallying her]

Sim-ple-ton! Do you expect stupid people to love you for shewing
them up? Do blundering old military dug-outs love the successful
young captains who supersede them? Do ambitious politicians   50
love the climbers who take the front seats from them? Do archbishops enjoy being played off their own altars, even by saints?
Why, I should be jealous of you myself if I were ambitious enough.

JOAN

You are the pick of the basket here, Jack: the only friend I have   55
among all these nobles. I'll wager your mother was from the
country. I will go back to the farm when I have taken Paris.

DUNOIS

I am not so sure that they will let you take Paris.

JOAN [startled]   60
What!

DUNOIS

I should have taken it myself before this if they had all been
sound about it. Some of them would rather Paris took you, I
think. So take care.   65

49   *dug-outs* retired officers recalled for temporary military service (*OED*)
60–1   JOAN *[startled] What!* SJ

71

JOAN

Jack: the world is too wicked for me. If the goddams and the
Burgundians do not make an end of me, the French will. Only
for my voices I should lose all heart. That is why I had to steal
away to pray here alone after the coronation. I'll tell you some-   70
thing, Jack. It is in the bells I hear my voices. Not today, when
they all rang: that was nothing but jangling. But here in this
corner, where the bells come down from heaven, and the echoes
linger, or in the fields, where they come from a distance through
the quiet of the countryside, my voices are in them. [*The cathe-*   75
dral clock chimes the quarter] Hark! [*She becomes rapt*] Do you
hear? 'Dear-child-of-God': just what you said. At the half-hour
they will say 'Be-brave-go-on'. At the three-quarters they will say
'I-am-thy-Help'. But it is at the hour, when the great bell goes
after 'God-will-save-France': it is then that St Margaret and   80
St Catherine and sometimes even the blessed Michael will say
things that I cannot tell beforehand. Then, oh then –

DUNOIS [*interrupting her kindly but not sympathetically*]

Then, Joan, we shall hear whatever we fancy in the booming of
the bell. You make me uneasy when you talk about your voices: I   85
should think you were a bit cracked if I hadnt noticed that you
give me very sensible reasons for what you do, though I hear you
telling others you are only obeying Madame Saint Catherine.

JOAN [*crossly*]

Well, I have to find reasons for you, because you do not believe   90
in my voices. But the voices come first; and I find the reasons
after: whatever you may choose to believe.

DUNOIS

Are you angry, Joan?

JOAN   95

Yes. [*Smiling*] No: not with you. I wish you were one of the
village babies.

DUNOIS

Why?

JOAN   100

I could nurse you for awhile.

DUNOIS

You are a bit of a woman after all.

69–70   *steal away* SJ (come here LC)

72

JOAN

No: not a bit: I am a soldier and nothing else. Soldiers always   105
nurse children when they get a chance.

DUNOIS

That is true. [*He laughs*]

KING CHARLES, *with* BLUEBEARD *on his left and* LA HIRE
on his right, comes from the vestry, where he has been disrobing.   110
JOAN *shrinks away behind the pillar.* DUNOIS *is left between*
CHARLES *and* LA HIRE.

DUNOIS

Well, your Majesty is an anointed king at last. How do you like it?

CHARLES   115

I would not go through it again to be emperor of the sun and
moon. The weight of those robes! I thought I should have
dropped when they loaded that crown on to me. And the
famous holy oil they talked so much about was rancid: phew!
The Archbishop must be nearly dead: his robes must have   120
weighed a ton: they are stripping him still in the vestry.

DUNOIS [*drily*]

Your majesty should wear armor oftener. That would accustom
you to heavy dressing.

CHARLES   125

Yes: the old jibe! Well, I am not going to wear armor: fighting is
not my job. Where is The Maid?

JOAN [*coming forward between* CHARLES *and* BLUEBEARD, *and
falling on her knee*]

Sire: I have made you king: my work is done. I am going back   130
to my father's farm.

CHARLES [*surprised, but relieved*]

Oh, are you? Well, that will be very nice.

JOAN *rises, deeply discouraged.*

CHARLES [*continuing heedlessly*]   135

A healthy life, you know.

DUNOIS

But a dull one.

BLUEBEARD

You will find the petticoats tripping you up after leaving them   140
off for so long.

135–49 CHARLES ... go In the equivalent scene in Taylor's play, only La Hire speaks out against
    Joan's return home.

73

LA HIRE

You will miss the fighting. It's a bad habit, but a grand one, and the hardest of all to break yourself of.

CHARLES [*anxiously*]   145

Still, we dont want you to stay if you would really rather go home.

JOAN [*bitterly*]

I know well that none of you will be sorry to see me go. [*She turns her shoulder to* CHARLES *and walks past him to the more*   150 *congenial neighborhood of* DUNOIS *and* LA HIRE]

LA HIRE

Well, I shall be able to swear when I want to. But I shall miss you at times.

JOAN   155

La Hire: in spite of all your sins and swears we shall meet in heaven; for I love you as I love Pitou, my old sheep dog. Pitou could kill a wolf. You will kill the English wolves until they go back to their country and become good dogs of God, will you not?   160

LA HIRE

You and I together: yes.

JOAN

No: I shall last only a year from the beginning.

ALL THE OTHERS   165

What!

JOAN

I know it somehow.

DUNOIS

Nonsense!   170

JOAN

Jack: do you think you will be able to drive them out?

DUNOIS [*with quiet conviction*]

Yes: I shall drive them out. They beat us because we thought battles were tournaments and ransom markets. We played the   175 fool while the goddams took war seriously. But I have learnt my lesson, and taken their measure. They have no roots here. I have beaten them before; and I shall beat them again.

149–51   s.d. *She . . .* LA HIRE SJ

164   *I . . . beginning* Cf. Alençon's deposition: 'Many times in my presence Jeanne told the king she would last but one year and no more' (Murray, p. 268).

165–71   ALL *. . .* JOAN SJ

JOAN

You will not be cruel to them, Jack?   180

DUNOIS

The goddams will not yield to tender handling. We did not begin it.

JOAN [*suddenly*]

Jack: before I go home, let us take Paris.   185

CHARLES [*terrified*]

Oh no no. We shall lose everything we have gained. Oh dont let us have any more fighting. We can make a very good treaty with the Duke of Burgundy.

JOAN   190

Treaty! [*She stamps with impatience*]

CHARLES

Well, why not, now that I am crowned and anointed? Oh, that oil!

THE ARCHBISHOP *comes from the vestry, and joins the group between* CHARLES *and* BLUEBEARD.   195

CHARLES

Archbishop: The Maid wants to start fighting again.

THE ARCHBISHOP

Have we ceased fighting, then? Are we at peace?

CHARLES   200

No: I suppose not; but let us be content with what we have done. Let us make a treaty. Our luck is too good to last; and now is our chance to stop before it turns.

JOAN

Luck! God has fought for us; and you call it luck! And you   205
would stop while there are still Englishmen on this holy earth of dear France!

THE ARCHBISHOP [*sternly*]

Maid: the king addressed himself to me, not to you. You forget yourself. You very often forget yourself.   210

JOAN [*unabashed, and rather roughly*]

Then speak, you; and tell him that it is not God's will that he should take his hand from the plough.

THE ARCHBISHOP

If I am not so glib with the name of God as you are, it is   215
because I interpret His will with the authority of the Church and of my sacred office. When you first came you respected it,

and would not have dared to speak as you are now speaking.
You came clothed with the virtue of humility; and because God
blessed your enterprises accordingly, you have stained yourself   220
with the sin of pride. The old Greek tragedy is rising among us.
It is the chastisement of hubris.

CHARLES

Yes: she thinks she knows better than everyone else.

JOAN [*distressed, but naïvely incapable of seeing the effect she is*   225
producing]

But I *do* know better than any of you seem to. And I am not
proud: I never speak unless I know I am right.

BLUEBEARD ⎱ [*exclaiming together*] ⎰ Ha ha!
CHARLES ⎰   ⎱ Just so.   230

THE ARCHBISHOP

How do you know you are right?

JOAN

I always know. My voices –

CHARLES   235

Oh, your voices, your voices. Why dont the voices come to me?
I am king, not you.

JOAN

They do come to you; but you do not hear them. You have not
sat in the field in the evening listening for them. When the   240
angelus rings you cross yourself and have done with it; but if
you prayed from your heart, and listened to the thrilling of the
bells in the air after they stop ringing, you would hear the
voices as well as I do. [*Turning brusquely from him*] But what
voices do you need to tell you what the blacksmith can tell you: 245
that you must strike while the iron is hot? I tell you we must
make a dash at Compiègne and relieve it as we relieved
Orleans. Then Paris will open its gates; or if not, we will break
through them. What is your crown worth without your capital?

LA HIRE   250

That is what I say too. We shall go through them like a red hot
shot through a pound of butter. What do you say, Bastard?

---

222   *hubris* overweening confidence or pride that, in Greek tragedy, brings down disaster as pun-
      ishment from the gods
241   *angelus* religious devotion said morning, noon and night in the Catholic church and, hence,
      the church bells announcing this
244   s.d. *Turning . . . him* SJ

76

DUNOIS

If our cannon balls were all as hot as your head, and we had
enough of them, we should conquer the earth, no doubt. Pluck   255
and impetuosity are good servants in war, but bad masters:
they have delivered us into the hands of the English every time
we have trusted to them. We never know when we are beaten:
that is our great fault.

JOAN   260

You never know when you are victorious: that is a worse fault. I
shall have to make you carry looking-glasses in battle to convince you that the English have not cut off all your noses. You
would have been besieged in Orleans still, you and your councils of war, if I had not made you attack. You should always   265
attack; and if you only hold on long enough the enemy will
stop first. You dont know how to begin a battle; and you dont
know how to use your cannons. And I do.

She squats down on the flags with crossed ankles, pouting.

DUNOIS   270

I know what you think of us, General Joan.

JOAN

Never mind that, Jack. Tell them what you think of me.

DUNOIS

I think that God was on your side; for I have not forgotten how   275
the wind changed, and how our hearts changed when you
came; and by my faith I shall never deny that it was in your sign
that we conquered. But I tell you as a soldier that God is no
man's daily drudge, and no maid's either. If you are worthy of it
He will sometimes snatch you out of the jaws of death and set   280
you on your feet again; but that is all: once on your feet you
must fight with all your might and all your craft. For He has to
be fair to your enemy too: dont forget that. Well, He set us on
our feet through you at Orleans; and the glory of it has carried
us through a few good battles here to the coronation. But if we   285
presume on it further, and trust to God to do the work we
should do ourselves, we shall be defeated; and serve us right!

JOAN

But –

267–8   *how to begin . . . use* SJ (how to use LC)
269   s.d. SJ

77

DUNOIS   290

Sh! I have not finished. Do not think, any of you, that these victories of ours were won without generalship. King Charles: you
have said no word in your proclamations of my part in this
campaign; and I make no complaint of that; for the people will
run after The Maid and her miracles and not after the Bastard's   295
hard work finding troops for her and feeding them. But I know
exactly how much God did for us through The Maid, and how
much He left me to do by my own wits; and I tell you that your
little hour of miracles is over, and that from this time on he
who plays the war game best will win – if the luck is on his side.   300

JOAN

Ah! if, if, if, if! If ifs and ans were pots and pans there'd be no
need of tinkers. [*Rising impetuously*] I tell *you*, Bastard, your
art of war is no use, because your knights are no good for real
fighting. War is only a game to them, like tennis and all their   305
other games: they make rules as to what is fair and what is not
fair, and heap armor on themselves and on their poor horses to
keep out the arrows; and when they fall they cant get up, and
have to wait for their squires to come and lift them to arrange
about the ransom with the man that has poked them off their   310
horse. Cant you see that all the like of that is gone by and done
with? What use is armor against gunpowder? And if it was, do
you think men that are fighting for France and for God will
stop to bargain about ransoms, as half your knights live by
doing? No: they will fight to win; and they will give up their   315
lives out of their own hand into the hand of God when they go
into battle, as I do. Common folks understand this. They
cannot afford armor and cannot pay ransoms; but they followed me half naked into the moat and up the ladder and over
the wall. With them it is my life or thine, and God defend the   320
right! You may shake your head, Jack; and Bluebeard may twirl
his billygoat's beard and cock his nose at me; but remember
the day your knights and captains refused to follow me to
attack the English at Orleans! You locked the gates to keep me
in; and it was the townsfolk and the common people that fol-   325
lowed me, and forced the gate, and shewed you the way to fight
in earnest.

BLUEBEARD [*offended*]

Not content with being Pope Joan, you must be Caesar and
Alexander as well.   330

THE ARCHBISHOP

Pride will have a fall, Joan.

JOAN

Oh, never mind whether it is pride or not: is it true? is it commonsense? 335

LA HIRE

It is true. Half of us are afraid of having our handsome noses
broken; and the other half are out for paying off their mortgages. Let her have her way, Dunois: she does not know
everything; but she has got hold of the right end of the stick. 340
Fighting is not what it was; and those who know least about it
often make the best job of it.

DUNOIS

I know all that. I do not fight in the old way: I have learnt the
lesson of Agincourt, of Poitiers and Crecy. I know how many 345
lives any move of mine will cost; and if the move is worth the
cost I make it and pay the cost. But Joan never counts the cost
at all: she goes ahead and trusts to God: she thinks she has God
in her pocket. Up to now she has had the numbers on her side;
and she has won. But I know Joan; and I see that some day she 350
will go ahead when she has only ten men to do the work of a
hundred. And then she will find that God is on the side of the
big battalions. She will be taken by the enemy. And the lucky
man that makes the capture will receive sixteen thousand
pounds from the Earl of Ouareek. 355

JOAN [flattered]

Sixteen thousand pounds! Eh, laddie, have they offered that for
me? There cannot be so much money in the world.

DUNOIS

There is, in England. And now tell me, all of you, which of you 360
will lift a finger to save Joan once the English have got her? I
speak first, for the army. The day after she has been dragged
from her horse by a goddam or a Burgundian, and he is not
struck dead: the day after she is locked in a dungeon, and the
bars and bolts do not fly open at the touch of St Peter's angel: 365
the day when the enemy finds out that she is as vulnerable as I
am and not a bit more invincible, she will not be worth the life

---

345   *of Agincourt, of Poitiers and Crecy* The speed and mobility of the infantry and long-
bowmen played a large part in the English victories of 1415, 1356 and 1346, respectively.
355   *Ouareek* Warwick

79

of a single soldier to us; and I will not risk that life, much as I
cherish her as a companion-in-arms.

JOAN   370

I dont blame you, Jack: you are right. I am not worth one soldier's life if God lets me be beaten; but France may think me
worth my ransom after what God has done for her through me.

CHARLES

I tell you I have no money; and this coronation, which is all   375
your fault, has cost me the last farthing I can borrow.

JOAN

The Church is richer than you. I put my trust in the Church.

THE ARCHBISHOP

Woman: they will drag you through the streets, and burn you   380
as a witch.

JOAN [running to him]

Oh, my lord, do not say that. It is impossible. I a witch!

THE ARCHBISHOP

Peter Cauchon knows his business. The University of Paris has   385
burnt a woman for saying that what you have done was well
done, and according to God.

JOAN [bewildered]

But why? What sense is there in it? What I have done is according to God. They could not burn a woman for speaking the   390
truth.

THE ARCHBISHOP

They did.

JOAN

But you know that she was speaking the truth. You would not   395
let them burn me.

THE ARCHBISHOP

How could I prevent them?

JOAN

You would speak in the name of the Church. You are a great   400
prince of the Church. I would go anywhere with your blessing
to protect me.

THE ARCHBISHOP

I have no blessing for you while you are proud and disobedient.

JOAN   405

Oh, why will you go on saying things like that? I am not proud
and disobedient. I am a poor girl, and so ignorant that I do not
know A from B. How could I be proud? And how can you say

that I am disobedient when I always obey my voices, because
they come from God.   410

THE ARCHBISHOP

The voice of God on earth is the voice of the Church Militant;
and all the voices that come to you are the echoes of your own
wilfulness.

JOAN   415

It is not true.

THE ARCHBISHOP [*flushing angrily*]

You tell the Archbishop in his cathedral that he lies; and yet you
say you are not proud and disobedient.

JOAN   420

I never said you lied. It was you that as good as said my voices lied.
When have they ever lied? If you will not believe in them: even if
they are only the echoes of my own commonsense, are they not
always right? and are not your earthly counsels always wrong?

THE ARCHBISHOP [*indignantly*]   425

It is waste of time admonishing you.

CHARLES

It always comes back to the same thing. She is right; and everyone else is wrong.

THE ARCHBISHOP   430

Take this as your last warning. If you perish through setting
your private judgment above the instructions of your spiritual
directors, the Church disowns you, and leaves you to whatever
fate your presumption may bring upon you. The Bastard has
told you that if you persist in setting up your military conceit   435
above the counsels of your commanders –

DUNOIS [*interposing*]

To put it quite exactly, if you attempt to relieve the garrison in
Compiègne without the same superiority in numbers you had
at Orleans –   440

THE ARCHBISHOP

The army will disown you, and will not rescue you. And His
Majesty the King has told you that the throne has not the
means of ransoming you.

CHARLES   445

Not a penny.

---

418   *You . . . lies* A note on this phrase from Shaw to Alfred Bruning [the Archbishop] stipulates:
'more outraged' (r.n. 1924, fo. 141).

THE ARCHBISHOP

You stand alone: absolutely alone, trusting to your own conceit,
your own ignorance, your own headstrong presumption, your
own impiety in hiding all these sins under the cloak of a trust in   450
God. When you pass through these doors into the sunlight, the
crowd will cheer you. They will bring you their little children
and their invalids to heal: they will kiss your hands and feet, and
do what they can, poor simple souls, to turn your head, and
madden you with the self-confidence that is leading you to your   455
destruction. But you will be none the less alone: they cannot
save you. We and we only can stand between you and the stake
at which our enemies have burnt that wretched woman in Paris.

JOAN [her eyes skyward]

I have better friends and better counsel than yours.   460

THE ARCHBISHOP

I see that I am speaking in vain to a hardened heart. You reject
our protection, and are determined to turn us all against you.
In future, then, fend for yourself; and if you fail, God have
mercy on your soul.   465

DUNOIS

That is the truth, Joan. Heed it.

JOAN

Where would you all have been now if I had heeded that sort of
truth? There is no help, no counsel, in any of you. Yes: I am alone   470
on earth: I have always been alone. My father told my brothers to
drown me if I would not stay to mind his sheep while France was
bleeding to death: France might perish if only our lambs were
safe. I thought France would have friends at the court of the king
of France; and I find only wolves fighting for pieces of her poor   475
torn body. [I thought God would have friends everywhere,
because He is the friend of everyone;] and in my innocence I
believed that you who now cast me out would be like strong
towers to keep harm from me. But I am wiser now; and nobody
is any the worse for being wiser. Do not think you can frighten   480
me by telling me that I am alone. France is alone; and God is
alone; and what is my loneliness before the loneliness of my

469–92   *Where ... me!* This speech, described as 'immensely fine' by James Agate in his review
(*Sunday Times*, 30 March 1924), is similarly singled out by a number of the actresses who have
played the role, including Siobhan McKenna, one of the great Joans from the 1950s (Hill, p. 50).

479–81   *But ... frighten me* ms rev. (You think you can terrify me typescript)

country and my God? I see now that the loneliness of God is His
strength: what would He be if He listened to your jealous little
counsels? Well, my loneliness shall be my strength too; it is better   485
to be alone with God: His friendship will not fail me, nor His
counsel, nor His love. In His strength I will dare, and dare, and
dare, until I die. I will go out now to the common people, and
let the love in their eyes comfort me for the hate in yours. You
will all be glad to see me burnt; but if I go through the fire I shall   490
go through it to their hearts for ever and ever. And so, God be
with me!

*She goes from them. They stare after her in glum silence for a
moment. Then* GILLES DE RAIS *twirls his beard.*

BLUEBEARD   495

You know, the woman is quite impossible. I dont dislike her,
really; but what are you to do with such a character?

DUNOIS

As God is my judge, if she fell into the Loire I would jump in in
full armor to fish her out. But if she plays the fool at   500
Compiègne, and gets caught, I must leave her to her doom.

LA HIRE

Then you had better chain me up; for I could follow her to hell
when the spirit rises in her like that.

THE ARCHBISHOP   505

She disturbs my judgment too: there is a dangerous power in
her outbursts. But the pit is open at her feet; and for good or
evil we cannot turn her from it.

CHARLES

If only she would keep quiet, or go home!   510

They follow her dispiritedly.

487–8   *I will . . . die* an echo of the declaration which won over Charles (II.670).
493–4   s.d. *They . . . moment* ms rev.
   503   *chain me up* La Hire, always a loyal supporter of Jeanne, was, in fact, a prisoner of the
         Burgundians at the time of her burning.
506–7   *She . . . outbursts* ms rev. (My heart bleeds for the poor girl typescript)

SCENE VI

Rouen, 30th May 1431. A great stone hall in the castle, arranged for
a trial-at-law, but not a trial-by-jury, the court being the Bishop's
court with the Inquisition participating: hence there are two raised
chairs side by side for the Bishop and the Inquisitor as judges. Rows
of chairs radiating from them at an obtuse angle are for the canons, 5
the doctors of law and theology, and the Dominican monks, who act
as assessors. In the angle is a table for the scribes, with stools. There is
also a heavy rough wooden stool for the prisoner. All these are at the
inner end of the hall. The further end is open to the courtyard
through a row of arches. The court is shielded from the weather by 10
screens and curtains.

Looking down the great hall from the middle of the inner end, the
judicial chairs and scribes' table are to the right. The prisoner's stool
is to the left. There are arched doors right and left. It is a fine sun-
shiny May morning. 15

WARWICK *comes in through the arched doorway on the judges'*
side, followed by his PAGE.

THE PAGE [*pertly*]

I suppose your lordship is aware that we have no business here.
This is an ecclesiastical court; and we are only the secular arm. 20

WARWICK

I am aware of that fact. Will it please your impudence to find
the Bishop of Beauvais for me, and give him a hint that he can
have a word with me here before the trial, if he wishes?

THE PAGE [*going*] 25

Yes, my lord.

0   *Scene VI* SJ (Act IV LC)

1–15   s.d. *Rouen . . . morning* LC indicates a more complicated set, with the inner end of the hall
raised by a few steps, the inclusion of a '*specially high*' chair decorated with the Bishop's
armorial bearings, and shadows so falling that '*the right half of the prospect is shut in, the*
left full of morning sunshine'.

1   s.d. *30th May 1431* Jeanne's trial began on 26 March 1431, concluding with her recantation
on 24 May. Public pronouncement of relapse and excommunication was made on 30 May
and death by burning followed. Shaw compresses events but retains the stages and preoccupations of the trial.

WARWICK

And mind you behave yourself. Do not address him as Pious
Peter.

THE PAGE   30

No, my lord. I shall be kind to him, because, when The Maid is
brought in, Pious Peter will have to pick a peck of pickled
pepper.

CAUCHON *enters through the same door with a* DOMINICAN
MONK *and a* CANON, *the latter carrying a brief.*   35

THE PAGE

The Right Reverend his lordship the Bishop of Beauvais. And
two other reverend gentlemen.

WARWICK

Get out; and see that we are not interrupted.   40

THE PAGE

Right, my lord [*he vanishes airily*].

CAUCHON

I wish your lordship good-morrow.

WARWICK   45

Good-morrow to your lordship. Have I had the pleasure of
meeting your friends before? I think not.

CAUCHON [*introducing* THE MONK, *who is on his right*]

This, my lord, is Brother John Lemaître, of the order of St
Dominic. He is acting as deputy for the Chief Inquisitor into   50
the evil of heresy in France. Brother John: the Earl of Warwick.

WARWICK

Your Reverence is most welcome. We have no Inquisitor in
England, unfortunately; though we miss him greatly, especially
on occasions like the present.   55

THE INQUISITOR *smiles patiently, and bows. He is a mild elderly gentleman, but has evident reserves of authority and firmness.*

CAUCHON [*introducing the* CANON, *who is on his left*]

This gentleman is Canon John D'Estivet, of the Chapter of
Bayeaux. He is acting as Promoter.   60

32–3   *Pious ... pepper* The Page gives his version of a common tongue-twister, substituting
        'Pious Peter' for the more usual 'Peter Piper'.

   56   s.d. *INQUISITOR* Shaw envisaged him as 'a quite pleasant elderly gentleman and a very
        good speaker, quietly incisive', 'very mild and silvery' (L3, pp. 856, 862). In 1930 he called
        him 'my infernal old scoundrel of an Inquisitor' (L4, p. 170).

WARWICK

Promoter?

CAUCHON

Prosecutor, you would call him in civil law.

WARWICK   65

Ah! prosecutor. Quite, quite. I am very glad to make your acquaintance, Canon D'Estivet.

D'ESTIVET *bows. He is on the young side of middle age, well mannered, but vulpine beneath his veneer.*

WARWICK   70

May I ask what stage the proceedings have reached? It is now more than nine months since The Maid was captured at Compiègne by the Burgundians. It is fully four months since I bought her from the Burgundians for a very handsome sum, solely that she might be brought to justice. It is very   75
nearly three months since I delivered her up to you, my Lord Bishop, as a person suspected of heresy. May I suggest that you are taking a rather unconscionable time to make up your minds about a very plain case? Is this trial never going to end?   80

THE INQUISITOR [*smiling*]

It has not yet begun, my lord.

WARWICK

Not yet begun! Why, you have been at it eleven weeks!

CAUCHON   85

We have not been idle, my lord. We have held fifteen examinations of The Maid: six public and nine private.

THE INQUISITOR [*always patiently smiling*]

You see, my lord, I have been present at only two of these examinations. They were proceedings of the Bishop's court   90
solely, and not of the Holy Office. I have only just decided to associate myself – that is, to associate the Holy Inquisition – with the Bishop's court. I did not at first think that this was a case of heresy at all. I regarded it as a political case, and The Maid as a prisoner of war. But having now been present at two   95
of the examinations, I must admit that this seems to be one of the gravest cases of heresy within my experience. Therefore everything is now in order, and we proceed to trial this morning. [*He moves towards the judicial chairs*]

CAUCHON   100

This moment, if your lordship's convenience allows.

WARWICK [*graciously*]

Well, that is good news, gentlemen. I will not attempt to conceal from you that our patience was becoming strained.

CAUCHON   105

So I gathered from the threats of your soldiers to drown those of our people who favor The Maid.

WARWICK

Dear me! At all events their intentions were friendly to *you*, my lord.   110

CAUCHON [*sternly*]

I hope not. I am determined that the woman shall have a fair hearing. The justice of the Church is not a mockery, my lord.

THE INQUISITOR [*returning*]

Never has there been a fairer examination within my experi-   115
ence, my lord. The Maid needs no lawyers to take her part: she will be tried by her most faithful friends, all ardently desirous to save her soul from perdition.

D'ESTIVET

Sir: I am the Promoter; and it has been my painful duty to pres-   120
ent the case against the girl; but believe me, I would throw up my case today and hasten to her defence if I did not know that men far my superiors in learning and piety, in eloquence and persuasiveness, have been sent to reason with her, to explain to her the danger she is running, and the ease with which she may   125
avoid it. [*Suddenly bursting into forensic eloquence, to the disgust of* CAUCHON *and* THE INQUISITOR, *who have listened to him so far with patronizing approval*] Men have dared to say that we are acting from hate; but God is our witness that they lie. Have we tortured her? No. Have we ceased to exhort her; to implore her   130
to have pity on herself; to come to the bosom of her Church as an erring but beloved child? Have we –

CAUCHON [*interrupting drily*]

Take care, Canon. All that you say is true; but if you make his lordship believe it I will not answer for your life, and hardly for   135
my own.

103–13   *I . . . lord* Historical information in Shaw's shorthand draft was considerably reduced here to sharpen the sense of distrust and give Cauchon moral superiority (Tyson, pp. 50–1).

112   *I hope not* SJ (I have given them no ground for any such intention LC)

126–8   s.d. *Suddenly . . . approval* SJ

WARWICK [*deprecating, but by no means denying*]

Oh, my lord, you are very hard on us poor English. But we certainly do not share your pious desire to save The Maid: in fact I tell you now plainly that her death is a political   140 necessity which I regret but cannot help. If the Church lets her go –

CAUCHON [*with fierce and menacing pride*]

If the Church lets her go, woe to the man, were he the Emperor himself, who dares lay a finger on her! The Church is not   145 subject to political necessity, my lord.

THE INQUISITOR [*interposing smoothly*]

You need have no anxiety about the result, my lord. You have an invincible ally in the matter: one who is far more determined than you that she shall burn.   150

WARWICK

And who is this very convenient partisan, may I ask?

THE INQUISITOR

The Maid herself. Unless you put a gag in her mouth you cannot prevent her from convicting herself ten times over every   155 time she opens it.

D'ESTIVET

That is perfectly true, my lord. My hair bristles on my head when I hear so young a creature utter such blasphemies.

WARWICK   160

Well, by all means do your best for her if you are quite sure it will be of no avail. [*Looking hard at* CAUCHON] I should be sorry to have to act without the blessing of the Church.

CAUCHON [*with a mixture of cynical admiration and contempt*]

And yet they say Englishmen are hypocrites! You play for your   165 side, my lord, even at the peril of your soul. I cannot but admire such devotion; but I dare not go so far myself. I fear damnation.

WARWICK

If we feared anything we could never govern England, my lord.   170 Shall I send your people in to you?

CAUCHON

Yes: it will be very good of your lordship to withdraw and allow the court to assemble.

    WARWICK *turns on his heel, and goes out through the court-*   175 *yard.* CAUCHON *takes one of the judicial seats; and* D'ESTIVET *sits at the scribes' table, studying his brief.*

CAUCHON [*casually, as he makes himself comfortable*]

What scoundrels these English nobles are!

THE INQUISITOR [*taking the other judicial chair on* CAUCHON'*s left*]   180

All secular power makes men scoundrels. They are not trained
for the work; and they have not the Apostolic Succession. Our
own nobles are just as bad.

THE BISHOP'S ASSESSORS *hurry into the hall, headed by*
CHAPLAIN DE STOGUMBER *and* CANON DE COURCELLES, *a*   185
young priest of 30. The scribes sit at the table, leaving a chair
vacant opposite D'ESTIVET. *Some of* THE ASSESSORS *take their*
seats: others stand chatting, waiting for the proceedings to begin
formally. DE STOGUMBER, *aggrieved and obstinate, will not take*
his seat: neither will the CANON, *who stands on his right.*   190

CAUCHON

Good morning, Master de Stogumber. [*To* THE INQUISITOR]
Chaplain to the Cardinal of England.

THE CHAPLAIN [*correcting him*]

Of Winchester, my lord. I have to make a protest, my lord.   195

CAUCHON

You make a great many.

THE CHAPLAIN

I am not without support, my lord. Here is Master de Courcelles,
Canon of Paris, who associates himself with me in my protest.   200

CAUCHON

Well, what is the matter?

THE CHAPLAIN [*sulkily*]

Speak you, Master de Courcelles, since I do not seem to enjoy
his lordship's confidence. [*He sits down in dudgeon next to* CAU-   205
CHON, *on his right*]

COURCELLES

My lord: we have been at great pains to draw up an indictment
of The Maid on sixty-four counts. We are now told that they
have been reduced, without consulting us.   210

---

182   *Apostolic Succession* the unbroken line of bishops from the Apostles, whose authority was
      granted by Christ

184–9   s.d. *hurry ... formally* SJ (*take their seats each one bobbing his head perfunctorily to*
      the Bishop before sitting down. The scribes sit at the table, leaving a chair vacant
      beside D'Estivet LC)

205–6   s.d. *He ... right* SJ

205   s.d. *in dudgeon* angrily, with resentment

210   *consulting us* SJ (consulting us to twelve articles, which must needs be insufficient LC)

THE INQUISITOR

Master de Courcelles: I am the culprit. I am overwhelmed with
admiration for the zeal displayed in your sixty-four counts; but
in accusing a heretic, as in other things, enough is enough. Also
you must remember that all the members of the court are not   215
so subtle and profound as you, and that some of your very
great learning might appear to them to be very great nonsense.
Therefore I have thought it well to have your sixty-four articles
cut down to twelve –

COURCELLES [*thunderstruck*]   220

Twelve!!!

THE INQUISITOR

Twelve will, believe me, be quite enough for your purpose.

THE CHAPLAIN

But some of the most important points have been reduced   225
almost to nothing. For instance, The Maid has actually declared
that the blessed saints Margaret and Catherine, and the holy
Archangel Michael, spoke to her in French. That is a vital point.

THE INQUISITOR

You think, doubtless, that they should have spoken in Latin?   230

CAUCHON

No: he thinks they should have spoken in English.

THE CHAPLAIN

Naturally, my lord.

THE INQUISITOR   235

Well, as we are all here agreed, I think, that these voices of The
Maid are the voices of evil spirits tempting her to her damnation, it would not be very courteous to you, Master de
Stogumber, or to the King of England, to assume that English is
the devil's native language. So let it pass. The matter is not   240
wholly omitted from the twelve articles. Pray take your places,
gentlemen; and let us proceed to business.

All who have not taken their seats, do so.

THE CHAPLAIN

Well, I protest. That is all.   245

220–2   *COURCELLES ... INQUISITOR* SJ

232   *he ... English* The claim to their speaking French was one of the twelve articles against
Jeanne at the trial: ' "Does not Saint Margaret speak English?" / "Why should she speak
English when she is not on the English side" ' (Murray, p. 42).

COURCELLES

I think it hard that all our work should go for nothing. It is
only another example of the diabolical influence which this
woman exercises over the court. [*He takes his chair, which is on*
THE CHAPLAIN'*s right*]   250

CAUCHON

Do you suggest that I am under diabolical influence?

COURCELLES

I suggest nothing, my lord. But it seems to me that there is a
conspiracy here to hush up the fact that The Maid stole the   255
Bishop of Senlis's horse.

CAUCHON [*keeping his temper with difficulty*]

This is not a police court. Are we to waste our time on such
rubbish?

COURCELLES [*rising, shocked*]   260

My lord: do you call the Bishop's horse rubbish?

THE INQUISITOR [*blandly*]

Master de Courcelles: The Maid alleges that she paid handsomely for the Bishop's horse, and that if he did not get the
money the fault was not hers. As that may be true, the point is 265
one on which The Maid may well be acquitted.

COURCELLES

Yes, if it were an ordinary horse. But the Bishop's horse! how
can she be acquitted for that? [*He sits down again, bewildered
and discouraged*]   270

THE INQUISITOR

I submit to you, with great respect, that if we persist in trying
The Maid on trumpery issues on which we may have to declare
her innocent, she may escape us on the great main issue of
heresy, on which she seems so far to insist on her own guilt. I will 275
ask you, therefore, to say nothing, when The Maid is brought
before us, of these stealings of horses, and dancings round fairy
trees with the village children, and prayings at haunted wells, and
a dozen other things which you were diligently inquiring into
until my arrival. There is not a village girl in France against   280
whom you could not prove such things: they all dance round

249–50   s.d. *on . . . right* SJ (*on the Inquisitor's left* LC). Shaw's left/right reorientation here had
consequences for his conception of the subsequent staging of the scene.

255–6   *The . . . horse* Accusations about the Bishop's horse were raised in the 15 March interrogation (Murray, pp. 72–3).

haunted trees, and pray at magic wells. Some of them would steal
the Pope's horse if they got the chance. Heresy, gentlemen, heresy
is the charge we have to try. The detection and suppression of
heresy is my peculiar business: I am here as an inquisitor, not as   285
an ordinary magistrate. Stick to the heresy, gentlemen; and leave
the other matters alone.

CAUCHON

I may say that we have sent to the girl's village to make inquiries
about her? and there is practically nothing serious against her.   290

THE CHAPLAIN   } [*rising and* } Nothing serious, my lord –
                 } *clamoring* }
COURCELLES   } *together*] } What! The fairy tree not –
CAUCHON [*out of patience*]

Be silent, gentlemen; or speak one at a time.   295

    COURCELLES *collapses into his chair, intimidated.*

THE CHAPLAIN [*sulkily resuming his seat*]

That is what The Maid said to us last Friday.

CAUCHON

I wish you had followed her counsel, sir. When I say nothing   300
serious, I mean nothing that men of sufficiently large mind to
conduct an inquiry like this would consider serious. I agree
with my colleague the Inquisitor that it is on the count of
heresy that we must proceed.

LADVENU [*a young but ascetically fine-drawn Dominican who is*   305
sitting next COURCELLES, *on his right*]

But is there any great harm in the girl's heresy? Is it not merely
her simplicity? Many saints have said as much as Joan.

THE INQUISITOR [*dropping his blandness and speaking very gravely*]

Brother Martin: if you had seen what I have seen of heresy,   310
you would not think it a light thing even in its most apparently
harmless and even lovable and pious origins. Heresy begins with
people who are to all appearance better than their neighbors. A
gentle and pious girl, or a young man who has obeyed the command of our Lord by giving all his riches to the poor, and putting   315
on the garb of poverty, the life of austerity, and the rule of humility and charity, may be the founder of a heresy that will wreck
both Church and Empire if not ruthlessly stamped out in time.

---

306   s.d. *sitting . . . right* SJ (*sitting in the chair nearest to the stool for the prisoner* LC)
310–87   *Brother . . . trial* Shaw regularly timed the speech, recording '7 minutes' (frequently noted,
        including r.n. 1936, fo. 302, and Hill, pp. 8, 35).

The records of the holy Inquisition are full of histories we dare
not give to the world, because they are beyond the belief of honest   320
men and innocent women; yet they all began with saintly simple-
tons. I have seen this again and again. Mark what I say: the
woman who quarrels with her clothes, and puts on the dress of a
man, is like the man who throws off his fur gown and dresses like
John the Baptist: they are followed, as surely as the night follows   325
the day, by bands of wild women and men who refuse to wear any
clothes at all. When maids will neither marry nor take regular
vows, and men reject marriage and exalt their lusts into divine
inspirations, then, as surely as the summer follows the spring,
they begin with polygamy, and end by incest. Heresy at first seems   330
innocent and even laudable; but it ends in such a monstrous
horror of unnatural wickedness that the most tender-hearted
among you, if you saw it at work as I have seen it, would clamor
against the mercy of the Church in dealing with it. For two hundred years the Holy Office has striven with these diabolical   335
madnesses; and it knows that they begin always by vain and ignorant persons setting up their own judgment against the Church,
and taking it upon themselves to be the interpreters of God's will.
You must not fall into the common error of mistaking these sim-
pletons for liars and hypocrites. They believe honestly and   340
sincerely that their diabolical inspiration is divine. Therefore you
must be on your guard against your natural compassion. You are
all, I hope, merciful men: how else could you have devoted your
lives to the service of our gentle Savior? You are going to see
before you a young girl, pious and chaste; for I must tell you, gen-   345
tlemen, that the things said of her by our English friends are
supported by no evidence, whilst there is abundant testimony
that her excesses have been excesses of religion and charity and
not of worldliness and wantonness. This girl is not one of those
whose hard features are the sign of hard hearts, and whose brazen   350
looks and lewd demeanor condemn them before they are
accused. The devilish pride that has led her into her present peril
has left no mark on her countenance. Strange as it may seem to
you, it has even left no mark on her character outside those special matters in which she is proud; so that you will see a diabolical   355
pride and a natural humility seated side by side in the selfsame
soul. Therefore be on your guard. God forbid that I should tell

330   *polygamy* marriage to several women simultaneously

93

you to harden your hearts; for her punishment if we condemn
her will be so cruel that we should forfeit our own hope of divine
mercy were there one grain of malice against her in our hearts.   360
But if you hate cruelty – and if any man here does not hate it I
command him on his soul's salvation to quit this holy court – I
say, if you hate cruelty, remember that nothing is so cruel in its
consequences as the toleration of heresy. Remember also that no
court of law can be so cruel as the common people are to those   365
whom they suspect of heresy. The heretic in the hands of the
Holy Office is safe from violence, is assured of a fair trial, and
cannot suffer death, even when guilty, if repentance follows sin.
Innumerable lives of heretics have been saved because the Holy
Office has taken them out of the hands of the people, and because   370
the people have yielded them up, knowing that the Holy Office
would deal with them. Before the Holy Inquisition existed, and
even now when its officers are not within reach, the unfortunate
wretch suspected of heresy, perhaps quite ignorantly and unjustly,
is stoned, torn in pieces, drowned, burned in his house with all   375
his innocent children, without a trial, unshriven, unburied save as
a dog is buried: all of them deeds hateful to God and most cruel
to man. Gentlemen: I am compassionate by nature as well as by
my profession; and though the work I have to do may seem cruel
to those who do not know how much more cruel it would be to   380
leave it undone, I would go to the stake myself sooner than do it if
I did not know its righteousness, its necessity, its essential mercy. I
ask you to address yourself to this trial in that conviction. Anger is
a bad counsellor: cast out anger. Pity is sometimes worse: cast out
pity. But do not cast out mercy. Remember only that justice   385
comes first. Have you anything to say, my lord, before we proceed
to trial?

CAUCHON

You have spoken for me, and spoken better than I could. I do
not see how any sane man could disagree with a word that has   390
fallen from you. But this I will add. The crude heresies of which
you have told us are horrible; but their horror is like that of the
black death: they rage for a while and then die out, because
sound and sensible men will not under any incitement be rec-
onciled to nakedness and incest and polygamy and the like. But   395

376 *unshriven* not having been absolved of sin, so without chance of heaven
393 *black death* the plague of 1347–50 that killed a third of Europe's population

we are confronted today throughout Europe with a heresy that
is spreading among men not weak in mind nor diseased in
brain: nay, the stronger the mind, the more obstinate the
heretic. It is neither discredited by fantastic extremes nor corrupted by the common lusts of the flesh; but it, too, sets up the   400
private judgment of the single erring mortal against the considered wisdom and experience of the Church. The mighty
structure of Catholic Christendom will never be shaken by
naked madmen or by the sins of Moab and Ammon. But it may
be betrayed from within, and brought to barbarous ruin and   405
desolation, by this arch heresy which the English Commander
calls Protestantism.

THE ASSESSORS [whispering]

Protestantism! What was that? What does the Bishop mean? Is
it a new heresy? The English Commander, he said. Did *you* ever   410
hear of Protestantism? etc., etc.

CAUCHON [continuing]

And that reminds me. What provision has the Earl of Warwick
made for the defence of the secular arm should The Maid prove
obdurate, and the people be moved to pity her?   415

THE CHAPLAIN

Have no fear on that score, my lord. The noble earl has eight
hundred men-at-arms at the gates. She will not slip through
our English fingers even if the whole city be on her side.

CAUCHON [revolted]   420

Will you not add, God grant that she repent and purge her sin?

THE CHAPLAIN

That does not seem to me to be consistent; but of course I
agree with your lordship.

CAUCHON [giving him up with a shrug of contempt]   425

The court sits.

THE INQUISITOR

Let the accused be brought in.

LADVENU [calling]

The accused. Let her be brought in.   430

---

399   *discredited* SJ (disgraced LC)

404   *Moab and Ammon* sons of the incestuous coupling of Lot with his daughters following the
      destruction of Sodom, whose descendants indulged in idolatry and human sacrifice, threat-
      ening the faith of Solomon (Genesis 19; 1 Kings 11: 1–10)

408–11   THE ASSESSORS ... *etc.* The responses of the Assessors here and at ll. 624, 665, 710, 996
      were added in SJ.

JOAN, *chained by the ankles, is brought in through the arched door behind the prisoner's stool by a guard of English* SOLDIERS. *With them is* THE EXECUTIONER *and his* ASSISTANTS. *They lead her to the prisoner's stool, and place themselves behind it after taking off her chain. She wears a page's black suit. Her long imprisonment and the strain of the examinations which have pre-ceded the trial have left their mark on her; but her vitality still holds: she confronts the court unabashed, without a trace of the awe which their formal solemnity seems to require for the com-plete success of its impressiveness.* 435

440

THE INQUISITOR [*kindly*]

Sit down, Joan. [*She sits on the prisoner's stool*] You look very pale today. Are you not well?

JOAN

Thank you kindly: I am well enough. But the Bishop sent me 445 some carp; and it made me ill.

CAUCHON

I am sorry. I told them to see that it was fresh.

JOAN

You meant to be good to me, I know; but it is a fish that does 450 not agree with me. The English thought you were trying to poison me –

CAUCHON   } [*together*] { What!
THE CHAPLAIN }   { No, my lord.

JOAN [*continuing*] 455

They are determined that I shall be burnt as a witch; and they sent their doctor to cure me; but he was forbidden to bleed me because the silly people believe that a witch's witchery leaves her if she is bled; so he only called me filthy names. Why do you leave me in the hands of the English? I should be in the 460 hands of the Church. And why must I be chained by the feet to a log of wood? Are you afraid I will fly away?

431–5   s.d. JOAN . . . *chain* Shaw to Wendy Hiller (Malvern, 1936): 'kick the chain from step to step instead of dragging it. Let the kicks be heard before you come in; and when they take it off do not rub your ankle pathetically; but bend your legs at the knee as if you were going to take on the whole court at all-in wrestling' (L4, p. 437).

435   s.d. *She . . . suit* Shaw cites Lang, p. 262, as source for this costume (ms file, fo. 56).

446   *carp . . . ill* The carp (a river fish) was believed to have caused Jeanne's sickness (Murray, p. 245).

457   *bleed* The medical practice of releasing excess blood, believed to restore the equilibrium of the body, was common from Ancient Greece to the nineteenth century.

D'ESTIVET [*harshly*]

Woman: it is not for you to question the court: it is for us to
question you.   465

COURCELLES

When you were left unchained, did you not try to escape by
jumping from a tower sixty feet high? If you cannot fly like a
witch, how is it that you are still alive?

JOAN   470

I suppose because the tower was not so high then. It has grown
higher every day since you began asking me questions about it.

D'ESTIVET

Why did you jump from the tower?

JOAN   475

How do you know that I jumped?

D'ESTIVET

You were found lying in the moat. Why did you leave the tower?

JOAN

Why would anybody leave a prison if they could get out?   480

D'ESTIVET

You tried to escape?

JOAN

Of course I did; and not for the first time either. If you leave the
door of the cage open the bird will fly out.   485

D'ESTIVET [*rising*]

That is a confession of heresy. I call the attention of the court
to it.

JOAN

Heresy, he calls it! Am I a heretic because I try to escape from   490
prison?

D'ESTIVET

Assuredly, if you are in the hands of the Church, and you
wilfully take yourself out of its hands, you are deserting the
Church; and that is heresy.   495

JOAN

It is great nonsense. Nobody could be such a fool as to think that.

D'ESTIVET

You hear, my lord, how I am reviled in the execution of my
duty by this woman. [*He sits down indignantly*]   500

CAUCHON

I have warned you before, Joan, that you are doing yourself no
good by these pert answers.

JOAN

But you will not talk sense to me. I am reasonable if you will be   505
reasonable.

THE INQUISITOR [*interposing*]

This is not yet in order. You forget, Master Promoter, that the
proceedings have not been formally opened. The time for questions is after she has sworn on the Gospels to tell us the whole   510
truth.

JOAN

You say this to me every time. I have said again and again that I
will tell you all that concerns this trial. But I cannot tell you the
whole truth: God does not allow the whole truth to be told. You   515
do not understand it when I tell it. It is an old saying that he
who tells too much truth is sure to be hanged. I am weary of
this argument: we have been over it nine times already. I have
sworn as much as I will swear; and I will swear no more.

COURCELLES   520

My lord: she should be put to the torture.

THE INQUISITOR

You hear, Joan? That is what happens to the obdurate. Think
before you answer. Has she been shewn the instruments?

THE EXECUTIONER   525

They are ready, my lord. She has seen them.

JOAN

If you tear me limb from limb until you separate my soul from
my body you will get nothing out of me beyond what I have
told you. What more is there to tell that you could understand?   530
Besides, I cannot bear to be hurt; and if you hurt me I will say
anything you like to stop the pain. But I will take it all back
afterwards; so what is the use of it?

LADVENU

There is much in that. We should proceed mercifully.   535

COURCELLES

But the torture is customary.

THE INQUISITOR

It must not be applied wantonly. If the accused will confess
voluntarily, then its use cannot be justified.   540

514–15   *I . . . told* 'I will not tell you all; I have not leave; my oath does not touch on that. My Voice
is good and to be honoured. I am not bound to answer you about it' (Murray, p. 24).

COURCELLES

But this is unusual and irregular. She refuses to take the oath.

LADVENU [*disgusted*]

Do you want to torture the girl for the mere pleasure of it?

COURCELLES [*bewildered*]   545

But it is not a pleasure. It is the law. It is customary. It is always ⎬
done.

THE INQUISITOR

That is not so, Master, except when the inquiries are carried on
by people who do not know their legal business.   550

COURCELLES

But the woman is a heretic. I assure you it is always done.

CAUCHON [*decisively*]

It will not be done today if it is not necessary. Let there be an
end of this. I will not have it said that we proceeded on forced   555
confessions. We have sent our best preachers and doctors to this
woman to exhort and implore her to save her soul and body
from the fire: we shall not now send the executioner to thrust
her into it.

COURCELLES   560

Your lordship is merciful, of course. But it is a great responsibility to depart from the usual practice.

JOAN

Thou art a rare noodle, Master. Do what was done last time is
thy rule, eh?   565

COURCELLES [*rising*]

Thou wanton: dost thou dare call me noodle?

THE INQUISITOR

Patience, Master, patience: I fear you will soon be only too
terribly avenged.   570

COURCELLES [*mutters*]

Noodle indeed! [*He sits down, much discontented*]

THE INQUISITOR

Meanwhile, let us not be moved by the rough side of a shepherd
lass's tongue.   575

---

554 *It ... necessary* Cauchon judged so, following advice from the Assessors (Murray,
     pp. 127–9).

564 *Thou ... Master* Shaw's invention; a rehearsal note to Sybil Thorndike reads 'play it more
     heartily', and to Wendy Hiller, 'here a flash of her old fun and fire' (r.n. 1924, fo. 161; r.n.
     1936, fo. 302).

JOAN

Nay: I am no shepherd lass, though I have helped with the sheep like anyone else. I will do a lady's work in the house – spin or weave – against any woman in Rouen.

THE INQUISITOR   580

This is not a time for vanity, Joan. You stand in great peril.

JOAN

I know it: have I not been punished for my vanity? If I had not worn my cloth of gold surcoat in battle like a fool, that Burgundian soldier would never have pulled me backwards off   585
my horse; and I should not have been here.

THE CHAPLAIN

If you are so clever at woman's work why do you not stay at home and do it?

JOAN   590

There are plenty of other women to do it; but there is nobody to do my work.

CAUCHON

Come! we are wasting time on trifles. Joan: I am going to put a most solemn question to you. Take care how you answer; for   595
your life and salvation are at stake on it. Will you for all you have said and done, be it good or bad, accept the judgment of God's Church on earth? More especially as to the acts and words that are imputed to you in this trial by the Promoter here, will you submit your case to the inspired interpretation of   600
the Church Militant?

JOAN

I am a faithful child of the Church. I will obey the Church –

CAUCHON [hopefully leaning forward]

You will?   605

JOAN

– provided it does not command anything impossible.

CAUCHON sinks back in his chair with a heavy sigh. THE
INQUISITOR purses his lips and frowns. LADVENU shakes his
head pitifully.   610

577   no shepherd lass Jeanne's insistence at the trial (Murray, pp. 17, 25, 212, 213). See Preface, p. 143.
584   surcoat cloth garment showing heraldic arms, worn over armour
600–1 will . . . Militant Cf. 'this Church regularly assembled cannot err, being ruled by the Holy
       Spirit. Will you refer yourself to this Church which we have thus defined for you?' (Murray,
       p. 79).
601   the Church Militant the church on earth, led by 'God's Vicar', the Pope

D'ESTIVET

She imputes to the Church the error and folly of commanding the impossible.

JOAN

If you command me to declare that all that I have done and said, and all the visions and revelations I have had, were not from God, then that is impossible: I will not declare it for anything in the world. What God made me do I will never go back on; and what He has commanded or shall command I will not fail to do in spite of any man alive. That is what I mean by impossible. And in case the Church should bid me do anything contrary to the command I have from God, I will not consent to it, no matter what it may be. 615 620

THE ASSESSORS [shocked and indignant]

Oh! The Church contrary to God! What do you say now? Flat heresy. This is beyond everything, etc., etc. 625

D'ESTIVET [throwing down his brief]

My lord: do you need anything more than this?

CAUCHON

Woman: you have said enough to burn ten heretics. Will you not be warned? Will you not understand? 630

THE INQUISITOR

If the Church Militant tells you that your revelations and visions are sent by the devil to tempt you to your damnation, will you not believe that the Church is wiser than you? 635

JOAN

I believe that God is wiser than I; and it is His commands that I will do. All the things that you call my crimes have come to me by the command of God. I say that I have done them by the order of God: it is impossible for me to say anything else. If any Churchman says the contrary I shall not mind him: I shall mind God alone, whose command I always follow. 640

LADVENU [pleading with her urgently]

You do not know what you are saying, child. Do you want to kill yourself? Listen. Do you not believe that you are subject to the Church of God on earth? 645

JOAN

Yes. When have I ever denied it?

633–5   If . . . you? Shaw asked Cecil Trouncer for 'despair in his voice' here (r.n. 1936, fo. 302).

101

LADVENU

Good. That means, does it not, that you are subject to our Lord   650
the Pope, to the cardinals, the archbishops, and the bishops for
whom his lordship stands here today?

JOAN

God must be served first.

D'ESTIVET   655

Then your voices command you not to submit yourself to the
Church Militant?

JOAN

My voices do not tell me to disobey the Church; but God must
be served first.   660

CAUCHON

And you, and not the Church, are to be the judge?

JOAN

What other judgment can I judge by but my own?

THE ASSESSORS [scandalized]   665

Oh! [They cannot find words]

CAUCHON

Out of your own mouth you have condemned yourself. We
have striven for your salvation to the verge of sinning ourselves:
we have opened the door to you again and again; and you have   670
shut it in our faces and in the face of God. Dare you pretend,
after what you have said, that you are in a state of grace?

JOAN

If I am not, may God bring me to it: if I am, may God keep me
in it!   675

LADVENU

That is a very good reply, my lord.

COURCELLES

Were you in a state of grace when you stole the Bishop's horse?

CAUCHON [rising in a fury]   680

Oh, devil take the Bishop's horse and you too! We are here to try
a case of heresy; and no sooner do we come to the root of the
matter than we are thrown back by idiots who understand nothing but horses. [Trembling with rage, he forces himself to sit down]

THE INQUISITOR   685

Gentlemen, gentlemen: in clinging to these small issues you are
The Maid's best advocates. I am not surprised that his lordship

674–5   If . . . it 'If I am not, may God place me there; if I am, may God so keep me' (Murray, p. 24).

has lost patience with you. What does the Promoter say? Does
he press these trumpery matters?

D'ESTIVET   690

I am bound by my office to press everything; but when the
woman confesses a heresy that must bring upon her the doom of
excommunication, of what consequence is it that she has been
guilty also of offences which expose her to minor penances? I
share the impatience of his lordship as to these minor charges.   695
Only, with great respect, I must emphasize the gravity of two very
horrible and blasphemous crimes which she does not deny. First,
she has intercourse with evil spirits, and is therefore a sorceress.
Second, she wears men's clothes, which is indecent, unnatural, and
abominable; and in spite of our most earnest remonstrances and   700
entreaties, she will not change them even to receive the sacrament.

JOAN

Is the blessed St Catherine an evil spirit? Is St Margaret? Is
Michael the Archangel?

COURCELLES   705

How do you know that the spirit which appears to you is an
archangel? Does he not appear to you as a naked man?

JOAN

Do you think God cannot afford clothes for him?

    THE ASSESSORS *cannot help smiling, especially as the joke is*   710
against COURCELLES.

LADVENU

Well answered, Joan.

THE INQUISITOR

It is, in effect, well answered. But no evil spirit would be so   715
simple as to appear to a young girl in a guise that would scandalize her when he meant her to take him for a messenger from
the Most High? Joan: the Church instructs you that these
apparitions are demons seeking your soul's perdition. Do you
accept the instruction of the Church?   720

JOAN

I accept the messenger of God. How could any faithful believer
in the Church refuse him?

CAUCHON

Wretched woman: again I ask you, do you know what you are   725
saying?

709   *Do . . . him?* 'Do you think God has not wherewithal to clothe him?' (Murray, p. 44).

THE INQUISITOR

You wrestle in vain with the devil for her soul, my lord: she will not be saved. Now as to this matter of the man's dress. For the last time, will you put off that impudent attire, and dress as   730 becomes your sex?

JOAN

I will not.

D'ESTIVET [*pouncing*]

The sin of disobedience, my lord.   735

JOAN [*distressed*]

But my voices tell me I must dress as a soldier.

LADVENU

Joan, Joan: does not that prove to you that the voices are the voices of evil spirits? Can you suggest to us one good reason   740 why an angel of God should give you such shameless advice?

JOAN

Why, yes: what can be plainer commonsense? I was a soldier living among soldiers. I am a prisoner guarded by soldiers. If I were to dress as a woman they would think of me as a woman;   745 and then what would become of me? If I dress as a soldier they think of me as a soldier, and I can live with them as I do at home with my brothers. That is why St Catherine tells me I must not dress as a woman until she gives me leave.

COURCELLES   750

When will she give you leave?

JOAN

When you take me out of the hands of the English soldiers. I have told you that I should be in the hands of the Church, and not left night and day with four soldiers of the Earl of Warwick.   755 Do you want me to live with them in petticoats?

LADVENU

My lord: what she says is, God knows, very wrong and shocking; but there is a grain of worldly sense in it such as might impose on a simple village maiden.   760

JOAN

If we were as simple in the village as you are in your courts and palaces, there would soon be no wheat to make bread for you.

746   *what would become of me?* Male dress defended against rape in the male dominated prison. Various depositions, including Ladvenu's, said Jeanne reported molestation (Murray, pp. 166, 189).

753–5   *I . . . Warwick* Despite the charge of heresy, she was held in a secular prison.

CAUCHON

That is the thanks you get for trying to save her, Brother Martin.   765

LADVENU

Joan: we are all trying to save you. His lordship is trying to save you. The Inquisitor could not be more just to you if you were his own daughter. But you are blinded by a terrible pride and self-sufficiency.   770

JOAN

Why do you say that? I have said nothing wrong. I cannot understand.

THE INQUISITOR

The blessed St Athanasius has laid it down in his creed that   775
those who cannot understand are damned. It is not enough to be simple. It is not enough even to be what simple people call good. The simplicity of a darkened mind is no better than the simplicity of a beast.

JOAN   780

There is great wisdom in the simplicity of a beast, let me tell you; and sometimes great foolishness in the wisdom of scholars.

LADVENU

We know that, Joan: we are not so foolish as you think us. Try   785
to resist the temptation to make pert replies to us. Do you see that man who stands behind you [*he indicates* THE EXECUTIONER]?

JOAN [*turning and looking at the man*]

Your torturer? But the Bishop said I was not to be tortured.   790

LADVENU

You are not to be tortured because you have confessed everything that is necessary to your condemnation. That man is not only the torturer: he is also the Executioner. Executioner: let The Maid hear your answers to my questions. Are you prepared   795
for the burning of a heretic this day?

THE EXECUTIONER

Yes, Master.

---

775   *St Athanasius* Bishop of Alexandria, elected Patriarch in 326. His creed is known as the '*Quicumque Vult*' from its all-inclusive opening, 'Whosoever wishes (to be saved)'. A condition for the licensing of Shaw's *Back to Methuselah*, 1920, had been the omission of a paraphrase of the Athanasian Creed.

LADVENU

Is the stake ready? 800

THE EXECUTIONER

It is. In the market-place. The English have built it too high for me to get near her and make the death easier. It will be a cruel death.

JOAN [horrified] 805

But you are not going to burn me now?

THE INQUISITOR

You realize it at last.

LADVENU

There are eight hundred English soldiers waiting to take you to 810 the market-place the moment the sentence of excommunication has passed the lips of your judges. You are within a few short moments of that doom.

JOAN [looking round desperately for rescue]

Oh God! 815

LADVENU

Do not despair, Joan. The Church is merciful. You can save yourself.

JOAN [hopefully]

Yes, my voices promised me I should not be burnt. St Catherine 820 bade me be bold.

CAUCHON

Woman: are you quite mad? Do you not yet see that your voices have deceived you?

JOAN 825

Oh no: that is impossible.

CAUCHON

Impossible! They have led you straight to your excommunication, and to the stake which is there waiting for you.

LADVENU [pressing the point hard] 830

Have they kept a single promise to you since you were taken at Compiègne? The devil has betrayed you. The Church holds out its arms to you.

JOAN [despairing]

Oh, it is true: it is true: my voices have deceived me. I have been 835 mocked by devils: my faith is broken. I have dared and dared; but only a fool will walk into a fire: God, who gave me my commonsense, cannot will me to do that.

LADVENU

Now God be praised that He has saved you at the eleventh hour!　840
[*He hurries to the vacant seat at the scribes' table, and snatches a
sheet of paper, on which he sets to work writing eagerly*]

CAUCHON

Amen!

JOAN　845

What must I do?

CAUCHON

You must sign a solemn recantation of your heresy.

JOAN

Sign? That means to write my name. I cannot write.　850

CAUCHON

You have signed many letters before.

JOAN

Yes; but someone held my hand and guided the pen. I can make
my mark.　855

THE CHAPLAIN [*who has been listening with growing alarm and
indignation*]

My lord: do you mean that you are going to allow this woman
to escape us?

THE INQUISITOR　860

The law must take its course, Master de Stogumber. And you
know the law.

THE CHAPLAIN [*rising, purple with fury*]

I know that there is no faith in a Frenchman. [*Tumult, which he
shouts down*] I know what my lord the Cardinal of Winchester　865
will say when he hears of this. I know what the Earl of Warwick
will do when he learns that you intend to betray him. There are
eight hundred men at the gate who will see that this abominable witch is burnt in spite of your teeth.

THE ASSESSORS [*meanwhile*]　870

What is this? What did he say? He accuses us of treachery! This
is past bearing. No faith in a Frenchman! Did you hear that?
This is an intolerable fellow. Who is he? Is this what English
Churchmen are like? He must be mad or drunk, etc., etc.

THE INQUISITOR [*rising*]　875

Silence, pray! Gentlemen: pray silence! Master Chaplain: bethink
you a moment of your holy office: of what you are, and where
you are. I direct you to sit down.

870　s.d. *meanwhile* SJ (*scandalised* LC)

THE CHAPLAIN [*folding his arms doggedly, his face working convulsively*]   880
I will NOT sit down.

CAUCHON
Master Inquisitor: this man has called me a traitor to my face before now.

THE CHAPLAIN   885
So you are a traitor. You are all traitors. You have been doing nothing but begging this damnable witch on your knees to recant all through this trial.

THE INQUISITOR [*placidly resuming his seat*]
If you will not sit, you must stand: that is all.   890

THE CHAPLAIN
I will NOT stand [*he flings himself back into his chair*].

LADVENU [*rising with the paper in his hand*]
My lord: here is the form of recantation for The Maid to sign.

CAUCHON   895
Read it to her.

JOAN
Do not trouble. I will sign it.

THE INQUISITOR
Woman: you must know what you are putting your hand to.   900
Read it to her, Brother Martin. And let all be silent.

LADVENU [*reading quietly*]
'I, Joan, commonly called The Maid, a miserable sinner, do confess that I have most grievously sinned in the following articles. I have pretended to have revelations from God and the angels and   905
the blessed saints, and perversely rejected the Church's warnings that these were temptations by demons. I have blasphemed abominably by wearing an immodest dress, contrary to the Holy Scripture and the canons of the Church. Also I have clipped my hair in the style of a man, and, against all the duties which have   910
made my sex specially acceptable in heaven, have taken up the sword, even to the shedding of human blood, inciting men to slay each other, invoking evil spirits to delude them, and stubbornly and most blasphemously imputing these sins to Almighty God. I confess to the sin of sedition, to the sin of idolatry, to the   915
sin of disobedience, to the sin of pride, and to the sin of heresy. All of which sins I now renounce and abjure and depart from, humbly thanking you Doctors and Masters who have brought me back to the truth and into the grace of our Lord. And I will

never return to my errors, but will remain in communion with   920
our Holy Church and in obedience to our Holy Father the Pope
of Rome. All this I swear by God Almighty and the Holy Gospels,
in witness whereto I sign my name to this recantation.'

THE INQUISITOR
You understand this, Joan?   925

JOAN [*listless*]
It is plain enough, sir.

THE INQUISITOR
And is it true?

JOAN   930
It may be true. If it were not true, the fire would not be ready
for me in the market-place.

LADVENU [*taking up his pen and a book, and going to her quickly
lest she should compromise herself again*]
Come, child: let me guide your hand. Take the pen. [*She does so;*   935
and they begin to write, using the book as a desk] J. E. H. A. N. E.
So. Now make your mark by yourself.

JOAN [*makes her mark, and gives him back the pen, tormented by
the rebellion of her soul against her mind and body*]
There!   940

LADVENU [*replacing the pen on the table, and handing the recantation to* CAUCHON *with a reverence*]
Praise be to God, my brothers, the lamb has returned to the
flock; and the shepherd rejoices in her more than in ninety and
nine just persons. [*He returns to his seat*]   945

THE INQUISITOR [*taking the paper from* CAUCHON]
We declare thee by this act set free from the danger of excommunication in which thou stoodest. [*He throws the paper down
to the table*]

JOAN   950
I thank you.

THE INQUISITOR
But because thou has sinned most presumptuously against God
and the Holy Church, and that thou mayst repent thy errors in
solitary contemplation, and be shielded from all temptation to   955
return to them, we, for the good of thy soul, and for a penance
that may wipe out thy sins and bring thee finally unspotted to

---

944–5   *shepherd . . . persons* 'joy shall be in heaven over one sinner that repenteth, more than over
ninety and nine just persons, which need no repentance' (Luke 15: 7)

the throne of grace, do condemn thee to eat the bread of sorrow
and drink the water of affliction to the end of thy earthly days in
perpetual imprisonment.   960

JOAN [rising in consternation and terrible anger]

Perpetual imprisonment! Am I not then to be set free?

LADVENU [mildly shocked]

Set free, child, after such wickedness as yours! What are you
dreaming of?   965

JOAN

Give me that writing. [She rushes to the table; snatches up the
paper; and tears it into fragments] Light your fire: do you think I
dread it as much as the life of a rat in a hole? My voices were right.

LADVENU   970

Joan! Joan!

JOAN

Yes: they told me you were fools [the word gives great offence],
and that I was not to listen to your fine words nor trust to your
charity. You promised me my life; but you lied [indignant excla-   975
mations]. You think that life is nothing but not being stone dead.
It is not the bread and water I fear: I can live on bread: when
have I asked for more? It is no hardship to drink water if the
water be clean. Bread has no sorrow for me, and water no affliction. But to shut me from the light of the sky and the sight of the   980
fields and flowers; to chain my feet so that I can never again ride
with the soldiers nor climb the hills; to make me breathe foul
damp darkness, and keep from me everything that brings me
back to the love of God when your wickedness and foolishness
tempt me to hate Him: all this is worse than the furnace in the   985
Bible that was heated seven times. I could do without my
warhorse; I could drag about in a skirt; I could let the banners
and the trumpets and the knights and soldiers pass me and leave
me behind as they leave the other women, if only I could still
hear the wind in the trees, the larks in the sunshine, the young   990
lambs crying through the healthy frost, and the blessed blessed
church bells that send my angel voices floating to me on the

968–95   Light . . . God Although the length and detail of this speech is entirely Shaw's, on 28 May,
         Jeanne declared 'I would rather do penance once for all – that is die – than endure any
         longer the suffering of a prison' (Murray, p. 141).
985–6   furnace . . . times reference to the faith of Shadrach, Meshach and Abednego who survived
         the fiery furnace to which Nebuchadnezzar sentenced them (Daniel 3)

wind. But without these things I cannot live; and by your wanting to take them away from me, or from any human creature, I
know that your counsel is of the devil, and that mine is of God.   995

THE ASSESSORS [*in great commotion*]

Blasphemy! blasphemy! She is possessed. She said our counsel
was of the devil. And hers of God. Monstrous! The devil is in
our midst, etc., etc.

D'ESTIVET [*shouting above the din*]   1000

She is a relapsed heretic, obstinate, incorrigible, and altogether
unworthy of the mercy we have shewn her. I call for her excommunication.

THE CHAPLAIN [*to* THE EXECUTIONER]

Light your fire, man. To the stake with her.   1005

    THE EXECUTIONER *and his* ASSISTANTS *hurry out through
    the courtyard.*

LADVENU

You wicked girl: if your counsel were of God would He not
deliver you?   1010

JOAN

His ways are not your ways. He wills that I go through the fire
to His bosom; for I am His child, and you are not fit that I
should live among you. That is my last word to you.

    THE SOLDIERS *seize her.*   1015

CAUCHON [*rising*]

Not yet.

    They wait. There is a dead silence. CAUCHON *turns to* THE
    INQUISITOR *with an inquiring look.* THE INQUISITOR *nods affir-
    matively. They rise solemnly, and intone the sentence antiphonally.*   1020

CAUCHON

We decree that thou art a relapsed heretic.

THE INQUISITOR

Cast out from the unity of the Church.

CAUCHON   1025

Sundered from her body.

THE INQUISITOR

Infected with the leprosy of heresy.

CAUCHON

A member of Satan.   1030

1020   s.d. *and . . . antiphonally* ms rev.

THE INQUISITOR

We declare that thou must be excommunicate.

CAUCHON

And now we do cast thee out, segregate thee, and abandon thee
to the secular power.   1035

THE INQUISITOR

Admonishing the same secular power that it moderate its judgment of thee in respect of death and division of the limbs. [*He
resumes his seat*]

CAUCHON   1040

And if any true sign of penitence appear in thee, to permit our
Brother Martin to administer to thee the sacrament of penance.

THE CHAPLAIN

Into the fire with the witch [*he rushes at her, and helps* THE
SOLDIERS *to push her out*].   1045

JOAN *is taken away through the courtyard.* THE ASSESSORS
rise in disorder, and follow THE SOLDIERS, *except* LADVENU, *who
has hidden his face in his hands.*

CAUCHON [*rising again in the act of sitting down*]

No, no: this is irregular. The representative of the secular arm   1050
should be here to receive her from us.

THE INQUISITOR [*also on his feet again*]

That man is an incorrigible fool.

CAUCHON

Brother Martin: see that everything is done in order.   1055

LADVENU

My place is at her side, my Lord. You must exercise your own
authority. [*He hurries out*]

CAUCHON

These English are impossible: they will thrust her straight into   1060
the fire. Look!

*He points to the courtyard, in which the glow and flicker of fire
can now be seen reddening the May daylight. Only* THE BISHOP
and THE INQUISITOR *are left in the court.*

CAUCHON [*turning to go*]   1065

We must stop that.

THE INQUISITOR [*calmly*]

Yes; but not too fast, my lord.

1032   *excommunicate* SJ (abandoned LC, following Murray, p. 143)
1045   s.d. *push* SJ (*drag* LC)

CAUCHON [*halting*]

But there is not a moment to lose. 1070

THE INQUISITOR

We have proceeded in perfect order. If the English choose to put themselves in the wrong, it is not our business to put them in the right. A flaw in the procedure may be useful later on: one never knows. And the sooner it is over, the better for that 1075 poor girl.

CAUCHON [*relaxing*]

That is true. But I suppose we must see this dreadful thing through.

THE INQUISITOR 1080

One gets used to it. Habit is everything. I am accustomed to the fire: it is soon over. But it is a terrible thing to see a young and innocent creature crushed between these mighty forces, the Church and the Law.

CAUCHON 1085

You call her innocent!

THE INQUISITOR

Oh, quite innocent. What does she know of the Church and the Law? She did not understand a word we were saying. It is the ignorant who suffer. Come, or we shall be late for the end. 1090

CAUCHON [*going with him*]

I shall not be sorry if we are: I am not so accustomed as you.

They are going out when WARWICK *comes in, meeting them.*

WARWICK

Oh, I am intruding. I thought it was all over. [*He makes a feint* 1095 *of retiring*]

CAUCHON

Do not go, my lord. It is all over.

THE INQUISITOR

The execution is not in our hands, my lord; but it is desirable 1100 that we should witness the end. So by your leave – [*He bows, and goes out through the courtyard*]

CAUCHON

There is some doubt whether your people have observed the forms of law, my lord. 1105

WARWICK

I am told that there is some doubt whether your authority runs in this city, my lord. It is not in your diocese. However, if you will answer for that I will answer for the rest.

CAUCHON 1110

It is to God that we both must answer. Good morning, my lord.

WARWICK

My lord: good morning.

They look at one another for a moment with unconcealed hos-
tility. Then CAUCHON *follows* THE INQUISITOR *out.* WARWICK 1115
looks round. Finding himself alone, he calls for attendance.

WARWICK

Hallo: some attendance here! [*Silence*] Hallo, there! [*Silence*]
Hallo! Brian, you young blackguard, where are you? [*Silence*]
Guard! [*Silence*] They have all gone to see the burning: even 1120
that child.

The silence is broken by someone frantically howling and sobbing.

WARWICK

What in the devil's name –?

THE CHAPLAIN *staggers in from the courtyard like a demented* 1125
creature, his face streaming with tears, making the piteous sounds
that WARWICK *has heard. He stumbles to the prisoner's stool and*
throws himself upon it with heartrending sobs.

WARWICK [*going to him and patting him on the shoulder*]

What is it, Master John? What is the matter? 1130

THE CHAPLAIN [*clutching at his hand*]

My lord, my lord: for Christ's sake pray for my wretched
guilty soul.

WARWICK [*soothing him*]

Yes, yes: of course I will. Calmly, gently – 1135

THE CHAPLAIN [*blubbering miserably*]

I am not a bad man, my lord.

WARWICK

No, no: not at all.

THE CHAPLAIN 1140

I meant no harm. I did not know what it would be like.

WARWICK [*hardening*]

Oh! You saw it, then?

THE CHAPLAIN

I did not know what I was doing. I am a hot-headed fool; and I 1145
shall be damned to all eternity for it.

1111 *It . . . answer* SJ (We have both a good deal to answer for LC)
1142 s.d. *hardening* SJ (*understanding* ms rev.)
1146 *shall* ms rev. (will typescript)

114

WARWICK

Nonsense! Very distressing, no doubt; but it was not your doing.

THE CHAPLAIN [*lamentably*]

I let them do it. If I had known, I would have torn her from   1150
their hands. You dont know: you havnt seen: it is so easy to talk
when you dont know. You madden yourself with words: you
damn yourself because it feels grand to throw oil on the flaming hell of your own temper. But when it is brought home to
you; when you see the thing you have done; when it is blinding   1155
your eyes, stifling your nostrils, tearing your heart, then – then
– [*Falling on his knees*] O God, take away this sight from me! O
Christ, deliver me from this fire that is consuming me! She
cried to Thee in the midst of it: Jesus! Jesus! Jesus! She is in Thy
bosom; and I am in hell for evermore.   1160

WARWICK [*summarily hauling him to his feet*]

Come come, man! you must pull yourself together. We shall
have the whole town talking of this. [*He throws him not too
gently into a chair at the table*] If you have not the nerve to see
these things, why do you not do as I do, and stay away?   1165

THE CHAPLAIN [*bewildered and submissive*]

She asked for a cross. A soldier gave her two sticks tied together.
Thank God he was an Englishman! I might have done it; but
I did not: I am a coward, a mad dog, a fool. But he was an
Englishman too.   1170

WARWICK

The fool! they will burn him too if the priests get hold of him.

THE CHAPLAIN [*shaken with a convulsion*]

Some of the people laughed at her. They would have laughed at
Christ. They were French people, my lord: I know they were   1175
French.

WARWICK

Hush! someone is coming. Control yourself.

LADVENU *comes back through the courtyard to* WARWICK's
right hand, carrying a bishop's cross which he has taken from a   1180
church. He is very grave and composed.

1148   *Very . . . but* ms rev.
1151   *dont . . . havnt* Only now, after the more formal language of the trial scene, do contractions
reappear, marking Stogumber's hysteria.
1161   s.d. *summarily* ms rev.
1167–8   *She . . . Englishman* 'An Englishman, who was there present, made a little cross of wood
with the ends of a stick, which he gave her' (Murray, p. 177).

WARWICK

I am informed that it is all over, Brother Martin.

LADVENU [*enigmatically*]

We do not know, my lord. It may have only just begun.   1185

WARWICK

What does that mean, exactly?

LADVENU

I took this cross from the church for her that she might see it to
the last: she had only two sticks that she put into her bosom. When   1190
the fire crept round us, and she saw that if I held the cross before
her I should be burnt myself, she warned me to get down and save
myself. My lord: a girl who could think of another's danger in such
a moment was not inspired by the devil. When I had to snatch the
cross from her sight, she looked up to heaven. And I do not believe   1195
that the heavens were empty. I firmly believe that her Savior
appeared to her then in His tenderest glory. She called to Him and
died. This is not the end for her, but the beginning.

WARWICK

I am afraid it will have a bad effect on the people.   1200

LADVENU

It had, my lord, on some of them. I heard laughter. Forgive me
for saying that I hope and believe it was English laughter.

THE CHAPLAIN [*rising frantically*]

No: it was not. There was only one Englishman there that dis-   1205
graced his country; and that was the mad dog, de Stogumber.
[*He rushes wildly out, shrieking*] Let them torture him. Let them
burn him. I will go pray among her ashes. I am no better than
Judas: I will hang myself.

WARWICK   1210

Quick, Brother Martin: follow him: he will do himself some
mischief. After him, quick.

     LADVENU *hurries out,* WARWICK *urging him.* THE EXECU-
TIONER *comes in by the door behind the judges' chairs; and*
WARWICK, *returning, finds himself face to face with him.*   1215

WARWICK

Well, fellow: who are you?

THE EXECUTIONER [*with dignity*]

I am not addressed as fellow, my lord. I am the Master
Executioner of Rouen: it is a highly skilled mystery. I am come   1220
to tell your lordship that your orders have been obeyed.

1220   *mystery* ms rev. (trade typescript)

WARWICK

I crave your pardon, Master Executioner; and I will see that you
lose nothing by having no relics to sell. I have your word, have
I, that nothing remains, not a bone, not a nail, not a hair?   1225

THE EXECUTIONER

Her heart would not burn, my lord; but everything that was left
is at the bottom of the river. You have heard the last of her.

WARWICK [*with a wry smile, thinking of what* LADVENU *said*]

The last of her? Hm! I wonder!   1230

1225   *not . . . hair* SJ (not a hair, not a nail, not a bone LC)
1227–8   *everything . . . river* 'Her ashes and all that remained of her were collected and thrown in
    the Seine' (Murray, p. 204).
1230   *Hm!* ms rev.

EPILOGUE

*A restless fitfully windy night in June 1456, full of summer lightning
after many days of heat.* KING CHARLES THE SEVENTH *of France,
formerly Joan's Dauphin, now Charles the Victorious, aged 51, is in
bed in one of his royal chateaux. The bed, raised on a dais of two
steps, is towards the side of the room so as to avoid blocking a tall*   5
*lancet window in the middle. Its canopy bears the royal arms in
embroidery. Except for the canopy and the huge down pillows there is
nothing to distinguish it from a broad settee with bed-clothes and a
valance. Thus its occupant is in full view from the foot.*

    CHARLES *is not asleep: he is reading in bed, or rather looking at*   10
*the pictures in Fouquet's Boccaccio with his knees doubled up to make
a reading-desk. Beside the bed on his left is a little table with a picture
of the Virgin, lighted by candles of painted wax. The walls are hung
from ceiling to floor with painted curtains which stir at times in the
draughts. At first glance the prevailing yellow and red in these hang-*   15
ing pictures is somewhat flamelike when the folds breathe in the wind.

    The door is on CHARLES's *left, but in front of him close to the
corner farthest from him. A large watchman's rattle, handsomely
designed and gaily painted, is in the bed under his hand.*

    CHARLES *turns a leaf. A distant clock strikes the half-hour softly.*   20
CHARLES *shuts the book with a clap; throws it aside; snatches up the
rattle; and whirls it energetically, making a deafening clatter.* LAD-
VENU *enters, 25 years older, strange and stark in bearing, and still
carrying the cross from Rouen.* CHARLES *evidently does not expect
him; for he springs out of bed on the farther side from the door.*   25

CHARLES

Who are you? Where is my gentleman of the bedchamber?
What do you want?

---

    0   *Epilogue* SJ (Act V: Epilogue LC)

 4–9   s.d. *bed . . . foot* A note in LC that the bed '*is not a four poster*' was removed in SJ.

    6   s.d. *lancet window* window rising to a pointed arch

  11   s.d. *Fouquet's Boccaccio* stories by the Italian writer illuminated by Jean Fouquet (1420–80),
          Court painter to Charles VII and Louis XI. Fouquet's portrait of Charles is in the Louvre.

12–13   s.d. *a little . . . Virgin* SJ. LC otherwise details essentially the same set.

  18   s.d. *rattle* Shaw told Ernest Thesiger, his 1924 Dauphin, 'the rattle is important because it
          makes such a mad noise; and it is the mad noises in dreams that do not waken the sleeper'
          (L3, p. 872).

LADVENU [*solemnly*]

    I bring you glad tidings of great joy. Rejoice, O king; for the   30
taint is removed from your blood, and the stain from your
crown. Justice, long delayed, is at last triumphant.

CHARLES

    What are you talking about? Who are you?

LADVENU   35

    I am Brother Martin.

CHARLES

    And who, saving your reverence, may Brother Martin be?

LADVENU

    I held this cross when The Maid perished in the fire. Twenty-   40
five years have passed since then: nearly ten thousand days. And
on every one of those days I have prayed God to justify His
daughter on earth as she is justified in heaven.

CHARLES [*reassured, sitting down on the foot of the bed*]

    Oh, I remember now. I have heard of you. You have a bee in   45
your bonnet about The Maid. Have you been at the inquiry?

LADVENU

    I have given my testimony.

CHARLES

    Is it over?   50

LADVENU

    It is over.

CHARLES

    Satisfactorily?

LADVENU   55

    The ways of God are very strange.

CHARLES

    How so?

LADVENU

    At the trial which sent a saint to the stake as a heretic and a sor-   60
ceress, the truth was told; the law was upheld; mercy was shewn
beyond all custom; no wrong was done but the final and dreadful wrong of the lying sentence and the pitiless fire. At this
inquiry from which I have just come, there was shameless per-
jury, courtly corruption, calumny of the dead who did their   65
duty according to their lights, cowardly evasion of the issue,
testimony made of idle tales that could not impose on a
ploughboy. Yet out of this insult to justice, this defamation of
the Church, this orgy of lying and foolishness, the truth is set in

119

the noonday sun on the hilltop; the white robe of innocence is   70
cleansed from the smirch of the burning faggots; the holy life is
sanctified; the true heart that lived through the flame is consecrated; a great lie is silenced for ever; and a great wrong is set
right before all men.

CHARLES   75

My friend: provided they can no longer say that I was crowned
by a witch and a heretic, I shall not fuss about how the trick has
been done. Joan would not have fussed about it if it came all
right in the end: she was not that sort: I knew her. Is her rehabilitation complete? I made it pretty clear that there was to   80
be no nonsense about it.

LADVENU

It is solemnly declared that her judges were full of corruption,
cozenage, fraud, and malice. Four falsehoods.

CHARLES   85

Never mind the falsehoods: her judges are dead.

LADVENU

The sentence on her is broken, annulled, annihilated, set aside
as non-existent, without value or effect.

CHARLES   90

Good. Nobody can challenge my consecration now, can they?

LADVENU

Not Charlemagne nor King David himself was more sacredly
crowned.

CHARLES [rising]   95

Excellent. Think of what that means to me!

LADVENU

I think of what it means to her!

CHARLES

You cannot. None of us ever knew what anything meant to her.   100
She was like nobody else; and she must take care of herself
wherever she is; for I cannot take care of her; and neither can
you, whatever you may think: you are not big enough. But I
will tell you this about her. If you could bring her back to life,
they would burn her again within six months, for all their pres-   105
ent adoration of her. And you would hold up the cross, too, just

---

93   *Charlemagne ... David* respectively, eighth-century Holy Roman Emperor and King of
Israel (2 Samuel 2: 4)

the same. So [*crossing himself*] let her rest; and let you and I mind our own business, and not meddle with hers.

LADVENU

God forbid that I should have no share in her, nor she in me! 110 [*He turns and strides out as he came, saying*] Henceforth my path will not lie through palaces, nor my conversation be with kings.

CHARLES [*following him towards the door, and shouting after him*]

Much good may it do you, holy man! [*He returns to the middle of* 115 *the chamber, where he halts, and says quizzically to himself*] That was a funny chap. How did he get in? Where are my people? [*He goes impatiently to the bed, and swings the rattle. A rush of wind through the open door sets the walls swaying agitatedly. The candles go out. He calls in the darkness*] Hallo! Someone come and shut 120 the windows: everything is being blown all over the place. [*A flash of summer lightning shews up the lancet window. A figure is seen in silhouette against it*] Who is there? Who is that? Help! Murder! [*Thunder. He jumps into bed, and hides under the clothes*] 125

JOAN'S VOICE

Easy, Charlie, easy. What art making all that noise for? No one can hear thee. Thourt asleep. [*She is dimly seen in a pallid greenish light by the bedside*]

CHARLES [*peeping out*] 130

Joan! Are you a ghost, Joan?

JOAN

Hardly even that, lad. Can a poor burnt-up lass have a ghost? I am but a dream that thourt dreaming. [*The light increases: they become plainly visible as he sits up*] Thou looks older, lad. 135

CHARLES

I *am* older. Am I really asleep?

JOAN

Fallen asleep over thy silly book.

CHARLES 140

That's funny.

JOAN

Not so funny as that I am dead, is it?

107 s.d. *crossing himself* SJ
124–5 s.d. *Thunder . . . clothes* SJ (*He rattles again; but a clap of thunder paralyses him* LC)

CHARLES

Are you really dead?   145

JOAN

As dead as anybody ever is, laddie. I am out of the body.

CHARLES

Just fancy! Did it hurt much?

JOAN   150

Did what hurt much?

CHARLES

Being burnt.

JOAN

Oh, *that*! I cannot remember very well. I think it did at first;   155
but then it all got mixed up; and I was not in my right mind
until I was free of the body. But do not thou go handling fire
and thinking it will not hurt thee. How hast been ever since?

CHARLES

Oh, not so bad. Do you know, I actually lead my army out and   160
win battles? Down into the moat up to my waist in mud and
blood. Up the ladders with the stones and hot pitch raining
down. Like you.

JOAN

No! Did I make a man of thee after all, Charlie?   165

CHARLES

I am Charles the Victorious now. I had to be brave because you
were. Agnes put a little pluck into me too.

JOAN

Agnes! Who was Agnes?   170

CHARLES

Agnes Sorel. A woman I fell in love with. I dream of her often. I
never dreamed of you before.

JOAN

Is she dead, like me?   175

CHARLES

Yes. But she was not like you. She was very beautiful.

---

167   *Charles the Victorious* Shaw to Sybil Thorndike: 'laugh at "the Victorious" ' (r.n. 1924, fo. 142)

172   *Agnes Sorel* Charles' mistress from 1444 until her sudden death in 1450, Agnès Sorel, *b*.1422, was the first person to be the officially acknowledged mistress of a French monarch. (In 2005, the European Synchroton Radiation Facility identified mercury poisoning in her remains.)

JOAN [*laughing heartily*]

Ha ha! I was no beauty: I was always a rough one: a regular soldier. I might almost as well have been a man. Pity I wasnt: I   180
should not have bothered you all so much then. But my head
was in the skies; and the glory of God was upon me; and, man
or woman, I should have bothered you as long as your noses
were in the mud. Now tell me what has happened since you
wise men knew no better than to make a heap of cinders of me?   185

CHARLES

Your mother and brothers have sued the courts to have your
case tried over again. And the courts have declared that your
judges were full of corruption and cozenage, fraud and malice.

JOAN   190

Not they. They were as honest a lot of poor fools as ever burned
their betters.

CHARLES

The sentence on you is broken, annihilated, annulled: null,
non-existent, without value or effect.   195

JOAN

I was burned, all the same. Can they unburn me?

CHARLES

If they could, they would think twice before they did it. But
they have decreed that a beautiful cross be placed where the   200
stake stood, for your perpetual memory and for your salvation.

JOAN

It is the memory and the salvation that sanctify the cross, not
the cross that sanctifies the memory and the salvation. [*She
turns away, forgetting him*] I shall outlast that cross. I shall be   205
remembered when men will have forgotten where Rouen stood.

CHARLES

There you go with your self-conceit, the same as ever! I think
you might say a word of thanks to me for having had justice
done at last.   210

CAUCHON [*appearing at the window between them*]

Liar!

---

180 *Pity I wasnt* SJ. This comment, made in rehearsal by Sybil Thorndike, was retained by Shaw.
      See Basil Langton, 'Interview with Sybil Thorndike and Lewis Casson', *Bernard Shaw
      Studies*, 21 (2001), 1–26 at 19.

185 *me?* SJ ('What has set you to dream of me this night of all nights?' included in LC was
      removed in SJ)

204–5 s.d. *She . . . him* SJ

CHARLES

Thank you.

JOAN   215

Why, if it isnt Peter Cauchon! How are you, Peter? What luck have you had since you burned me?

CAUCHON

None. I arraign the justice of Man. It is not the justice of God.

JOAN   220

Still dreaming of justice, Peter? See what justice came to with me! But what has happened to thee? Art dead or alive?

CAUCHON

Dead. Dishonored. They pursued me beyond the grave. They excommunicated my dead body: they dug it up and flung it   225 into the common sewer.

JOAN

Your dead body did not feel the spade and the sewer as my live body felt the fire.

CAUCHON   230

But this thing that they have done against me hurts justice; destroys faith; saps the foundation of the Church. The solid earth sways like the treacherous sea beneath the feet of men and spirits alike when the innocent are slain in the name of law, and their wrongs are undone by slandering the pure of heart.   235

JOAN

Well, well, Peter, I hope men will be the better for remembering me; and they would not remember me so well if you had not burned me.

CAUCHON   240

They will be the worse for remembering me: they will see in me evil triumphing over good, falsehood over truth, cruelty over mercy, hell over heaven. Their courage will rise as they think of you, only to faint as they think of me. Yet God is my witness I was just: I was merciful: I was faithful to my light: I could do no   245 other than I did.

CHARLES [scrambling out of the sheets and enthroning himself on the side of the bed]

Yes: it is always you good men that do the big mischiefs. Look at me! I am not Charles the Good, nor Charles the Wise, nor   250

247–8   s.d scrambling . . . bed SJ (chuckling LC)

124

Charles the Bold. Joan's worshippers may even call me Charles
the Coward because I did not pull her out of the fire. But I have
done less harm than any of you. You people with your heads in
the sky spend all your time trying to turn the world upside
down; but I take the world as it is, and say that top-side-up is   255
right-side-up; and I keep my nose pretty close to the ground.
And I ask you, what king of France has done better, or been a
better fellow in his little way?

JOAN

Art really king of France, Charlie? Be the English gone?   260

DUNOIS [*coming through the tapestry on* JOAN'*s left, the candles
relighting themselves at the same moment, and illuminating his
armor and surcoat cheerfully*]

I have kept my word: the English are gone.   265

JOAN

Praised be God! now is fair France a province in heaven. Tell
me all about the fighting, Jack. Was it thou that led them? Wert
thou God's captain to thy death?

DUNOIS

I am not dead. My body is very comfortably asleep in my bed at   270
Chateaudun; but my spirit is called here by yours.

JOAN

And you fought them *my* way, Jack: eh? Not the old way, chaf-
fering for ransoms; but The Maid's way: staking life against
death, with the heart high and humble and void of malice, and   275
nothing counting under God but France free and French. Was
it my way, Jack?

DUNOIS

Faith, it was any way that would win. But the way that won was
always your way. I give you best, lassie. I wrote a fine letter to   280
set you right at the new trial. Perhaps I should never have let
the priests burn you; but I was busy fighting; and it was the
Church's business, not mine. There was no use in both of us
being burned, was there?

CAUCHON   285

Ay! put the blame on the priests. But I, who am beyond praise
and blame, tell you that the world is saved neither by its priests
nor its soldiers, but by God and His Saints. The Church
Militant sent this woman to the fire; but even as she burned,

288–93   *but . . . tune* ms rev.

the flames whitened into the radiance of the Church   290
Triumphant.

The clock strikes the third quarter. A rough MALE VOICE *is
heard trolling an improvised tune.*

    Rum tum trumpledum,   295
    Bacon fat and rumpledum,
    Old Saint mumpledum,
    Pull his tail and stumpledum
    O my Ma——ry Ann!

A ruffianly ENGLISH SOLDIER *comes through the curtains*   300
and marches between DUNOIS *and* JOAN.

DUNOIS
What villainous troubadour taught you that doggrel?

THE SOLDIER
No troubadour. We made it up ourselves as we marched. We   305
were not gentlefolks and troubadours. Music straight out of the
heart of the people, as you might say. Rum tum trumpledum,
Bacon fat and rumpledum, Old Saint mumpledum, Pull his tail
and stumpledum: that dont mean anything, you know; but it
keeps you marching. Your servant, ladies and gentlemen. Who   310
asked for a saint?

JOAN
Be you a saint?

THE SOLDIER
Yes, lady, straight from hell.   315

DUNOIS
A saint, and from hell!

THE SOLDIER
Yes, noble captain: I have a day off. Every year, you know. Thats
my allowance for my one good action.   320

   294 An undated note on the typescript in Shaw's hand reads: 'This key signature in D flat is
      wrong. It should be G flat. The mistake ran through several editions before I noticed and
      corrected it' – it is corrected, as here, in the Constable pocket edition of 1929.
299–301 *O . . . JOAN* ms rev.
  302–3 DUNOIS *. . . doggrel* LC (CHARLES: What sort of song is that? DUNOIS: What troubadour
      perpetrated it? typescript; ms rev. retains typescript version but adds 'villainous')

CAUCHON

Wretch! In all the years of your life did you do only one good action?

THE SOLDIER

I never thought about it: it came natural like. But they scored it up for me. 325

CHARLES

What was it?

THE SOLDIER

Why, the silliest thing you ever heard of. I – 330

JOAN [interrupting him by strolling across to the bed, where she sits beside CHARLES]

He tied two sticks together, and gave them to a poor lass that was going to be burned.

THE SOLDIER 335

Right. Who told you that?

JOAN

Never mind. Would you know her if you saw her again?

THE SOLDIER

Not I. There are so many girls! and they all expect you to 340
remember them as if there was only one in the world. This one
must have been a prime sort; for I have a day off every year for
her; and so, until twelve o'clock punctually, I am a saint, at your
service, noble lords and lovely ladies.

CHARLES 345

And after twelve?

THE SOLDIER

After twelve, back to the only place fit for the likes of me.

JOAN [rising]

Back there! You! that gave the lass the cross! 350

THE SOLDIER [excusing his unsoldierly conduct]

Well, she asked for it; and they were going to burn her. She had
as good a right to a cross as they had; and they had dozens of
them. It was her funeral, not theirs. Where was the harm in it?

331–2 s.d. interrupting . . . CHARLES SJ

333–4 He . . . burned Shaw proposed in 1913, 'I should have God about to damn the English . . .
and Joan producing an end of burnt stick in arrest of judgement. "What's that? Is it one of
the faggots?" says God. "No," says Joan, "It's what's left of the two sticks a common English
soldier tied together and gave me as I went to the stake . . . you cannot damn the common
people of England . . . because a poor cowardly riff-raff of barons and bishops were too
futile to resist the devil" ' (L3, pp. 201–2).

JOAN   355

Man: I am not reproaching you. But I cannot bear to think of
you in torment.

THE SOLDIER [*cheerfully*]

No great torment, lady. You see I was used to worse.

CHARLES   360

What! worse than hell?

THE SOLDIER

Fifteen years' service in the French wars. Hell was a treat after
that.

> JOAN *throws up her arms, and takes refuge from despair of*   365
> *humanity before the picture of the Virgin.*

THE SOLDIER [*continuing*]

– Suits me somehow. The day off was dull at first, like a wet
Sunday. I dont mind it so much now. They tell me I can have as
many as I like as soon as I want them.   370

CHARLES

What is hell like?

THE SOLDIER

You wont find it so bad, sir. Jolly. Like as if you were always
drunk without the trouble and expense of drinking. Tip top   375
company too: emperors and popes and kings and all sorts.
They chip me about giving that young judy the cross; but I
dont care: I stand up to them proper, and tell them that if she
hadnt a better right to it than they, she'd be where they are.
That dumbfounds them, that does. All they can do is gnash   380
their teeth, hell fashion; and I just laugh, and go off singing the
old chanty: Rum tum trumple – Hullo! Who's that knocking at
the door?

> *They listen. A long gentle knocking is heard.*

CHARLES   385

Come in.

> *The door opens; and an old* PRIEST, *white-haired, bent, with*
> *a silly but benevolent smile, comes in and trots over to* JOAN.

THE NEWCOMER

Excuse me, gentle lords and ladies. Do not let me disturb you. 390
Only a poor old harmless English rector. Formerly chaplain to
the cardinal: to my lord of Winchester. John de Stogumber, at

---

377   *chip* tease
       judy slang for woman (from the puppet-show 'Punch and Judy')

your service. [*He looks at them inquiringly*] Did you say anything? I am a little deaf, unfortunately. Also a little – well, not
always in my right mind, perhaps; but still, it is a small village   395
with a few simple people. I suffice: I suffice: they love me there;
and I am able to do a little good. I am well connected, you see;
and they indulge me.

JOAN

Poor old John! What brought thee to this state?   400

DE STOGUMBER

I tell my folks they must be very careful. I say to them, 'If you
only saw what you think about you would think quite differently about it. It would give you a great shock. Oh, a great
shock.' And they all say 'Yes, Parson: we all know you are a kind   405
man, and would not harm a fly.' That is a great comfort to me.
For I am not cruel by nature, you know.

THE SOLDIER

Who said you were?

DE STOGUMBER   410

Well, you see, I did a very cruel thing once because I did not
know what cruelty was like. I had not seen it, you know. That is
the great thing: you must see it. And then you are redeemed
and saved.

CAUCHON   415

Were not the sufferings of our Lord Christ enough for you?

DE STOGUMBER

No. Oh no: not at all. I had seen them in pictures, and read of
them in books, and been greatly moved by them, as I thought.
But it was no use: it was not our Lord that redeemed me, but a   420
young woman whom I saw actually burned to death. It was
dreadful: oh, most dreadful. But it saved me. I have been a different man ever since, though a little astray in my wits sometimes.

CAUCHON

Must then a Christ perish in torment in every age to save those   425
that have no imagination?

JOAN

Well, if I saved all those he would have been cruel to if he had
not been cruel to me, I was not burnt for nothing, was I?

DE STOGUMBER   430

Oh no; it was not you. My sight is bad: I cannot distinguish
your features: but you are not she: oh no: she was burned to a
cinder: dead and gone, dead and gone.

THE EXECUTIONER [*stepping from behind the bed curtains on* CHARLES's *right, the bed being between them*]   435

She is more alive than you, old man. Her heart would not burn; and it would not drown. I was a master at my craft: better than the master of Paris, better than the master of Toulouse; but I could not kill The Maid. She is up and alive everywhere.   440

THE EARL OF WARWICK [*sallying from the bed curtains on the other side, and coming to* JOAN's *left hand*]

Madam: my congratulations on your rehabilitation. I feel that I owe you an apology.

JOAN   445

Oh, please dont mention it.

WARWICK [*pleasantly*]

The burning was purely political. There was no personal feeling against you, I assure you.

JOAN   450

I bear no malice, my lord.

WARWICK

Just so. Very kind of you to meet me in that way: a touch of true breeding. But I must insist on apologizing very amply. The truth is, these political necessities sometimes turn out to be   455 political mistakes; and this one was a veritable howler; for your spirit conquered us, madam, in spite of our faggots. History will remember me for your sake, though the incidents of the connection were perhaps a little unfortunate.

JOAN   460

Ay, perhaps just a little, you funny man.

WARWICK

Still, when they make you a saint, you will owe your halo to me, just as this lucky monarch owes his crown to you.

JOAN [*turning from him*]   465

I shall owe nothing to any man: I owe everything to the spirit of God that was within me. But fancy me a saint! What would St Catherine and St Margaret say if the farm girl was cocked up beside them!

435   s.d. *right* SJ (*left* LC)
457   *conquered us* SJ (walks LC)

A clerical-looking GENTLEMAN *in black frockcoat and* 470
trousers, and tall hat, in the fashion of the year 1920, suddenly
appears before them in the corner on their right. They all stare at
him. Then they burst into uncontrollable laughter.

THE GENTLEMAN

Why this mirth, gentlemen? 475

WARWICK

I congratulate you on having invented a most extraordinarily
comic dress.

THE GENTLEMAN

I do not understand. You are all in fancy dress: I am properly 480
dressed.

DUNOIS

All dress is fancy dress, is it not, except our natural skins?

THE GENTLEMAN

Pardon me: I am here on serious business, and cannot engage 485
in frivolous discussions. [*He takes out a paper, and assumes a*
dry official manner] I am sent to announce to you that Joan of
Arc, formerly known as The Maid, having been the subject of
an inquiry instituted by the Bishop of Orleans –

JOAN [*interrupting*] 490

Ah! They remember me still in Orleans.

THE GENTLEMAN [*emphatically, to mark his indignation at the*
interruption]

– by the Bishop of Orleans into the claim of the said Joan of
Arc to be canonized as a saint – 495

JOAN [*again interrupting*]

But I never made any such claim.

THE GENTLEMAN [*as before*]

– the Church has examined the claim exhaustively in the usual
course, and, having admitted the said Joan successively to the 500
ranks of Venerable and Blessed, –

JOAN [*chuckling*]

Me venerable!

471–3   s.d. *suddenly . . . him* SJ (*comes in through the door and attracts attention by shutting*
it sharply behind him. They all crowd together to stare at him from the opposite side of
the room LC)
492–3   s.d. *emphatically . . . interruption* SJ (*ignoring the interruption* LC)

THE GENTLEMAN

    – has finally declared her to have been endowed with heroic   505
virtues and favored with private revelations, and calls the said
Venerable and Blessed Joan to the communion of the Church
Triumphant as Saint Joan.

JOAN [*rapt*]

    Saint Joan!   510

THE GENTLEMAN

    On every thirtieth day of May, being the anniversary of the death
of the said most blessed daughter of God, there shall in every
Catholic church to the end of time be celebrated a special office
in commemoration of her; and it shall be lawful to dedicate a   515
special chapel to her, and to place her image on its altar in every
such church. And it shall be lawful and laudable for the faithful
to kneel and address their prayers through her to the Mercy Seat.

JOAN

    Oh no. It is for the saint to kneel. [*She falls on her knees, still rapt*]   520

THE GENTLEMAN [*putting up his paper, and retiring beside* THE
EXECUTIONER]

    In Basilica Vaticana, the sixteenth day of May, nineteen hun-
dred and twenty.

DUNOIS [*raising* JOAN]   525

    Half an hour to burn you, dear Saint: and four centuries to find
out the truth about you!

DE STOGUMBER

    Sir: I was chaplain to the Cardinal of Winchester once. They
always would call him the Cardinal of England. It would be a   530
great comfort to me and to my master to see a fair statue to The
Maid in Winchester Cathedral. Will they put one there, do you
think?

THE GENTLEMAN

    As the building is temporarily in the hands of the Anglican   535
heresy, I cannot answer for that.

    *A vision of the statue in Winchester Cathedral is seen through
the window.*

DE STOGUMBER

    Oh look! look! that is Winchester.   540

518   *Mercy Seat* throne of God
523   *Basilica Vaticana* St Peter's in the Vatican
525   s.d. *raising* JOAN SJ

JOAN

Is that meant to be me? I was stiffer on my feet.

The vision fades.

THE GENTLEMAN

I have been requested by the temporal authorities of France to   545
mention that the multiplication of public statues to The Maid
threatens to become an obstruction to traffic. I do so as a
matter of courtesy to the said authorities, but must point out
on behalf of the Church that The Maid's horse is no greater
obstruction to traffic than any other horse.   550

JOAN

Eh! I am glad they have not forgotten my horse.

A vision of the statue before Rheims Cathedral appears.

JOAN

Is that funny little thing me too?   555

CHARLES

That is Rheims Cathedral where you had me crowned. It must
be you.

JOAN

Who has broken my sword? My sword was never broken. It is   560
the sword of France.

DUNOIS

Never mind. Swords can be mended. Your soul is unbroken;
and you are the soul of France.

The vision fades. THE ARCHBISHOP *and* THE INQUISITOR   565
are now seen on the right and left of CAUCHON.

JOAN

My sword shall conquer yet: the sword that never struck a blow.
Though men destroyed my body, yet in my soul I have seen
God.   570

CAUCHON [*kneeling to her*]

The girls in the field praise thee; for thou hast raised their eyes;
and they see that there is nothing between them and heaven.

---

541   JOAN SJ (JOAN *rises from her knees still rapt, and turns to the window* LC)

545–7   *temporal . . . traffic* Following Jeanne's canonisation, the French authorities nominated the
second Sunday in May a National holiday, but were concerned when Jeanne's statues became
a focus for opposing political demonstrations on that day. Feeling generated by the cancella-
tion of the holiday in 1925 has been suggested as one reason for the popularity of Shaw's
play in France that year (Craig Hamilton, 'Constructing a Cultural Icon: Nomos and Shaw's
Saint Joan in Paris', *Modern Drama*, 43 (Fall 2000), 359–75 at 367).

DUNOIS [*kneeling to her*]

The dying soldiers praise thee, because thou art a shield of   575
glory between them and the judgment.

THE ARCHBISHOP [*kneeling to her*]

The princes of the Church praise thee, because thou hast
redeemed the faith their worldlinesses have dragged through
the mire.   580

WARWICK [*kneeling to her*]

The cunning counsellors praise thee, because thou hast cut the
knots in which they have tied their own souls.

DE STOGUMBER [*kneeling to her*]

The foolish old men on their deathbeds praise thee, because   585
their sins against thee are turned into blessings.

THE INQUISITOR [*kneeling to her*]

The judges in the blindness and bondage of the law praise thee,
because thou hast vindicated the vision and the freedom of the
living soul.   590

THE SOLDIER [*kneeling to her*]

The wicked out of hell praise thee, because thou hast shewn
them that the fire that is not quenched is a holy fire.

THE EXECUTIONER [*kneeling to her*]

The tormentors and executioners praise thee, because thou hast 595
shewn that their hands are guiltless of the death of the soul.

CHARLES [*kneeling to her*]

The unpretending praise thee, because thou hast taken upon
thyself the heroic burdens that are too heavy for them.

JOAN   600

Woe unto me when all men praise me! I bid you remember that
I am a saint, and that saints can work miracles. And now tell
me: shall I rise from the dead, and come back to you a living
woman?

A sudden darkness blots out the walls of the room as they all 605
spring to their feet in consternation. Only the figures and the bed
remain visible.

587–607 THE INQUISITOR ... *visible* Shaw considerably developed this sequence in ms rev. of
August 1923. The speeches of the Inquisitor and the Executioner were expanded; Charles
was included among those kneeling; 'I bid you remember that I am a saint and that saints
can work miracles. And now tell me' added to Joan's response; and the darkness-effect, with
the figures illuminated, introduced.

601   *Woe ... me!* 'Woe unto you when all men shall speak well of you!' (Luke 6: 26).

JOAN

What! Must I burn again? Are none of you ready to receive me?

CAUCHON 610

The heretic is always better dead. And mortal eyes cannot distinguish the saint from the heretic. Spare them. [*He goes out as he came*]

DUNOIS

Forgive us, Joan: we are not yet good enough for you. I shall go 615 back to my bed. [*He also goes*]

WARWICK

We sincerely regret our little mistake; but political necessities, though occasionally erroneous, are still imperative; so if you will be good enough to excuse me – [*He steals discreetly away*] 620

THE ARCHBISHOP

Your return would not make me the man you once thought me. The utmost I can say is that though I dare not bless you, I hope I may one day enter into your blessedness. Meanwhile, however – [*He goes*] 625

THE INQUISITOR

I who am of the dead, testified that day that you were innocent. But I do not see how The Inquisition could possibly be dispensed with under existing circumstances. Therefore – [*He goes*]

DE STOGUMBER 630

Oh, do not come back: you must not come back. I must die in peace. Give us peace in our time, O Lord! [*He goes*]

THE GENTLEMAN

The possibility of your resurrection was not contemplated in the recent proceedings for your canonization. I must return to 635 Rome for fresh instructions. [*He bows formally, and withdraws*]

THE EXECUTIONER

As a master in my profession I have to consider its interests. And, after all, my first duty is to my wife and children. I must have time to think over this. [*He goes*] 640

CHARLES

Poor old Joan! They have all run away from you except this blackguard who has to go back to hell at twelve o'clock. And

---

610–12 CAUCHON ... *them* ms rev. (CHARLES: I told brother Martin that they would burn you again if you came back. THE SOLDIER [*rising*]: What's the odds. Some chap would give you a couple of sticks all the same. CAUCHON: The [illegible] of the judge might again be redeemed by the sacrifice of the priest typescript)

what can I do but follow Jack Dunois' example, and go back to
bed too? [*He does so*]   645

JOAN [*sadly*]

Goodnight, Charlie.

CHARLES [*mumbling in his pillows*]

Goo ni. [*He sleeps. The darkness envelops the bed*]

JOAN [*to* THE SOLDIER]   650

And you, my one faithful? What comfort have you for Saint
Joan?

THE SOLDIER

Well, what do they all amount to, these kings and captains and
bishops and lawyers and such like? They just leave you in the   655
ditch to bleed to death; and the next thing is, you meet them
down there, for all the airs they give themselves. What I say is,
you have as good a right to your notions as they have to theirs,
and perhaps better. [*Settling himself for a lecture on the subject*]
You see, it's like this. If – [*the first stroke of midnight is heard*   660
softly from a distant bell]. Excuse me: a pressing appointment –
[*He goes on tiptoe*]

    The last remaining rays of light gather into a white radiance
descending on JOAN. *The hour continues to strike.*

JOAN   665

O God that madest this beautiful earth, when will it be ready to
receive Thy saints? How long, O Lord, how long?

662–4 s.d. *He . . . strike* ms rev. (*He goes. A white radiance descends on Joan as she stands*
    alone except for the sleeping king, hidden in his bedclothes typescript)

PREFACE

Joan the Original and Presumptuous

Joan of Arc, a village girl from the Vosges, was born about 1412; burnt for heresy, witchcraft, and sorcery in 1431; rehabilitated after a fashion in 1456; designated Venerable in 1904; declared Blessed in 1908; and finally canonized in 1920. She is the most notable Warrior Saint in the Christian calendar, and the queerest fish among the eccentric worthies of the Middle Ages. Though a professed and most pious Catholic, and the projector of a Crusade against the Husites,[1] she was in fact one of the first Protestant martyrs. She was also one of the first apostles of Nationalism, and the first French practitioner of Napoleonic realism in warfare as distinguished from the sporting ransom-gambling chivalry of her time. She was the pioneer of rational dressing for women, and, like Queen Christina of Sweden[2] two centuries later, to say nothing of Catalina de Erauso[3] and innumerable obscure heroines who have disguised themselves as men to serve as soldiers and sailors, she refused to accept the specific woman's lot, and dressed and fought and lived as men did.

As she contrived to assert herself in all these ways with such force that she was famous throughout western Europe before she was out of her teens (indeed she never got out of them), it is hardly surprising that she was judicially burnt, ostensibly for a number of capital crimes which we no longer punish as such, but essentially for what we call unwomanly and insufferable presumption. At eighteen Joan's pretensions were beyond those of the proudest Pope or the haughtiest emperor. She claimed to be the ambassador and plenipotentiary of God, and to be, in effect, a

---

1 John Hus, or Huss (1373–1415), a Bohemian priest, protested against clerical abuses and a papal bull (order) that demanded destruction of all Wycliffe's writings (see p. 161, n. 53). Despite a safe-conduct to defend his *De Ecclesia*, he was convicted of heresy by the Council of Constance, and burnt. A bull of 14 March 1420, that proclaimed a crusade 'for the destruction of Wycliffites, Hussites and all other heretics in Bohemia' (*Enc. Brit.*, vol. XIV, p. 8), was endorsed in a letter signed by Jeanne, 23 March 1430, appealing to the Hussites to return to the true church.

2 Queen Christina, who ruled Sweden from 1644 to her abdication in 1654, was educated as a prince by her father, Gustavus Adolphus, and frequently adopted male dress.

3 Catalina, a seventeenth-century Basque woman, fled the convent and, disguised as a man, fought with the Spanish army in the New World, eventually gaining papal dispensation to wear men's clothing. Shaw originally wrote 'Chevalier D'Eon' (1924) but substituted Catalina in subsequent editions (from the 1929 reprint onwards) when he realised that the Chevalier was, in fact, a man who used both male and female disguise.

member of the Church Triumphant whilst still in the flesh on earth. She patronized her own king, and summoned the English king to repentance and obedience to her commands. She lectured, talked down, and overruled statesmen and prelates. She poohpoohed the plans of generals, leading their troops to victory on plans of her own. She had an unbounded and quite unconcealed contempt for official opinion, judgment, and authority, and for War Office tactics and strategy. Had she been a sage and monarch in whom the most venerable hierarchy and the most illustrious dynasty converged, her pretensions and proceedings would have been as trying to the official mind as the pretensions of Caesar were to Cassius.[4] As her actual condition was pure upstart, there were only two opinions about her. One was that she was miraculous: the other that she was unbearable.

Joan and Socrates

If Joan had been malicious, selfish, cowardly, or stupid, she would have been one of the most odious persons known to history instead of one of the most attractive. If she had been old enough to know the effect she was producing on the men whom she humiliated by being right when they were wrong, and had learned to flatter and manage them, she might have lived as long as Queen Elizabeth. But she was too young and rustical and inexperienced to have any such arts. When she was thwarted by men whom she thought fools, she made no secret of her opinion of them or her impatience with their folly; and she was naïve enough to expect them to be obliged to her for setting them right and keeping them out of mischief. Now it is always hard for superior wits to understand the fury roused by their exposures of the stupidities of comparative dullards. Even Socrates, for all his age and experience, did not defend himself at his trial like a man who understood the long accumulated fury that had burst on him, and was clamoring for his death.[5] His accuser, if born 2300 years later, might have been picked out of any first class carriage on a suburban railway during the evening or morning rush from or to the City; for he had really nothing to say except that he and his like could not endure being shewn up as idiots every time Socrates opened his mouth. Socrates, unconscious of this, was paralyzed by his sense that somehow he was missing the point of

---

4 Cassius was a leader of the assassins of Caesar who, already dictator, had become increasingly absolute. See *Julius Caesar*, 1.2.80–177.
5 Socrates, Greek philosopher of the fifth century BC, accused of denying the gods and cor-
    ~upting youth, defied the court, scorning to answer the charges, and was condemned to
    ` `(by drinking hemlock).

the attack. He petered out after he had established the fact that he was an old soldier and a man of honorable life, and that his accuser was a silly snob. He had no suspicion of the extent to which his mental superiority had roused fear and hatred against him in the hearts of men towards whom he was conscious of nothing but good will and good service.

Contrast with Napoleon

If Socrates was as innocent as this at the age of seventy, it may be imagined how innocent Joan was at the age of seventeen. Now Socrates was a man of argument, operating slowly and peacefully on men's minds, whereas Joan was a woman of action, operating with impetuous violence on their bodies. That, no doubt, is why the contemporaries of Socrates endured him so long, and why Joan was destroyed before she was fully grown. But both of them combined terrifying ability with a frankness, personal modesty, and benevolence which made the furious dislike to which they fell victims absolutely unreasonable, and therefore inapprehensible by themselves. Napoleon,[6] also possessed of terrifying ability, but neither frank nor disinterested, had no illusions as to the nature of his popularity. When he was asked how the world would take his death, he said it would give a gasp of relief. But it is not so easy for mental giants who neither hate nor intend to injure their fellows to realize that nevertheless their fellows hate mental giants and would like to destroy them, not only enviously because the juxtaposition of a superior wounds their vanity, but quite humbly and honestly because it frightens them. Fear will drive men to any extreme; and the fear inspired by a superior being is a mystery which cannot be reasoned away. Being immeasurable it is unbearable when there is no presumption or guarantee of its benevolence and moral responsibility: in other words, when it has no official status. The legal and conventional superiority of Herod and Pilate, and of Annas and Caiaphas,[7] inspires fear; but the fear, being a reasonable fear of measurable and avoidable consequences which seem salutary and protective, is bearable; whilst the strange superiority of Christ and the fear it inspires elicit a shriek of Crucify Him from all who cannot divine its benevolence. Socrates has to drink the hemlock, Christ to hang on the cross, and Joan to burn at the stake, whilst Napoleon, though

---

6 Napoleon Bonaparte, a brilliant soldier, became First Consul of France (1799) then Emperor (1804–14), and following his final defeat was imprisoned on the remote island of Saint Helena until his death. He is the central character of Shaw's first history play, *The Man of Destiny*, 1895.

7 At the time of Jesus' trial and execution these were, respectively, Herod, the king of the Israelites; Pontius Pilate, the Roman judge; and Annas and Caiaphas, the Jewish high priests.

he ends in St Helena, at least dies in his bed there; and many terrifying but quite comprehensible official scoundrels die natural deaths in all the glory of the kingdoms of this world, proving that it is far more dangerous to be a saint than to be a conqueror. Those who have been both, like Mahomet and Joan, have found that it is the conqueror who must save the saint, and that defeat and capture mean martyrdom. Joan was burnt without a hand lifted on her own side to save her. The comrades she had led to victory and the enemies she had disgraced and defeated, the French king she had crowned and the English king whose crown she had kicked into the Loire, were equally glad to be rid of her.

Was Joan Innocent or Guilty?

As this result could have been produced by a crapulous inferiority as well as by a sublime superiority, the question which of the two was operative in Joan's case has to be faced. It was decided against her by her contemporaries after a very careful and conscientious trial; and the reversal of the verdict twentyfive years later, in form a rehabilitation of Joan, was really only a confirmation of the validity of the coronation of Charles VII. It is the more impressive reversal by a unanimous Posterity, culminating in her canonization, that has quashed the original proceedings, and put her judges on their trial, which, so far, has been much more unfair than their trial of her. Nevertheless the rehabilitation of 1456, corrupt job as it was, really did produce evidence enough to satisfy all reasonable critics that Joan was not a common termagant,[8] not a harlot, not a witch, not a blasphemer, no more an idolater than the Pope himself, and not ill conducted in any sense apart from her soldiering, her wearing of men's clothes, and her audacity, but on the contrary good-humored, an intact virgin, very pious, very temperate (we should call her meal of bread soaked in the common wine which is the drinking water of France ascetic), very kindly, and, though a brave and hardy soldier, unable to endure loose language or licentious conduct. She went to the stake without a stain on her character except the overweening presumption, the superbity as they called it, that led her thither. It would therefore be waste of time now to prove that the Joan of the first part of the Elizabethan chronicle play of Henry VI (supposed to have been tinkered by Shakespear)[9] grossly libels her in its

---

8 A virago or scold.

9 A major reason for the identification by nineteenth-century scholars of *Henry VI, Part 1,* as one of the plays on which Shakespeare collaborated was the change in tone from the serious treatment of Joan in the early scenes to the jingoistic scurrility of her later representation when she conjures evil spirits and claims to be with child to escape death.

concluding scenes in deference to Jingo patriotism. The mud that was thrown at her has dropped off by this time so completely that there is no need for any modern writer to wash up after it. What is far more difficult to get rid of is the mud that is being thrown at her judges, and the white-wash which disfigures her beyond recognition. When Jingo scurrility had done its worst to her, sectarian scurrility (in this case Protestant scurrility) used her stake to beat the Roman Catholic Church and the Inquisition. The easiest way to make these institutions the villains of a melodrama was to make The Maid its heroine. That melodrama may be dismissed as rubbish. Joan got a far fairer trial from the Church and the Inquisition than any prisoner of her type and in her situation gets nowadays in any official secular court; and the decision was strictly according to law. And she was not a melodramatic heroine: that is, a physically beautiful lovelorn parasite on an equally beautiful hero, but a genius and a saint, about as completely the opposite of a melodramatic heroine as it is possible for a human being to be.

Let us be clear about the meaning of the terms. A genius is a person who, seeing farther and probing deeper than other people, has a different set of ethical valuations from theirs, and has energy enough to give effect to this extra vision and its valuations in whatever manner best suits his or her specific talents. A saint is one who having practised heroic virtues, and enjoyed revelations or powers of the order which The Church classes technically as supernatural, is eligible for canonization. If a historian is an Anti-Feminist, and does not believe women to be capable of genius in the traditional masculine departments, he will never make anything of Joan, whose genius was turned to practical account mainly in soldiering and politics. If he is Rationalist enough to deny that saints exist, and to hold that new ideas cannot come otherwise than by conscious ratiocination, he will never catch Joan's likeness. Her ideal biographer must be free from nineteenth century prejudices and biases; must understand the Middle Ages, the Roman Catholic Church, and the Holy Roman Empire much more intimately than our Whig historians have ever understood them; and must be capable of throwing off sex partialities and their romance, and regarding woman as the female of the human species, and not as a different kind of animal with specific charms and specific imbecilities.

Joan's Good Looks
To put the last point roughly, any book about Joan which begins by describing her as a beauty may be at once classed as a romance. Not one of Joan's comrades, in village, court, or camp, even when they were straining themselves to please the king by praising her, ever claimed that

she was pretty. All the men who alluded to the matter declared most emphatically that she was unattractive sexually to a degree that seemed to them miraculous, considering that she was in the bloom of youth, and neither ugly, awkward, deformed, nor unpleasant in her person. The evident truth is that like most women of her hardy managing type she seemed neutral in the conflict of sex because men were too much afraid of her to fall in love with her. She herself was not sexless: in spite of the virginity she had vowed up to a point, and preserved to her death, she never excluded the possibility of marriage for herself. But marriage, with its preliminary of the attraction, pursuit, and capture of a husband, was not her business: she had something else to do. Byron's formula, 'Man's love is of man's life a thing apart: 'tis woman's whole existence',[10] did not apply to her any more than to George Washington or any other masculine worker on the heroic scale. Had she lived in our time, picture postcards might have been sold of her as a general: they would not have been sold of her as a sultana. Nevertheless there is one reason for crediting her with a very remarkable face. A sculptor of her time in Orleans made a statue of a helmeted young woman with a face that is unique in art in point of being evidently not an ideal face but a portrait, and yet so uncommon as to be unlike any real woman one has ever seen. It is surmised that Joan served unconsciously as the sculptor's model. There is no proof of this; but those extraordinarily spaced eyes raise so powerfully the question 'If this woman be not Joan, who is she?' that I dispense with further evidence, and challenge those who disagree with me to prove a negative. It is a wonderful face, but quite neutral from the point of view of the operatic beauty fancier.

Such a fancier may perhaps be finally chilled by the prosaic fact that Joan was the defendant in a suit for breach of promise of marriage, and that she conducted her own case and won it.

Joan's Social Position

By class Joan was the daughter of a working farmer who was one of the headmen of his village, and transacted its feudal business for it with the neighbouring squires and their lawyers. When the castle in which the villagers were entitled to take refuge from raids became derelict, he organized a combination of half a dozen farmers to obtain possession of it so as to occupy it when there was any danger of invasion. As a child, Joan could please herself at times with being the young lady of this castle.

10 Byron, *Don Juan*, Canto 1, verse 194.

Her mother and brothers were able to follow and share her fortune at court without making themselves notably ridiculous. These facts leave us no excuse for the popular romance that turns every heroine into either a princess or a beggar maid. In the somewhat similar case of Shakespear a whole inverted pyramid of wasted research has been based on the assumption that he was an illiterate laborer, in the face of the plainest evidence that his father was a man of business, and at one time a very prosperous one, married to a woman of some social pretensions. There is the same tendency to drive Joan into the position of a hired shepherd girl, though a hired shepherd girl in Domrémy would have deferred to her as the young lady of the farm.

The difference between Joan's case and Shakespear's is that Shakespear was not illiterate. He had been to school, and knew as much Latin and Greek as most university passmen retain: that is, for practical purposes, none at all. Joan was absolutely illiterate. 'I do not know A from B' she said. But many princesses at that time and for long after might have said the same. Marie Antoinette,[11] for instance, at Joan's age could not spell her own name correctly. But this does not mean that Joan was an ignorant person, or that she suffered from the diffidence and sense of social disadvantage now felt by people who cannot read or write. If she could not write letters, she could and did dictate them and attach full and indeed excessive importance to them. When she was called a shepherd lass to her face she very warmly resented it, and challenged any woman to compete with her in the household arts of the mistresses of well furnished houses. She understood the political and military situation in France much better than most of our newspaper fed university women-graduates understand the corresponding situation of their own country today. Her first convert was the neighboring commandant at Vaucouleurs; and she converted him by telling him about the defeat of the Dauphin's troops at the Battle of Herrings[12] so long before he had official news of it that he concluded she must have had a divine revelation. This knowledge of and interest in public affairs was nothing extraordinary among farmers in a war-swept countryside. Politicians came to the door too often sword in hand to be disregarded: Joan's people could not afford to be ignorant of what was going on in the feudal world. They were not rich; and Joan worked on the farm as her father

11 Marie Antoinette was the Austrian consort of Louis XVI of France.
12 In February 1429, the French suffered a humiliating defeat, known as the Battle of Herrings, when they intercepted a convoy, escorted by 1000 archers, bringing fish to feed the besieging English at Orleans.

did, driving the sheep to pasture and so forth; but there is no evidence or suggestion of sordid poverty, and no reason to believe that Joan had to work as a hired servant works, or indeed to work at all when she preferred to go to confession, or dawdle about waiting for visions and listening to the church bells to hear voices in them. In short, much more of a young lady, and even of an intellectual, than most of the daughters of our petty bourgeoisie.

Joan's Voices and Visions

Joan's voices and visions have played many tricks with her reputation. They have been held to prove that she was mad, that she was a liar and impostor, that she was a sorceress (she was burned for this), and finally that she was a saint. They do not prove any of these things; but the variety of the conclusions reached shew how little our matter-of-fact historians know about other people's minds, or even about their own. There are people in the world whose imagination is so vivid that when they have an idea it comes to them as an audible voice, sometimes uttered by a visual figure. Criminal lunatic asylums are occupied largely by murderers who have obeyed voices. Thus a woman may hear voices telling her that she must cut her husband's throat and strangle her child as they lie asleep; and she may feel obliged to do what she is told. By a medico-legal superstition it is held in our courts that criminals whose temptations present themselves under these illusions are not responsible for their actions, and must be treated as insane. But the seers of visions and the hearers of revelations are not always criminals. The inspirations and intuitions and unconsciously reasoned conclusions of genius sometimes assume similar illusions. Socrates, Luther, Swedenborg, Blake[13] saw visions and heard voices just as Saint Francis and Saint Joan did. If Newton's imagination had been of the same vividly dramatic kind he might have seen the ghost of Pythagoras walk into the orchard and explain why the apples were falling. Such an illusion would have invalidated neither the theory of gravitation nor Newton's general sanity. What is more, the visionary method of making the discovery would not be a whit more miraculous than the normal method. The test of sanity is not the normality of the method but the reasonableness of the discovery. If Newton had been informed by Pythagoras that the moon was made of

13 These, all radical thinkers, were, respectively, Martin Luther (1483–1546), the German monk whose ideas launched the Reformation; Emmanuel Swedenborg (1688–1782), the Swedish scientist who became a mystic in later life and against whom heresy charges were also brought; William Blake (1757–1827), the English poet and artist.

144

green cheese, then Newton would have been locked up. Gravitation, being a reasoned hypothesis which fitted remarkably well into the Copernican version of the observed physical facts of the universe,[14] established Newton's reputation for extraordinary intelligence, and would have done so no matter how fantastically he had arrived at it. Yet his theory of gravitation is not so impressive a mental feat as his astounding chronology,[15] which establishes him as the king of mental conjurors, but a Bedlamite[16] king whose authority no one now accepts. On the subject of the eleventh horn of the beast seen by the prophet Daniel[17] he was more fantastic than Joan, because his imagination was not dramatic but mathematical and therefore extraordinarily susceptible to numbers: indeed if all his works were lost except his chronology we should say that he was as mad as a hatter. As it is, who dares diagnose Newton as a madman?

In the same way Joan must be judged a sane woman in spite of her voices because they never gave her any advice that might not have come to her from her mother wit exactly as gravitation came to Newton. We can all see now, especially since the late war threw so many of our women into military life, that Joan's campaigning could not have been carried on in petticoats. This was not only because she did a man's work, but because it was morally necessary that sex should be left out of the question as between her and her comrades-in-arms. She gave this reason herself when she was pressed on the subject; and the fact that this entirely reasonable necessity came to her imagination first as an order from God delivered through the mouth of Saint Catherine does not prove that she was mad. The soundness of the order proves that she was unusually sane; but its form proves that her dramatic imagination played tricks with her senses. Her policy was also quite sound: nobody disputes that the relief of Orleans, followed up by the coronation at Rheims of the Dauphin as a counterblow to the suspicions then current of his legitimacy and consequently of his title, were military and political masterstrokes that saved France. They might have been planned by Napoleon or any other illusionproof genius. They came to Joan as an instruction from her

---

14 The argument of the Polish astronomer Copernicus (1473–1543) that the earth moved round the sun was fiercely rejected by the church.

15 Isaac Newton (1642–1727) used astrology when dating the Greek, Egyptian, Assyrian, Babylonian and Persian empires. The *Chronology* had been presented to Cambridge University Library in 1888 (MS add. 3988, fo. 102).

16 Lunatic. Founded in 1247, Bethlehem or 'Bedlam' was the London hospital for the insane.

17 Daniel 7: 7–28.

Counsel, as she called her visionary saints; but she was none the less an able leader of men for imagining her ideas in this way.

The Evolutionary Appetite

What then is the modern view of Joan's voices and visions and messages from God? The nineteenth century said that they were delusions, but that as she was a pretty girl, and had been abominably ill-treated and finally done to death by a superstitious rabble of medieval priests hounded on by a corrupt political bishop, it must be assumed that she was the innocent dupe of these delusions. The twentieth century finds this explanation too vapidly commonplace, and demands something more mystic. I think the twentieth century is right, because an explanation which amounts to Joan being mentally defective instead of, as she obviously was, mentally excessive, will not wash. I cannot believe, nor, if I could, could I expect all my readers to believe, as Joan did, that three ocularly visible well dressed persons, named respectively Saint Catherine, Saint Margaret, and Saint Michael, came down from heaven and gave her certain instructions with which they were charged by God for her. Not that such a belief would be more improbable or fantastic than some modern beliefs which we all swallow; but there are fashions and family habits in belief, and it happens that, my fashion being Victorian and my family habit Protestant, I find myself unable to attach any such objective validity to the form of Joan's visions.

But that there are forces at work which use individuals for purposes far transcending the purpose of keeping these individuals alive and prosperous and respectable and safe and happy in the middle station in life, which is all any good bourgeois can reasonably require, is established by the fact that men will, in the pursuit of knowledge and of social readjustments for which they will not be a penny the better, and are indeed often many pence the worse, face poverty, infamy, exile, imprisonment, dreadful hardship, and death. Even the selfish pursuit of personal power does not nerve men to the efforts and sacrifices which are eagerly made in pursuit of extensions of our power over nature, though these extensions may not touch the personal life of the seeker at any point. There is no more mystery about this appetite for knowledge and power than about the appetite for food: both are known as facts and as facts only, the difference between them being that the appetite for food is necessary to the life of the hungry man and is therefore a personal appetite, whereas the other is an appetite for evolution, and therefore a superpersonal need.

The diverse manners in which our imaginations dramatize the approach of the superpersonal forces is a problem for the psychologist, not for the historian. Only, the historian must understand that visionaries are neither impostors nor lunatics. It is one thing to say that the figure Joan recognized as St Catherine was not really St Catherine, but the dramatization by Joan's imagination of that pressure upon her of the driving force that is behind evolution which I have just called the evolutionary appetite. It is quite another to class her visions with the vision of two moons seen by a drunken person, or with Brocken spectres,[18] echoes and the like. Saint Catherine's instructions were far too cogent for that; and the simplest French peasant who believes in apparitions of celestial personages to favored mortals is nearer to the scientific truth about Joan than the Rationalist and Materialist historians and essayists who feel obliged to set down a girl who saw saints and heard them talking to her as either crazy or mendacious. If Joan was mad, all Christendom was mad too; for people who believe devoutly in the existence of celestial personages are every whit as mad in that sense as the people who think they see them. Luther, when he threw his inkhorn at the devil, was no more mad than any other Augustinian monk:[19] he had a more vivid imagination, and had perhaps eaten and slept less: that was all.

The Mere Iconography does not Matter

All the popular religions in the world are made apprehensible by an array of legendary personages, with an Almighty Father, and sometimes a mother and divine child, as the central figures. These are presented to the mind's eye in childhood; and the result is a hallucination which persists strongly throughout life when it has been well impressed. Thus all the thinking of the hallucinated adult about the fountain of inspiration which is continually flowing in the universe, or about the promptings of virtue and the revulsions of shame: in short, about aspiration and conscience, both of which forces are matters of fact more obvious than electro-magnetism, is thinking in terms of the celestial vision. And when in the case of exceptionally imaginative persons, especially those practising certain appropriate austerities, the hallucination extends from the mind's eye to the body's, the visionary sees Krishna or the Buddha[20] or the Blessed Virgin or St Catherine as the case may be.

---

18 An optical illusion of a huge haloed figure, encountered in the Brocken mountains in Germany, created by a shadow cast when the sun shines from behind a person looking from a ridge into mist.

19 Popular tradition, taking literally a metaphor about the force of Luther's writing, has held, at least since the sixteenth century, that Luther, while translating the Bible into German, saw the Devil and vanquished him by hurling his inkwell at him. A stain on the wall of Luther's study at Wartburg Castle, in Germany, is said to bear witness to this event.

20 Respectively a major Hindu deity and the founder of Buddhism.

The Modern Education which Joan Escaped

It is important to everyone nowadays to understand this, because modern science is making short work of the hallucinations without regard to the vital importance of the things they symbolize. If Joan were reborn today she would be sent, first to a convent school in which she would be mildly taught to connect inspiration and conscience with St Catherine and St Michael exactly as she was in the fifteenth century, and then finished up with a very energetic training in the gospel of Saints Louis Pasteur and Paul Bert,[21] who would tell her (possibly in visions but more probably in pamphlets) not to be a superstitious little fool, and to empty out St Catherine and the rest of the Catholic hagiology[22] as an obsolete iconography of exploded myths. It would be rubbed into her that Galileo[23] was a martyr, and his persecutors incorrigible ignoramuses, and that St Teresa's[24] hormones had gone astray and left her incurably hyperpituitary or hyperadrenal or hysteroid or epileptoid or anything but asteroid. She would have been convinced by precept and experiment that baptism and receiving the body of her Lord were contemptible superstitions, and that vaccination and vivisection were enlightened practices. Behind her new Saints Louis and Paul there would be not only Science purifying Religion and being purified by it, but hypochondria, melancholia, cowardice, stupidity, cruelty, muckraking curiosity, knowledge without wisdom, and everything that the eternal soul in Nature loathes, instead of the virtues of which St Catherine was the figure head. As to the new rites, which would be the saner Joan? the one who carried little children to be baptized of water and the spirit, or the one who sent the police to force their parents to have the most villainous racial poison we know thrust into their veins? the one who told them the story of the angel and Mary, or the one who questioned them as to their experiences of the Edipus complex? the one to whom the consecrated wafer was the very body of the virtue that was her salvation, or the one who looked forward to a precise and convenient regulation of her health and her desires by a nicely calculated diet of thyroid extract, adrenalin, thymin,

---

21 Shaw cites exemplary nineteenth-century French scientists. Louis Pasteur invented pasteurisation and developed the rabies anti-toxin; Paul Bert worked on the physiological effects of air pressure and was fiercely anti-clerical.

22 Accounts of the lives of the saints.

23 Galileo Galilei (1564–1642) was under effective house arrest by the church after his observations endorsed Copernicus' hypotheses. The smuggling out of Italy and publication in Holland of his *Discoursi*, one of the founding documents of modern physics, led to charges of heresy.

24 St Teresa, a sixteenth-century Carmelite nun, experienced mystic visions and her teaching and writing created a surge of religious fervour in Spain.

pituitrin, and insulin, with pick-me-ups of hormone stimulants, the blood being first carefully fortified with antibodies against all possible infections by inoculations of infected bacteria and serum from infected animals, and against old age by surgical extirpation of the reproductive ducts or weekly doses of monkey gland?

It is true that behind all these quackeries there is a certain body of genuine scientific physiology. But was there any the less a certain body of genuine psychology behind St Catherine and the Holy Ghost? And which is the healthier mind? the saintly mind or the monkey gland mind? Does not the present cry of Back to the Middle Ages, which has been incubating ever since the pre-Raphaelite movement[25] began, mean that it is no longer our Academy pictures that are intolerable, but our credulities that have not the excuse of being superstitions, our cruelties that have not the excuse of barbarism, our persecutions that have not the excuse of religious faith, our shameless substitution of successful swindlers and scoundrels and quacks for saints as objects of worship, and our deafness and blindness to the calls and visions of the inexorable power that made us, and will destroy us if we disregard it? To Joan and her contemporaries we should appear as a drove of Gadarene swine,[26] possessed by all the unclean spirits cast out by the faith and civilization of the Middle Ages, running violently down a steep place into a hell of high explosives. For us to set up our condition as a standard of sanity, and declare Joan mad because she never condescended to it, is to prove that we are not only lost but irredeemable. Let us then once for all drop all nonsense about Joan being cracked, and accept her as at least as sane as Florence Nightingale, who also combined a very simple iconography of religious belief with a mind so exceptionally powerful that it kept her in continual trouble with the medical and military panjandrums of her time.

Failures of the Voices

That the voices and visions were illusory, and their wisdom all Joan's own, is shewn by the occasions on which they failed her, notably during her trial, when they assured her that she would be rescued. Here her

---

25 The Pre-Raphaelites were a group of mid-nineteenth-century artists, including Dante Gabriel Rosetti and John Everett Millais, who sought to revitalise painting by imbuing it with the colour and spirituality of the early medieval period. Major collections can be found in London's Tate Britain and the Birmingham Art Gallery.
26 Gadarene swine, possessed by evil spirits, rushed together down a steep hill to their doom (Matthew 8: 30–2).

hopes flattered her; but they were not unreasonable: her military colleague La Hire was in command of a considerable force not so very far off; and if the Armagnacs, as her party was called, had really wanted to rescue her, and had put anything like her own vigor into the enterprise, they could have attempted it with very fair chances of success. She did not understand that they were glad to be rid of her, nor that the rescue of a prisoner from the hands of the Church was a much more serious business for a medieval captain, or even a medieval king, than its mere physical difficulty as a military exploit suggested. According to her lights her expectation of a rescue was reasonable; therefore she heard Madame Saint Catherine assuring her it would happen, that being her way of finding out and making up her own mind. When it became evident that she had miscalculated: when she was led to the stake, and La Hire was not thundering at the gates of Rouen nor charging Warwick's men at arms, she threw over Saint Catherine at once, and recanted. Nothing could be more sane or practical. It was not until she discovered that she had gained nothing by her recantation but close imprisonment for life that she withdrew it, and deliberately and explicitly chose burning instead: a decision which shewed not only the extraordinary decision of her character, but also a Rationalism carried to its ultimate human test of suicide. Yet even in this the illusion persisted; and she announced her relapse as dictated to her by her voices.

Joan a Galtonic Visualizer

The most sceptical scientific reader may therefore accept as a flat fact, carrying no implication of unsoundness of mind, that Joan was what Francis Galton[27] and other modern investigators of human faculty call a visualizer. She saw imaginary saints just as some other people see imaginary diagrams and landscapes with numbers dotted about them, and are thereby able to perform feats of memory and arithmetic impossible to non-visualizers. Visualizers will understand this at once. Non-visualizers who have never read Galton will be puzzled and incredulous. But a very little inquiry among their acquaintances will reveal to them that the mind's eye is more or less a magic lantern, and that the street is full of normally sane people who have hallucinations of all sorts which they believe to be part of the normal permanent equipment of all human beings.

27 Now best known for his work on eugenics, Francis Galton (1822–1911) was also an influential psychologist whose paper on 'The Visions of Sane Persons' was published in 1881.

Joan's Manliness and Militarism

Joan's other abnormality, too common among uncommon things to be properly called a peculiarity, was her craze for soldiering and the masculine life. Her father tried to frighten her out of it by threatening to drown her if she ran away with the soldiers, and ordering her brothers to drown her if he were not on the spot. This extravagance was clearly not serious: it must have been addressed to a child young enough to imagine that he was in earnest. Joan must therefore as a child have wanted to run away and be a soldier. The awful prospect of being thrown into the Meuse and drowned by a terrible father and her big brothers kept her quiet until the father had lost his terrors and the brothers yielded to her natural leadership; and by that time she had sense enough to know that the masculine and military life was not a mere matter of running away from home. But the taste for it never left her, and was fundamental in determining her career.

If anyone doubts this, let him ask himself why a maid charged with a special mission from heaven to the Dauphin (this was how Joan saw her very able plan for retrieving the desperate situation of the uncrowned king) should not have simply gone to the court as a maid, in woman's dress, and urged her counsel upon him in a woman's way, as other women with similar missions had come to his mad father and his wise grandfather. Why did she insist on having a soldier's dress and arms and sword and horse and equipment, and on treating her escort of soldiers as comrades, sleeping side by side with them on the floor at night as if there were no difference of sex between them? It may be answered that this was the safest way of travelling through a country infested with hostile troops and bands of marauding deserters from both sides. Such an answer has no weight because it applies to all the women who travelled in France at that time, and who never dreamt of travelling otherwise than as women. But even if we accept it, how does it account for the fact that when the danger was over, and she could present herself at court in feminine attire with perfect safety and obviously with greater propriety, she presented herself in her man's dress, and instead of urging Charles, like Queen Victoria urging the War Office to send Roberts to the Transvaal,[28] to send D'Alençon,[29] De Rais, La Hire and the rest to the relief of Dunois at Orleans, insisted that she must go herself and lead the assault in person? Why did she give exhibitions of her dexterity in handling a lance, and of

---

28 Lord Roberts changed British fortunes in the Boer War when, sent to take command of the army, he captured Pretoria, capital of the Transvaal on 5 June 1900.

29 John, Duke of Alençon, born 1407, commanded Charles' army in the Loire campaign, was co-commander at Patay and supported Jeanne's attempt on Paris.

her seat as a rider? Why did she accept presents of armor and chargers and masculine surcoats, and in every action repudiate the conventional character of a woman? The simple answer to all these questions is that she was the sort of woman that wants to lead a man's life. They are to be found wherever there are armies on foot or navies on the seas, serving in male disguise, eluding detection for astonishingly long periods, and sometimes, no doubt, escaping it entirely. When they are in a position to defy public opinion they throw off all concealment. You have your Rosa Bonheur painting in male blouse and trousers, and George Sand living a man's life and almost compelling her Chopins and De Mussets to live women's lives to amuse her. Had Joan not been one of those 'unwomanly women',[30] she might have been canonized much sooner.

But it is not necessary to wear trousers and smoke big cigars to live a man's life any more than it is necessary to wear petticoats to live a woman's. There are plenty of gowned and bodiced women in ordinary civil life who manage their own affairs and other people's, including those of their menfolk, and are entirely masculine in their tastes and pursuits. There always were such women, even in the Victorian days when women had fewer legal rights than men, and our modern women magistrates, mayors, and members of Parliament were unknown. In reactionary Russia in our own century a woman soldier organized an effective regiment of amazons, which disappeared only because it was Aldershottian[31] enough to be against the Revolution. The exemption of women from military service is founded, not on any natural inaptitude that men do not share, but on the fact that communities cannot reproduce themselves without plenty of women. Men are more largely dispensable, and are sacrificed accordingly.

Was Joan Suicidal?

These two abnormalities were the only ones that were irresistibly prepotent in Joan; and they brought her to the stake. Neither of them was peculiar to her. There was nothing peculiar about her except the vigor and scope of her mind and character, and the intensity of her vital energy. She was accused of a suicidal tendency; and it is a fact that when

30 The phrase 'unwomanly women', in popular use at the end of the nineteenth century, and dramatised in Shaw's *The Philanderer*, 1893, indicated feminists who asserted their art and lifestyle against contemporary convention. The novelist Aurore Dupin (Georges Sand) and the painter Rose Bonheur were notable French examples.

31 i.e. dedicated to the political and military status quo. A permanent military camp having been established at Aldershot in 1854, the village grew rapidly into the town, known as the 'Home of the British Army'.

she attempted to escape from Beaurevoir Castle by jumping from a tower said to be sixty feet high, she took a risk beyond reason, though she recovered from the crash after a few days fasting. Her death was deliberately chosen as an alternative to life without liberty. In battle she challenged death as Wellington did at Waterloo, and as Nelson habitually did when he walked his quarter deck during his battles with all his decorations in full blaze. As neither Nelson nor Wellington nor any of those who have performed desperate feats, and preferred death to captivity, has been accused of suicidal mania, Joan need not be suspected of it. In the Beaurevoir affair there was more at stake than her freedom. She was distracted by the news that Compiègne was about to fall; and she was convinced that she could save it if only she could get free. Still, the leap was so perilous that her conscience was not quite easy about it; and she expressed this, as usual, by saying that Saint Catherine had forbidden her to do it, but forgave her afterwards for her disobedience.

Joan Summed up

We may accept and admire Joan, then, as a sane and shrewd country girl of extraordinary strength of mind and hardihood of body. Everything she did was thoroughly calculated; and though the process was so rapid that she was hardly conscious of it, and ascribed it all to her voices, she was a woman of policy and not of blind impulse. In war she was as much a realist as Napoleon: she had his eye for artillery and his knowledge of what it could do. She did not expect besieged cities to fall Jerichowise at the sound of her trumpet,[32] but, like Wellington, adapted her methods of attack to the peculiarities of the defence; and she anticipated the Napoleonic calculation that if you only hold on long enough the other fellow will give in: for example, her final triumph at Orleans was achieved after her commander Dunois had sounded the retreat at the end of a day's fighting without a decision. She was never for a moment what so many romancers and playwrights have pretended: a romantic young lady. She was a thorough daughter of the soil in her peasantlike matter-of-factness and doggedness, and her acceptance of great lords and kings and prelates as such without idolatry or snobbery, seeing at a glance how much they were individually good for. She had the respectable countrywoman's sense of the value of public decency, and would not tolerate foul language and neglect of religious observances, nor allow disreputable women to hang about her soldiers. She had one pious ejaculation 'En

32 The walls of the Canaanite city of Jericho fell miraculously to the besieging Israelites at a blast from Joshua's trumpet (Joshua 6: 1–27).

nom Dé!' and one meaningless oath 'Par mon martin';[33] and this much swearing she allowed to the incorrigibly blasphemous La Hire equally with herself. The value of this prudery was so great in restoring the self-respect of the badly demoralized army that, like most of her policy, it justified itself as soundly calculated. She talked to and dealt with people of all classes, from laborers to kings, without embarrassment or affectation, and got them to do what she wanted when they were not afraid or corrupt. She could coax and she could hustle, her tongue having a soft side and a sharp edge. She was very capable: a born boss.

Joan's Immaturity and Ignorance

All this, however, must be taken with one heavy qualification. She was only a girl in her teens. If we could think of her as a managing woman of fifty we should seize her type at once; for we have plenty of managing women among us of that age who illustrate perfectly the sort of person she would have become had she lived. But she, being only a lass when all is said, lacked their knowledge of men's vanities and of the weight and proportion of social forces. She knew nothing of iron hands in velvet gloves: she just used her fists. She thought political changes much easier than they are, and, like Mahomet in his innocence of any world but the tribal world, wrote letters to kings calling on them to make millennial rearrangements. Consequently it was only in the enterprises that were really simple and compassable by swift physical force, like the coronation and the Orleans campaign, that she was successful.

Her want of academic education disabled her when she had to deal with such elaborately artificial structures as the great ecclesiastical and social institutions of the Middle Ages. She had a horror of heretics without suspecting that she was herself a heresiarch, one of the precursors of a schism that rent Europe in two, and cost centuries of bloodshed that is not yet staunched. She objected to foreigners on the sensible ground that they were not in their proper place in France; but she had no notion of how this brought her into conflict with Catholicism and Feudalism, both essentially international. She worked by commonsense; and where scholarship was the only clue to institutions she was in the dark, and broke her shins against them, all the more rudely because of her enormous self-confidence, which made her the least cautious of human beings in civil affairs.

33 MFr = 'In the name of God!' . . . 'By my staff'. See Murray, pp. 2, 291, 295.

This combination of inept youth and academic ignorance with great natural capacity, push, courage, devotion, originality and oddity, fully accounts for all the facts in Joan's career, and makes her a credible historical and human phenomenon; but it clashes most discordantly both with the idolatrous romance that has grown up around her, and the belittling scepticism that reacts against that romance.

The Maid in Literature

English readers would probably like to know how these idolizations and reactions have affected the books they are most familiar with about Joan. There is the first part of the Shakespearean, or pseudo-Shakespearean trilogy of Henry VI, in which Joan is one of the leading characters. This portrait of Joan is not more authentic than the descriptions in the London papers of George Washington in 1780, of Napoleon in 1803, of the German Crown Prince in 1915, or of Lenin in 1917.[34] It ends in mere scurrility. The impression left by it is that the playwright, having begun by an attempt to make Joan a beautiful and romantic figure,[35] was told by his scandalized company that English patriotism would never stand a sympathetic representation of a French conqueror of English troops, and that unless he at once introduced all the old charges against Joan of being a sorceress and harlot, and assumed her to be guilty of all of them, his play could not be produced. As likely as not, this is what actually happened: indeed there is only one other apparent way of accounting for the sympathetic representation of Joan as a heroine culminating in her eloquent appeal to the Duke of Burgundy, followed by the blackguardly scurrility of the concluding scenes. That other way is to assume that the original play was wholly scurrilous, and that Shakespear touched up the earlier scenes. As the work belongs to a period at which he was only beginning his practice as a tinker of old works, before his own style was fully formed and hardened, it is impossible to verify this guess. His finger is not unmistakably evident in the play, which is poor and base in its moral tone; but he may have tried to redeem it from downright infamy by shedding a momentary glamor on the figure of The Maid.

---

34 All figures demonised by the British press for opposing British interests: Washington led the American Independence campaign; Napoleon commanded in the French Revolutionary wars; the Kaiser's son, the Crown Prince, represented the Germany of the recent World War; and Lenin led the Russian Bolshevik Revolution.

35 Cf. *Henry VI, Part 1*, 1.2.51–4: 'DUNOIS A holy maid hither with me I bring, / Which by a vision sent to her from heaven / Ordained is to raise this tedious siege / And drive the English forth the bounds of France.'

When we jump over two centuries to Schiller, we find Die Jungfrau von Orleans[36] drowned in a witch's caldron of raging romance. Schiller's Joan has not a single point of contact with the real Joan, nor indeed with any mortal woman that ever walked this earth. There is really nothing to be said of his play but that it is not about Joan at all, and can hardly be said to pretend to be; for he makes her die on the battlefield, finding her burning unbearable. Before Schiller came Voltaire, who burlesqued Homer in a mock epic called La Pucelle.[37] It is the fashion to dismiss this with virtuous indignation as an obscene libel; and I certainly cannot defend it against the charge of extravagant indecorum. But its purpose was not to depict Joan, but to kill with ridicule everything that Voltaire righteously hated in the institutions and fashions of his own day. He made Joan ridiculous, but not contemptible nor (comparatively) unchaste; and as he also made Homer and St Peter and St Denis and the brave Dunois ridiculous, and the other heroines of the poem very unchaste indeed, he may be said to have let Joan off very easily. But indeed the personal adventures of the characters are so outrageous, and so Homerically free from any pretence at or even possibility of historical veracity, that those who affect to take them seriously only make themselves Pecksniffian.[38] Samuel Butler believed The Iliad to be a burlesque of Greek Jingoism and Greek religion, written by a hostage or a slave;[39] and La Pucelle makes Butler's theory almost convincing. Voltaire represents Agnes Sorel, the Dauphin's mistress, whom Joan never met, as a woman with a consuming passion for the chastest concubinal fidelity, whose fate it was to be continually falling into the hands of licentious foes and suffering the worst extremities of rapine. The combats in which Joan rides a flying donkey, or in which, taken unaware with no clothes on, she defends Agnes with her sword, and inflicts appropriate mutilations on her assailants, can be laughed at as they are intended to be without scruple; for no sane person could mistake them for sober history; and it may be that their ribald irreverence is more wholesome than the beglamored sentimentality of Schiller. Certainly

---

36 Die Jungfrau von Orleans, written in 1801, was Johan Christoph Friedrich von Schiller's most performed play in his lifetime. Its five acts dramatise Jeanne's life, ending with her trial and execution. Among numerous translations was Lewis Filmore, The maid of Orleans: A Romantic Tragedy, 1882.

37 The first authorised edition of Voltaire's satirical poem on Jeanne's story, La Pucelle, was published in 1762.

38 Hypocritical, after Pecksniff, a character in Charles Dickens' Martin Chuzzlewit.

39 Samuel Butler (1835–1902) is best known for his novel The Way of All Flesh, 1874. He advanced his claims about the identity of Homer in The Authoress of the Odyssey, 1897, and his introduction to his translation of The Iliad, 1898.

Voltaire should not have asserted that Joan's father was a priest; but when he was out to *écraser l'infâme*[40] (the French Church) he stuck at nothing.

So far, the literary representations of The Maid were legendary. But the publication by Quicherat[41] in 1841 of the reports of her trial and rehabilitation placed the subject on a new footing. These entirely realistic documents created a living interest in Joan which Voltaire's mock Homerics and Schiller's romantic nonsense missed. Typical products of that interest in America and England are the histories of Joan by Mark Twain and Andrew Lang.[42] Mark Twain was converted to downright worship of Joan directly by Quicherat. Later on, another man of genius, Anatole France,[43] reacted against the Quicheratic wave of enthusiasm, and wrote a Life of Joan in which he attributed Joan's ideas to clerical prompting and her military success to an adroit use of her by Dunois as a *mascotte*: in short, he denied that she had any serious military or political ability. At this Andrew saw red, and went for Anatole's scalp in a rival Life of her which should be read as a corrective to the other. Lang had no difficulty in shewing that Joan's ability was not an unnatural fiction to be explained away as an illusion manufactured by priests and soldiers, but a straightforward fact.

It has been lightly pleaded in explanation that Anatole France is a Parisian of the art world, into whose scheme of things the able, hard-headed, hardhanded female, though she dominates provincial France and business Paris, does not enter; whereas Lang was a Scot, and every Scot knows that the grey mare is as likely as not to be the better horse. But this explanation does not convince me. I cannot believe that Anatole France does not know what everybody knows. I wish everybody knew all that he knows. One feels antipathies at work in his book. He is not anti-Joan; but he is anti-clerical, anti-mystic, and fundamentally unable to believe that there ever was any such person as the real Joan.

Mark Twain's Joan, skirted to the ground, and with as many petticoats as Noah's wife in a toy ark, is an attempt to combine Bayard[44] with Esther

---

40 Meaning 'to crush infamy', this phrase was used by Voltaire above his signature, sometimes shortened to '*écrelinf*'.

41 Jules Quicherat's publication, *Le Procès de Jeanne d'Arc*, 1841–9, made available the extensive documentation associated with Jeanne.

42 Mark Twain's fictional memoir, supposedly by Jeanne's page, *Personal Recollections of Joan of Arc, by the Sieur Louis de Conte*, 1899, and Andrew Lang's retelling of Jeanne's story, *The Maid of France*, 1908, both drew on Quicherat.

43 France's *La Vie de Jeanne D'Arc*, 1908, is a sceptical dismissal of Jeanne's claim to mystic inspiration and honour.

44 Pierre Terrail, Seigneur de Bayard (1473–1524), known as 'The Good Knight' or 'The Fearless and Blameless', was considered the epitome of French Chivalry.

Summerson[45] from Bleak House into an unimpeachable American school teacher in armor. Like Esther Summerson she makes her creator ridiculous, and yet, being the work of a man of genius, remains a credible human goodygoody in spite of her creator's infatuation. It is the description rather than the valuation that is wrong. Andrew Lang and Mark Twain are equally determined to make Joan a beautiful and most ladylike Victorian; but both of them recognize and insist on her capacity for leadership, though the Scots scholar is less romantic about it than the Mississippi pilot.[46] But then Lang was, by lifelong professional habit, a critic of biographies rather than a biographer, whereas Mark Twain writes his biography frankly in the form of a romance.

Protestant Misunderstandings of the Middle Ages

They had, however, one disability in common. To understand Joan's history it is not enough to understand her character: you must understand her environment as well. Joan in a nineteenth-twentieth century environment is as incongruous a figure as she would appear were she to walk down Piccadilly today in her fifteenth century armor. To see her in her proper perspective you must understand Christendom and the Catholic Church, the Holy Roman Empire and the Feudal System, as they existed and were understood in the Middle Ages. If you confuse the Middle Ages with the Dark Ages, and are in the habit of ridiculing your aunt for wearing 'medieval clothes', meaning those in vogue in the eighteen-nineties, and are quite convinced that the world has progressed enormously, both morally and mechanically, since Joan's time, then you will never understand why Joan was burnt, much less feel that you might have voted for burning her yourself if you had been a member of the court that tried her; and until you feel that you know nothing essential about her.

That the Mississippi pilot should have broken down on this misunderstanding is natural enough. Mark Twain, the Innocent Abroad, who saw the lovely churches of the Middle Ages without a throb of emotion, author of A Yankee at the Court of King Arthur, in which the heroes and heroines of medieval chivalry are guys seen through the eyes of a street arab, was clearly out of court from the beginning. Andrew Lang was better read; but, like Walter Scott, he enjoyed medieval history as a string of Border romances rather than as the record of a high European civilization based on a catholic faith. Both of them were baptized as Protestants, and impressed by all their schooling and most of their reading with the

---

45 The selfless heroine, and first person narrator, of Dickens' novel, Bleak House, 1852–3.
46 Mark Twain.

belief that Catholic bishops who burnt heretics were persecutors capable of any villainy; that all heretics were Albigensians[47] or Husites or Jews or Protestants of the highest character; and that the Inquisition was a Chamber of Horrors invented expressly and exclusively for such burnings. Accordingly we find them representing Peter Cauchon, Bishop of Beauvais, the judge who sent Joan to the stake, as an unconscionable scoundrel, and all the questions put to her as 'traps' to ensnare and destroy her. And they assume unhesitatingly that the two or three score of canons and doctors of law and divinity who sat with Cauchon as assessors, were exact reproductions of him on slightly less elevated chairs and with a different headdress.

Comparative Fairness of Joan's Trial

The truth is that Cauchon was threatened and insulted by the English for being too considerate to Joan. A recent French writer denies that Joan was burnt, and holds that Cauchon spirited her away and burnt somebody or something else in her place, and that the pretender who subsequently personated her at Orleans and elsewhere was not a pretender but the real authentic Joan. He is able to cite Cauchon's pro-Joan partiality in support of his view. As to the assessors, the objection to them is not that they were a row of uniform rascals, but that they were political partisans of Joan's enemies. This is a valid objection to all such trials; but in the absence of neutral tribunals they are unavoidable. A trial by Joan's French partisans would have been as unfair as the trial by her French opponents; and an equally mixed tribunal would have produced a deadlock. Such recent trials as those of Edith Cavell by a German tribunal and Roger Casement by an English one[48] were open to the same objection; but they went forward to the death nevertheless, because neutral tribunals were not available. Edith, like Joan, was an arch heretic: in the middle of the war she declared before the world that 'Patriotism is not enough.' She nursed enemies back to health, and assisted their prisoners to escape, making it abundantly clear that she would help any fugitive or distressed person without asking whose side he was on, and acknowledging no distinction before Christ between Tommy and Jerry

---

47 The Albigensians, or Cathars, were an eleventh-century French religious sect against whom the Catholic church waged a twenty-year military crusade.

48 Cavell, a nurse with the Red Cross, was tried by the Germans for helping allied soldiers escape from occupied Belgium. Casement, an Irishman in the British diplomatic service, was arrested in 1916 for negotiating German arms for the Irish Independence movement. Convicted of treason and executed in August 1916, he became a popular hero in Ireland where his exhumed body was given a state funeral in 1965. Shaw was among his most vocal defenders.

and Pitou the *poilu*.[49] Well might Edith have wished that she could bring the Middle Ages back, and have fifty civilians, learned in the law or vowed to the service of God, to support two skilled judges in trying her case according to the Catholic law of Christendom, and to argue it out with her at sitting after sitting for many weeks. The modern military Inquisition was not so squeamish. It shot her out of hand; and her countrymen, seeing in this a good opportunity for lecturing the enemy on his intolerance, put up a statue to her, but took particular care not to inscribe on the pedestal 'Patriotism is not enough', for which omission, and the lie it implies, they will need Edith's intercession when they are themselves brought to judgment, if any heavenly power thinks such moral cowards capable of pleading to an intelligible indictment.[50]

The point need be no further labored. Joan was persecuted essentially as she would be persecuted today. The change from burning to hanging or shooting may strike us as a change for the better. The change from careful trial under ordinary law to recklessly summary military terrorism may strike us as a change for the worse. But as far as toleration is concerned the trial and execution in Rouen in 1431 might have been an event of today; and we may charge our consciences accordingly. If Joan had to be dealt with by us in London she would be treated with no more toleration than Miss Sylvia Pankhurst,[51] or the Peculiar People,[52] or the parents who keep their children from the elementary school, or any of the others who cross the line we have to draw, rightly or wrongly, between the tolerable and the intolerable.

Joan not Tried as a Political Offender

Besides, Joan's trial was not, like Casement's, a national political trial. Ecclesiastical courts and the courts of the Inquisition (Joan was tried by a combination of the two) were Courts Christian: that is, international courts; and she was tried, not as a traitress, but as a heretic, blasphemer, sorceress, and idolater. Her alleged offences were not political offences against England, nor against the Burgundian faction in France, but

---

49 A familiar World War One nickname for a French infantryman (*poilu* (Fr) = hairy), as was 'Tommy' for an English and 'Jerry' for a German soldier.

50 Cavell's statue in London now bears the words spoken before her execution in October 1915, 'Patriotism is not enough, I must have no hatred or bitterness towards anyone'.

51 The most radical of the Pankhurst women who were active in the suffragette movement, Sylvia was concerned with the situation of working-class women. She was a founder member of the British Communist Party and, like Shaw, a pacifist in the First War.

52 The Peculiar People, a Christian sect, that flourished in Essex in the 1850s, relied on prayer and faith for healing, rather than medicine.

against God and against the common morality of Christendom. And although the idea we call Nationalism was so foreign to the medieval conception of Christian society that it might almost have been directly charged against Joan as an additional heresy, yet it was not so charged; and it is unreasonable to suppose that the political bias of a body of Frenchmen like the assessors would on this point have run strongly in favor of the English foreigners (even if they had been making themselves particularly agreeable in France instead of just the contrary) against a Frenchwoman who had vanquished them.

The tragic part of the trial was that Joan, like most prisoners tried for anything but the simplest breaches of the ten commandments, did not understand what they were accusing her of. She was much more like Mark Twain than like Peter Cauchon. Her attachment to the Church was very different from the Bishop's, and does not, in fact, bear close examination from his point of view. She delighted in the solaces the Church offers to sensitive souls: to her, confession and communion were luxuries beside which the vulgar pleasures of the senses were trash. Her prayers were wonderful conversations with her three saints. Her piety seemed superhuman to the formally dutiful people whose religion was only a task to them. But when the Church was not offering her her favorite luxuries, but calling on her to accept its interpretation of God's will, and to sacrifice her own, she flatly refused, and made it clear that her notion of a Catholic Church was one in which the Pope was Pope Joan. How could the Church tolerate that, when it had just destroyed Hus, and had watched the career of Wycliffe[53] with a growing anger that would have brought him, too, to the stake, had he not died a natural death before the wrath fell on him in his grave? Neither Hus nor Wycliffe was as bluntly defiant as Joan: both were reformers of the Church like Luther; whilst Joan, like Mrs Eddy,[54] was quite prepared to supersede St Peter as the rock on which the Church was built, and, like Mahomet, was always ready with a private revelation from God to settle every question and fit every occasion.

The enormity of Joan's pretension was proved by her own unconsciousness of it, which we call her innocence, and her friends called her simplicity. Her solutions of the problems presented to her seemed, and

53 The English reformist theologian, John Wycliffe (1320–84), excoriated clerical corruption and preached the individual relationship of each Christian with God, to which end he made the first English translation of the Bible and was accused of heresy. His 'forty-five articles' of faith and reform influenced Huss and, through him, Luther.

54 Mary Baker Eddy was the nineteenth-century founder of the Christian Science Movement.

indeed mostly were, the plainest commonsense, and their revelation to her by her Voices was to her a simple matter of fact. How could plain commonsense and simple fact seem to her to be that hideous thing, heresy? When rival prophetesses came into the field, she was down on them at once for liars and humbugs; but she never thought of them as heretics. She was in a state of invincible ignorance as to the Church's view; and the Church could not tolerate her pretensions without either waiving its authority or giving her a place beside the Trinity during her lifetime and in her teens, which was unthinkable. Thus an irresistible force met an immovable obstacle, and developed the heat that consumed poor Joan.

Mark and Andrew would have shared her innocence and her fate had they been dealt with by the Inquisition: that is why their accounts of the trial are as absurd as hers might have been could she have written one. All that can be said for their assumption that Cauchon was a vulgar villain, and that the questions put to Joan were traps, is that it has the support of the inquiry which rehabilitated her twenty-five years later. But this rehabilitation was as corrupt as the contrary proceeding applied to Cromwell[55] by our Restoration reactionaries. Cauchon had been dug up, and his body thrown into the common sewer. Nothing was easier than to accuse him of cozenage,[56] and declare the whole trial void on that account. That was what everybody wanted, from Charles the Victorious, whose credit was bound up with The Maid's, to the patriotic Nationalist populace, who idolized Joan's memory. The English were gone; and a verdict in their favour would have been an outrage on the throne and on the patriotism which Joan had set on foot.

We have none of these overwhelming motives of political convenience and popularity to bias us. For us the first trial stands valid; and the rehabilitation would be negligible but for the mass of sincere testimony it produced as to Joan's engaging personal character. The question then arises: how did The Church get over the verdict at the first trial when it canonized Joan five hundred years later?

The Church Uncompromised by its Amends
Easily enough. In the Catholic Church, far more than in law, there is no wrong without a remedy. It does not defer to Joanesque private judgment as such, the supremacy of private judgment for the individual being the

55 Oliver Cromwell led the forces opposing Charles I and was Lord Protector from 1653 to his death in 1658. At the Restoration of the monarchy in 1660 his corpse was dug up, hung in chains and beheaded.

56 Fraud.

quintessence of Protestantism; nevertheless it finds a place for private judgment *in excelsis*[57] by admitting that the highest wisdom may come as a divine revelation to an individual. On sufficient evidence it will declare that individual a saint. Thus, as revelation may come by way of an enlightenment of the private judgment no less than by the words of a celestial personage appearing in a vision, a saint may be defined as a person of heroic virtue whose private judgment is privileged. Many innovating saints, notably Francis and Clare, have been in conflict with the Church during their lives, and have thus raised the question whether they were heretics or saints. Francis might have gone to the stake had he lived longer. It is therefore by no means impossible for a person to be excommunicated as a heretic, and on further consideration canonized as a saint. Excommunication by a provincial ecclesiastical court is not one of the acts for which the Church claims infallibility. Perhaps I had better inform my Protestant readers that the famous Dogma of Papal Infallibility is by far the most modest pretension of the kind in existence. Compared with our infallible democracies, our infallible medical councils, our infallible astronomers, our infallible judges, and our infallible parliaments, the Pope is on his knees in the dust confessing his ignorance before the throne of God, asking only that as to certain historical matters on which he has clearly more sources of information open to him than anyone else his decision shall be taken as final. The Church may, and perhaps some day will, canonize Galileo without compromising such infallibility as it claims for the Pope, if not without compromising the infallibility claimed for the Book of Joshua by simple souls whose rational faith in more important things has become bound up with a quite irrational faith in the chronicle of Joshua's campaigns as a treatise on physics. Therefore the Church will probably not canonize Galileo yet awhile, though it might do worse. But it has been able to canonize Joan without any compromise at all. She never doubted that the sun went round the earth: she had seen it do so too often.

Still, there was a great wrong done to Joan and to the conscience of the world by her burning. *Tout comprendre, c'est tout pardonner*,[58] which is the Devil's sentimentality, cannot excuse it. When we have admitted that the tribunal was not only honest and legal, but exceptionally merciful in respect of sparing Joan the torture which was customary when she was obdurate as to taking the oath, and that Cauchon was far more self-disciplined and conscientious both as priest and lawyer than

57 Lat = 'in the highest'.
58 Fr = 'to understand all is to pardon all'.

163

any English judge ever dreams of being in a political case in which his party and class prejudices are involved, the human fact remains that the burning of Joan of Arc was a horror, and that a historian who would defend it would defend anything. The final criticism of its physical side is implied in the refusal of the Marquesas islanders[59] to be persuaded that the English did not eat Joan. Why, they ask, should anyone take the trouble to roast a human being except with that object? They cannot conceive its being a pleasure. As we have no answer for them that is not shameful to us, let us blush for our more complicated and pretentious savagery before we proceed to unravel the business further, and see what other lessons it contains for us.

Cruelty, Modern and Medieval

First, let us get rid of the notion that the mere physical cruelty of the burning has any special significance. Joan was burnt just as dozens of less interesting heretics were burnt in her time. Christ, in being crucified, only shared the fate of thousands of forgotten malefactors. They have no pre-eminence in mere physical pain: much more horrible executions than theirs are on record, to say nothing of the agonies of so-called natural death at its worst.

Joan was burnt more than five hundred years ago. More than three hundred years later: that is, only about a hundred years before I was born, a woman was burnt on Stephen's Green in my native city of Dublin for coining,[60] which was held to be treason. In my preface to the recent volume on English Prisons under Local Government, by Sidney and Beatrice Webb,[61] I have mentioned that when I was already a grown man I saw Richard Wagner conduct two concerts, and that when Richard Wagner was a young man he saw and avoided a crowd of people hastening to see a soldier broken on the wheel by the more cruel of the two ways of carrying out that hideous method of execution.[62] Also that the penalty of hanging, drawing, and quartering, unmentionable in its details, was abolished so recently that there are men living who have been sentenced to it. We are still flogging criminals, and clamoring for more flogging. Not even the most sensationally frightful of these atrocities inflicted on its victim

---

59 The inhabitants of the Marquesas Islands in the Pacific were believed to be cannibals.

60 Forging money.

61 Social reformers, economists, prolific writers and founders of the London School of Economics, the husband and wife team, Beatrice (1858–1943) and Sidney (1859–1947) Webb, like Shaw, were active Fabians.

62 Wagner (1813–83), the German composer, is cited in demonstration of how recently such horrible torments were practised.

the misery, degradation, and conscious waste and loss of life suffered in our modern prisons, especially the model ones, without, as far as I can see, rousing any more compunction than the burning of heretics did in the Middle Ages. We have not even the excuse of getting some fun out of our prisons as the Middle Ages did out of their stakes and wheels and gibbets. Joan herself judged this matter when she had to choose between imprisonment and the stake, and chose the stake. And thereby she deprived The Church of the plea that it was guiltless of her death, which was the work of the secular arm. The Church should have confined itself to excommunicating her. There it was within its rights: she had refused to accept its authority or comply with its conditions; and it could say with truth 'You are not one of us: go forth and find the religion that suits you, or found one for yourself.' It had no right to say 'You may return to us now that you have recanted; but you shall stay in a dungeon all the rest of your life.' Unfortunately, The Church did not believe that there was any genuine soul saving religion outside itself; and it was deeply corrupted, as all the Churches were and still are, by primitive Calibanism (in Browning's sense),[63] or the propitiation of a dreaded deity by suffering and sacrifice. Its method was not cruelty for cruelty's sake, but cruelty for the salvation of Joan's soul. Joan, however, believed that the saving of her soul was her own business, and not that of *les gens d'église*.[64] By using that term as she did, mistrustfully and contemptuously, she announced herself as, in germ, an anti-Clerical as thoroughgoing as Voltaire or Anatole France. Had she said in so many words 'To the dustbin with the Church Militant and its blackcoated officials: I recognize only the Church Triumphant in heaven,' she would hardly have put her view more plainly.

Catholic Anti-Clericalism

I must not leave it to be inferred here that one cannot be an anti-Clerical and a good Catholic too. All the reforming Popes have been vehement anti-Clericals, veritable scourges of the clergy. All the great Orders arose from dissatisfaction with the priests: that of the Franciscans with priestly snobbery, that of the Dominicans with priestly laziness and Laodiceanism,[65] that of the Jesuits with priestly apathy and ignorance and indiscipline. The

---

63 Shaw refers to 'Caliban on Setebos', a poem by the nineteenth-century English poet, Robert Browning, in which Shakespeare's character, Caliban (from *The Tempest*), a representative of the primitive imagination, ascribes to his god, Setebos, his own arbitrary and jealous impulses.

64 Fr = 'churchmen'.

65 Worldliness. The complacency and self-indulgence of the inhabitants of the ancient city of Laodicea (sited in modern Turkey) are denounced in the Bible (Revelation 3: 14–16).

most bigoted Ulster Orangeman or Leicester Low Church bourgeois (as described by Mr Henry Nevinson)[66] is a mere Gallio[67] compared to Machiavelli,[68] who, though no Protestant, was a fierce anti-Clerical. Any Catholic may, and many Catholics do, denounce any priest or body of priests, as lazy, drunken, idle, dissolute, and unworthy of their great Church and their function as the pastors of their flocks of human souls. But to say that the souls of the people are no business of the Churchmen is to go a step further, a step across the Rubicon.[69] Joan virtually took that step.

Catholicism not yet Catholic enough

And so, if we admit, as we must, that the burning of Joan was a mistake, we must broaden Catholicism sufficiently to include her in its charter. Our Churches must admit that no official organization of mortal men whose vocation does not carry with it extraordinary mental powers (and this is all that any Church Militant can in the face of fact and history pretend to be), can keep pace with the private judgment of persons of genius except when, by a very rare accident, the genius happens to be Pope, and not even then unless he is an exceedingly overbearing Pope. The Churches must learn humility as well as teach it. The Apostolic Succession cannot be secured or confined by the laying on of hands: the tongues of fire have descended on heathens and outcasts too often for that, leaving anointed Churchmen to scandalize History as worldly rascals. When the Church Militant behaves as if it were already the Church Triumphant, it makes these appalling blunders about Joan and Bruno[70] and Galileo and the rest which make it so difficult for a Freethinker to join it; and a Church which has no place for Freethinkers: nay, which does not inculcate and encourage freethinking with a complete belief that thought, when really free, must by its own law take the path that leads to The Church's bosom, not only has no future in modern culture, but obviously has no faith in the valid science of its own tenets, and is guilty of the heresy that theology and science are two different and opposite impulses, rivals for human allegiance.

66 Henry Nevinson (1856–1941) was a social activist and journalist.
67 The Roman judge who dismissed the charges brought against the Apostle Paul by his religious enemies (Acts 18: 12–17).
68 Niccolo Machiavelli (1469–1527), an Italian, was famous for the political realism advanced in his treatise *The Prince*.
69 The idiom, which means to pass the point of no return, derives from Caesar's deliberate act of war when, in 49 BC, he crossed the River Rubicon which marked the Roman boundary between Gaul and Italy.
70 Giordano Bruno, a Dominican monk, expounded the ideas of Copernicus and, after eight years' imprisonment, was excommunicated for heresy and burnt in 1600.

I have before me the letter of a Catholic priest. 'In your play,' he writes, 'I see the dramatic presentation of the conflict of the Regal, sacerdotal, and Prophetical powers, in which Joan was crushed. To me it is not the victory of any one of them over the others that will bring peace and the Reign of the Saints in the Kingdom of God, but their fruitful interaction in a costly but noble state of tension.' The Pope himself could not put it better; nor can I. We must accept the tension, and maintain it nobly without letting ourselves be tempted to relieve it by burning the thread. This is Joan's lesson to The Church; and its formulation by the hand of a priest emboldens me to claim that her canonization was a magnificently Catholic gesture as the canonization of a Protestant saint by the Church of Rome. But its special value and virtue cannot be apparent until it is known and understood as such. If any simple priest for whom this is too hard a saying tells me that it was not so intended, I shall remind him that the Church is in the hands of God, and not, as simple priests imagine, God in the hands of the Church; so if he answers too confidently for God's intentions he may be asked 'Hast thou entered into the springs of the sea? or hast thou walked in the recesses of the deep?'[71] And Joan's own answer is also the answer of old: 'Though He slay me, yet will I trust in Him; *but I will maintain my own ways before Him.*'[72]

The Law of Change is the Law of God

When Joan maintained her own ways she claimed, like Job, that there was not only God and the Church to be considered, but the Word made Flesh: that is, the unaveraged individual, representing life possibly at its highest actual human evolution and possibly at its lowest, but never at its merely mathematical average. Now there is no deification of the democratic average in the theory of the Church: it is an avowed hierarchy in which the members are sifted until at the end of the process an individual stands supreme as the Vicar of Christ. But when the process is examined it appears that its successive steps of selection and election are of the superior by the inferior (the cardinal vice of democracy), with the result that great popes are as rare and accidental as great kings, and that it has sometimes been safer for an aspirant to the Chair and the Keys to pass as a moribund dotard than as an energetic saint. At best very few popes have been canonized, or could be without letting down the standard of sanctity set by the self-elected saints.

---

71 Job 38: 16.
72 Shaw used this quotation (Job 13: 15) as the epigraph to LC, removing it when the Preface was included for publication in June 1924.

No other result could have been reasonably expected; for it is not possible that an official organization of the spiritual needs of millions of men and women, mostly poor and ignorant, should compete successfully in the selection of its principals with the direct choice of the Holy Ghost as it flashes with unerring aim upon the individual. Nor can any College of Cardinals pray effectively that its choice may be inspired. The conscious prayer of the inferior may be that his choice may light on a greater than himself; but the sub-conscious intention of his self-preserving individuality must be to find a trustworthy servant for his own purposes. The saints and prophets, though they may be accidentally in this or that official position or rank, are always really self-selected, like Joan. And since neither Church nor State, by the secular necessities of its constitution, can guarantee even the recognition of such self-chosen missions, there is nothing for us but to make it a point of honor to privilege heresy to the last bearable degree on the simple ground that all evolution in thought and conduct must at first appear as heresy and misconduct. In short, though all society is founded on intolerance, all improvement is founded on tolerance, or the recognition of the fact that the law of evolution is Ibsen's law of change.[73] And as the law of God in any sense of the word which can now command a faith proof against science is a law of evolution, it follows that the law of God is a law of change, and that when the Churches set themselves against change as such, they are setting themselves against the law of God.

Credulity, Modern and Medieval

When Abernethy,[74] the famous doctor, was asked why he indulged himself with all the habits he warned his patients against as unhealthy, he replied that his business was that of a direction post, which points out the way to a place, but does not go thither itself. He might have added that neither does it compel the traveller to go thither, nor prevent him from seeking some other way. Unfortunately our clerical direction posts always do coerce the traveller when they have the political power to do so. When the Church was a temporal as well as a spiritual power, and for long after to the full extent to which it could control or influence the temporal power, it enforced conformity by persecutions that were all the more ruthless because their intention was so excellent. Today, when

---

73 Henrik Ibsen (1828–1906) coined the phrase 'law of change' in his play *Little Eyolf*, 1894, to express his view of the human condition.

74 The eighteenth-century Scottish surgeon was also creator of the – nutritious – Abernethy biscuit.

the doctor has succeeded to the priest, and can do practically what he likes with parliament and the press through the blind faith in him which has succeeded to the far more critical faith in the parson, legal compulsion to take the doctor's prescription, however poisonous, is carried to an extent that would have horrified the Inquisition and staggered Archbishop Laud.[75] Our credulity is grosser than that of the Middle Ages, because the priest had no such direct pecuniary interest in our sins as the doctor has in our diseases: he did not starve when all was well with his flock, nor prosper when they were perishing, as our private commercial doctors must. Also the medieval cleric believed that something extremely unpleasant would happen to him after death if he was unscrupulous, a belief now practically extinct among persons receiving a dogmatically materialist education. Our professional corporations are Trade Unions without souls to be damned; and they will soon drive us to remind them that they have bodies to be kicked. The Vatican was never soulless: at worst it was a political conspiracy to make the Church supreme temporally as well as spiritually. Therefore the question raised by Joan's burning is a burning question still, though the penalties involved are not so sensational. That is why I am probing it. If it were only an historical curiosity I would not waste my readers' time and my own on it for five minutes.

Toleration, Modern and Medieval

The more closely we grapple with it the more difficult it becomes. At first sight we are disposed to repeat that Joan should have been excommunicated and then left to go her own way, though she would have protested vehemently against so cruel a deprivation of her spiritual food; for confession, absolution, and the body of her Lord were first necessaries of life to her. Such a spirit as Joan's might have got over that difficulty as the Church of England got over the Bulls of Pope Leo, by making a Church of her own, and affirming it to be the temple of the true and original faith from which her persecutors had strayed.[76] But as such a proceeding was, in the eyes of both Church and State at that time, a spreading of damnation and anarchy, its toleration involved a greater strain on faith in

---

75 As Charles I's Archbishop of Canterbury (1633–45), William Laud sought to impose conformity of belief and worship and was notably intolerant of Presbyterianism and Puritanism.

76 Pope Leo X, having in his Bull *Exsurge Domine*, 1520, unsuccessfully demanded Luther's recantation of his teachings, excommunicated him. He awarded Henry VIII the title 'Defender of the Faith' for his treatise denouncing Luther's ideas. Henry, excommunicated, in his turn, when he proceeded with his divorce from Katherine of Aragon, broke with Rome and founded the Church of England (1536), continued to use this title.

freedom than political and ecclesiastical human nature could bear. It is easy to say that the Church should have waited for the alleged evil results instead of assuming that they would occur, and what they would be. That sounds simple enough; but if a modern Public Health Authority were to leave people entirely to their own devices in the matter of sanitation, saying, 'We have nothing to do with drainage or your views about drainage; but if you catch smallpox or typhus we will prosecute you and have you punished very severely like the authorities in Butler's Erewhon,'[77] it would either be removed to the County Asylum or reminded that A's neglect of sanitation may kill the child of B two miles off, or start an epidemic in which the most conscientious sanitarians may perish.

We must face the fact that society is founded on intolerance. There are glaring cases of the abuse of intolerance; but they are quite as characteristic of our own age as of the Middle Ages. The typical modern example and contrast is compulsory inoculation replacing what was virtually compulsory baptism. But compulsion to inoculate is objected to as a crudely unscientific and mischievous anti-sanitary quackery, not in the least because we think it wrong to compel people to protect their children from disease. Its opponents would make it a crime, and will probably succeed in doing so; and that will be just as intolerant as making it compulsory. Neither the Pasteurians nor their opponents the Sanitarians would leave parents free to bring up their children naked, though that course also has some plausible advocates. We may prate of toleration as we will; but society must always draw a line somewhere between allowable conduct and insanity or crime, in spite of the risk of mistaking sages for lunatics and saviors for blasphemers. We must persecute, even to the death; and all we can do to mitigate the danger of persecution is, first, to be very careful what we persecute, and second, to bear in mind that unless there is a large liberty to shock conventional people, and a well informed sense of the value of originality, individuality, and eccentricity, the result will be apparent stagnation covering a repression of evolutionary forces which will eventually explode with extravagant and probably destructive violence.

Variability of Toleration

The degree of tolerance attainable at any moment depends on the strain under which society is maintaining its cohesion. In war, for instance, we suppress the gospels and put Quakers in prison, muzzle the newspapers,

---

77 Samuel Butler's novel *Erewhon* (an anagram of 'Nowhere'), published 1872, presents a satirical utopia.

and make it a serious offence to shew a light at night. Under the strain of invasion the French Government in 1792 struck off 4000 heads, mostly on grounds that would not in time of settled peace have provoked any Government to chloroform a dog; and in 1920 the British Government slaughtered and burnt in Ireland to persecute the advocates of a constitutional change which it had presently to effect itself.[78] Later on the Fascisti in Italy did everything that the Black and Tans[79] did in Ireland, with some grotesquely ferocious variations, under the strain of an unskilled attempt at industrial revolution by Socialists who understood Socialism even less than Capitalists understand Capitalism. In the United States an incredibly savage persecution of Russians took place during the scare spread by the Russian Bolshevik revolution after 1917. These instances could easily be multiplied; but they are enough to shew that between a maximum of indulgent toleration and a ruthlessly intolerant Terrorism there is a scale through which toleration is continually rising or falling, and that there was not the smallest ground for the self-complacent conviction of the nineteenth century that it was more tolerant than the fifteenth, or that such an event as the execution of Joan could not possibly occur in what we call our own more enlightened times. Thousands of women, each of them a thousand times less dangerous and terrifying to our Governments than Joan was to the Government of her day, have within the last ten years been slaughtered, starved to death, burnt out of house and home, and what not that Persecution and Terror could do to them, in the course of Crusades far more tyrannically pretentious than the medieval Crusades which proposed nothing more hyperbolical than the rescue of the Holy Sepulchre from the Saracens. The Inquisition, with its English equivalent the Star Chamber, are gone in the sense that their names are now disused; but can any of the modern substitutes for the Inquisition, the Special Tribunals and Commissions, the punitive expeditions, the suspensions of the Habeas Corpus Act, the proclamations of martial law and of minor states of siege, and the rest of them, claim that their victims have as fair a trial, as well considered a body of law to govern their cases, or as conscientious a judge to insist on strict legality of procedure as Joan had from the Inquisition and from the spirit of the Middle Ages even when her country was under the heaviest strain of civil and foreign war? From us she would have had no trial and no law except

78 i.e. the granting of Home Rule.
79 The British auxiliary force, named for the colour of their uniforms, hastily recruited in 1920 to augment the Royal Irish Constabulary during the Irish independence struggles, had a reputation for drunkenness and brutality in their fight against the Irish Republican activists.

a Defence of The Realm Act suspending all law; and for judge she would have had, at best, a bothered major, and at worst a promoted advocate in ermine and scarlet to whom the scruples of a trained ecclesiastic like Cauchon would seem ridiculous and ungentlemanly.

The Conflict between Genius and Discipline

Having thus brought the matter home to ourselves, we may now consider the special feature of Joan's mental constitution which made her so unmanageable. What is to be done on the one hand with rulers who will not give any reason for their orders, and on the other with people who cannot understand the reasons when they are given? The government of the world, political, industrial, and domestic, has to be carried on mostly by the giving and obeying of orders under just these conditions. 'Dont argue: do as you are told' has to be said not only to children and soldiers, but practically to everybody. Fortunately most people do not want to argue: they are only too glad to be saved the trouble of thinking for themselves. And the ablest and most independent thinkers are content to understand their own special department. In other departments they will unhesitatingly ask for and accept the instructions of a policeman or the advice of a tailor without demanding or desiring explanations.

Nevertheless, there must be some ground for attaching authority to an order. A child will obey its parents, a soldier his officer, a philosopher a railway porter, and a workman a foreman, all without question, because it is generally accepted that those who give the orders understand what they are about, and are duly authorized and even obliged to give them, and because, in the practical emergencies of daily life, there is no time for lessons and explanations, or for arguments as to their validity. Such obediences are as necessary to the continuous operation of our social system as the revolutions of the earth are to the succession of night and day. But they are not so spontaneous as they seem: they have to be very carefully arranged and maintained. A bishop will defer to and obey a king; but let a curate venture to give him an order, however necessary and sensible, and the bishop will forget his cloth and damn the curate's impudence. The more obedient a man is to accredited authority the more jealous he is of allowing any unauthorized person to order him about.

With all this in mind, consider the career of Joan. She was a village girl, in authority over sheep and pigs, dogs and chickens, and to some extent over her father's hired laborers when he hired any, but over no one else on earth. Outside the farm she had no authority, no prestige, no claim to the smallest deference. Yet she ordered everybody about, from her uncle to the king, the archbishop, and the military General Staff. Her uncle obeyed her like a sheep, and took her to the castle of the local commander, who, on being ordered about, tried to assert himself, but soon collapsed and obeyed. And so on up to the king, as we have seen. This would have been unbearably irritating even if her orders had been offered as rational solutions of the desperate difficulties in which her social superiors found themselves just then. But they were not so offered. Nor were they offered as the expression of Joan's arbitrary will. It was never 'I say so', but always 'God says so'.

Joan as Theocrat

Leaders who take that line have no trouble with some people, and no end of trouble with others. They need never fear a lukewarm reception. Either they are messengers of God, or they are blasphemous impostors. In the Middle Ages the general belief in witchcraft greatly intensified this contrast, because when an apparent miracle happened (as in the case of the wind changing at Orleans) it proved the divine mission to the credulous, and proved a contract with the devil to the sceptical. All through, Joan had to depend on those who accepted her as an incarnate angel against those who added to an intense resentment of her presumption a bigoted abhorrence of her as a witch. To this abhorrence we must add the extreme irritation of those who did not believe in the voices, and regarded her as a liar and impostor. It is hard to conceive anything more infuriating to a statesman or a military commander, or to a court favorite, than to be overruled at every turn, or to be robbed of the ear of the reigning sovereign, by an impudent young upstart practising on the credulity of the populace and the vanity and silliness of an immature prince by exploiting a few of those lucky coincidences which pass as miracles with uncritical people. Not only were the envy, snobbery, and competitive ambition of the baser natures exacerbated by Joan's success, but among the friendly ones that were clever enough to be critical a quite reasonable scepticism and mistrust of her ability, founded on a fair observation of her obvious ignorance and temerity, were at work against her. And as she met all remonstrances and all criticisms, not with arguments or persuasion, but with a flat appeal to the authority of God and a claim to be in God's special confidence, she must have seemed, to all who were not infatuated by her, so insufferable that nothing but an unbroken chain of overwhelming successes in the military and political field could have saved her from the wrath that finally destroyed her.

Unbroken Success Essential in Theocracy

To forge such a chain she needed to be the King, the Archbishop of Rheims, the Bastard of Orleans, and herself into the bargain; and that was impossible. From the moment when she failed to stimulate Charles to follow up his coronation with a swoop on Paris she was lost. The fact that she insisted on this whilst the king and the rest timidly and foolishly thought they could square the Duke of Burgundy, and effect a combination with him against the English, made her a terrifying nuisance to them; and from that time onward she could do nothing but prowl about the battlefields waiting for some lucky chance to sweep the captains into a big move. But it was to the enemy that the chance came: she was taken prisoner by the Burgundians fighting before Compiègne, and at once discovered that she had not a friend in the political world. Had she escaped she would probably have fought on until the English were gone, and then had to shake the dust of the court off her feet, and retire to Domrémy as Garibaldi had to retire to Caprera.[80]

Modern Distortions of Joan's History

This, I think, is all that we can now pretend to say about the prose of Joan's career. The romance of her rise, the tragedy of her execution, and the comedy of the attempts of posterity to make amends for that execution, belong to my play and not to my preface, which must be confined to a sober essay on the facts. That such an essay is badly needed can be ascertained by examining any of our standard works of reference. They give accurately enough the facts about the visit to Vaucouleurs, the annunciation to Charles at Chinon, the raising of the siege of Orleans and the subsequent battles, the coronation at Rheims, the capture at Compiègne, and the trial and execution at Rouen, with their dates and the names of the people concerned; but they all break down on the melodramatic legend of the wicked bishop and the entrapped maiden and the rest of it. It would be far less misleading if they were wrong as to the facts, and right in their view of the facts. As it is, they illustrate the too little considered truth that the fashion in which we think changes like the fashion of our clothes, and that it is difficult, if not impossible, for most people to think otherwise than in the fashion of their own period.

---

80 Giuseppe Garibaldi (1807–82), the leader of Italian unification, retired to the island of Caprera after his victories had made Victor Emmanuel King of Italy in 1860. His two expeditions from there to liberate Rome from Papal rule in 1862 and 1867 were not successful.

History always out of Date

This, by the way, is why children are never taught contemporary history. Their history books deal with periods of which the thinking has passed out of fashion, and the circumstances no longer apply to active life. For example, they are taught history about Washington, and told lies about Lenin. In Washington's time they were told lies (the same lies) about Washington, and taught history about Cromwell. In the fifteenth and sixteenth centuries they were told lies about Joan, and by this time might very well be told the truth about her. Unfortunately the lies did not cease when the political circumstances became obsolete. The Reformation, which Joan had unconsciously anticipated, kept the questions which arose in her case burning up to our own day (you can see plenty of the burnt houses still in Ireland), with the result that Joan has remained the subject of anti-Clerical lies, of specifically Protestant lies, and of Roman Catholic evasions of her unconscious Protestantism. The truth sticks in our throats with all the sauces it is served with: it will never go down until we take it without any sauce at all.

The Real Joan not Marvellous enough for us

But even in its simplicity, the faith demanded by Joan is one which the anti-metaphysical temper of nineteenth century civilization, which remains powerful in England and America, and is tyrannical in France, contemptuously refuses her. We do not, like her contemporaries, rush to the opposite extreme in a recoil from her as from a witch self-sold to the devil, because we do not believe in the devil nor in the possibility of commercial contracts with him. Our credulity, though enormous, is not boundless; and our stock of it is quite used up by our mediums, clairvoyants, hand readers, slate writers, Christian Scientists, psycho-analysts, electronic vibration diviners, therapeutists of all schools registered and unregistered, astrologers, astronomers who tell us that the sun is nearly a hundred million miles away and that Betelgeuse[81] is ten times as big as the whole universe, physicists who balance Betelgeuse by describing the incredible smallness of the atom, and a host of other marvel mongers whose credulity would have dissolved the Middle Ages in a roar of sceptical merriment. In the Middle Ages people believed that the earth was flat, for which they had at least the evidence of their senses: we believe it to be round, not because as many as one per cent of us could give the physical reasons for so quaint a belief, but because modern science has

---

81 'yellowish-red star of the first magnitude, the brightest star in the constellation of Orion' (*OED*).

convinced us that nothing that is obvious is true, and that everything that is magical, improbable, extraordinary, gigantic, microscopic, heartless, or outrageous is scientific.

I must not, by the way, be taken as implying that the earth is flat, or that all or any of our amazing credulities are delusions or impostures. I am only defending my own age against the charge of being less imaginative than the Middle Ages. I affirm that the nineteenth century, and still more the twentieth, can knock the fifteenth into a cocked hat in point of susceptibility to marvels and miracles and saints and prophets and magicians and monsters and fairy tales of all kinds. The proportion of marvel to immediately credible statement in the latest edition of the Encyclopaedia Britannica is enormously greater than in the Bible. The medieval doctors of divinity who did not pretend to settle how many angels could dance on the point of a needle cut a very poor figure as far as romantic credulity is concerned beside the modern physicists who have settled to the billionth of a millimetre every movement and position in the dance of the electrons. Not for worlds would I question the precise accuracy of these calculations or the existence of electrons (whatever they may be). The fate of Joan is a warning to me against such heresy. But why the men who believe in electrons should regard themselves as less credulous than the men who believed in angels is not apparent to me. If they refuse to believe, with the Rouen assessors of 1431, that Joan was a witch, it is not because that explanation is too marvellous, but because it is not marvellous enough.

The Stage Limits of Historical Representation

For the story of Joan I refer the reader to the play which follows. It contains all that need be known about her; but as it is for stage use I have had to condense into three and a half hours a series of events which in their historical happening were spread over four times as many months; for the theatre imposes unities of time and place from which Nature in her boundless wastefulness is free. Therefore the reader must not suppose that Joan really put Robert de Baudricourt in her pocket in fifteen minutes, nor that her excommunication, recantation, relapse, and death at the stake were a matter of half an hour or so. Neither do I claim more for my dramatizations of Joan's contemporaries than that some of them are probably slightly more like the originals than those imaginary portraits of all the Popes from Saint Peter onward through the Dark Ages which are still gravely exhibited in the Uffizi in Florence (or were when I was there last). My Dunois would do equally well for the Duc d'Alençon. Both left descriptions of Joan so similar that, as a man always describes himself unconsciously whenever he describes anyone else, I have inferred that these goodnatured young men were very like one another in mind; so I have lumped the twain into a single figure, thereby saving the theatre manager a salary and a suit of armor. Dunois' face, still on record at Châteaudun, is a suggestive help. But I really know no more about these men and their circle than Shakespear knew about Falconbridge and the Duke of Austria, or about Macbeth and Macduff.[82] In view of things they did in history, and have to do again in the play, I can only invent appropriate characters for them in Shakespear's manner.

A Void in the Elizabethan Drama

I have, however, one advantage over the Elizabethans. I write in full view of the Middle Ages, which may be said to have been rediscovered in the middle of the nineteenth century after an eclipse of about four hundred and fifty years. The Renascence of antique literature and art in the sixteenth century, and the lusty growth of Capitalism, between them buried the Middle Ages; and their resurrection is a second Renascence. Now there is not a breath of medieval atmosphere in Shakespear's histories. His John of Gaunt is like a study of the old age of Drake.[83] Although he was a Catholic by family tradition, his figures are all intensely Protestant, individualist, sceptical, self-centred in everything but their love affairs, and completely personal and selfish even in them. His kings are not statesmen: his cardinals have no religion: a novice can read his plays from one end to the other without learning that the world is finally governed by forces expressing themselves in religions and laws which make epochs rather than by vulgarly ambitious individuals who make rows. The divinity which shapes our ends, rough hew them how we will,[84] is mentioned fatalistically only to be forgotten immediately like a passing vague apprehension. To Shakespear as to Mark Twain, Cauchon would have been a tyrant and a bully instead of a Catholic, and the inquisitor Lemaître would have been a Sadist instead of a lawyer. Warwick would have had no more feudal quality than his successor the King Maker has in the play of Henry VI. We should have seen them all completely satisfied that if they would only to their own selves be true they could not then be false to any man[85] (a precept which represents the

---

82 See Shakespeare's *King John* and *Macbeth*, respectively.

83 See *Richard II*.

84 'HAMLET: There's a divinity that shapes our ends, / Rough-hew them how we will –' (*Hamlet*, 5.2.10–11).

85 'POLONIUS: This above all – to thine own self be true, / And it must follow, as the night the day, / Thou canst not then be false to any man' (*Hamlet*, 1.3.78–80).

reaction against medievalism at its intensest) as if they were beings in the air, without public responsibilities of any kind. All Shakespear's characters are so: that is why they seem natural to our middle classes, who are comfortable and irresponsible at other people's expense, and are neither ashamed of that condition nor even conscious of it. Nature abhors this vacuum in Shakespear; and I have taken care to let the medieval atmosphere blow through my play freely. Those who see it performed will not mistake the startling event it records for a mere personal accident. They will have before them not only the visible and human puppets, but the Church, the Inquisition, the Feudal System, with divine inspiration always beating against their too inelastic limits: all more terrible in their dramatic force than any of the little mortal figures clanking about in plate armor or moving silently in the frocks and hoods of the order of St Dominic.

Tragedy, not Melodrama

There are no villains in the piece. Crime, like disease, is not interesting: it is something to be done away with by general consent, and that is all about it. It is what men do at their best, with good intentions, and what normal men and women find that they must and will do in spite of their intentions, that really concern us. The rascally bishop and the cruel inquisitor of Mark Twain and Andrew Lang are as dull as pickpockets; and they reduce Joan to the level of the even less interesting person whose pocket is picked. I have represented both of them as capable and eloquent exponents of The Church Militant and The Church Litigant, because only by doing so can I maintain my drama on the level of high tragedy and save it from becoming a mere police court sensation. A villain in a play can never be anything more than a *diabolus ex machina*, possibly a more exciting expedient than a *deus ex machina*,[86] but both equally mechanical, and therefore interesting only as mechanism. It is, I repeat, what normally innocent people do that concerns us; and if Joan had not been burnt by normally innocent people in the energy of their righteousness her death at their hands would have no more significance than the Tokyo earthquake,[87] which burnt a great many maidens. The tragedy of such murders is that they are not committed by murderers. They are judicial murders, pious murders; and this contradiction at once

---

86 Shaw here substitutes *diabolus*, 'devil', for *deus*, 'god', in the Latin expression used to describe the arrival on stage of a deity, for example in a chariot lowered from above, to rescue the hero or to dispense justice (literally, 'god from the machine').

87 An earthquake measuring 8.5 on the Richter scale devastated Tokyo on 1 September 1923, killing some 100,000 and making many more homeless in the fires that raged following the quake.

brings an element of comedy into the tragedy: the angels may weep at the murder, but the gods laugh at the murderers.

The Inevitable Flatteries of Tragedy

Here then we have a reason why my drama of Saint Joan's career, though it may give the essential truth of it, gives an inexact picture of some accidental facts. It goes almost without saying that the old Jeanne d'Arc melodramas, reducing everything to a conflict of villain and hero, or in Joan's case villain and heroine, not only miss the point entirely, but falsify the characters, making Cauchon a scoundrel, Joan a prima donna, and Dunois a lover. But the writer of high tragedy and comedy, aiming at the innermost attainable truth, must needs flatter Cauchon nearly as much as the melodramatist vilifies him. Although there is, as far as I have been able to discover, nothing against Cauchon that convicts him of bad faith or exceptional severity in his judicial relations with Joan, or of as much anti-prisoner, pro-police, class and sectarian bias as we now take for granted in our own courts, yet there is hardly more warrant for classing him as a great Catholic churchman, completely proof against the passions roused by the temporal situation. Neither does the inquisitor Lemaître, in such scanty accounts of him as are now recoverable, appear quite so able a master of his duties and of the case before him as I have given him credit for being. But it is the business of the stage to make its figures more intelligible to themselves than they would be in real life; for by no other means can they be made intelligible to the audience. And in this case Cauchon and Lemaître have to make intelligible not only themselves but the Church and the Inquisition, just as Warwick has to make the feudal system intelligible, the three between them having thus to make a twentieth-century audience conscious of an epoch fundamentally different from its own. Obviously the real Cauchon, Lemaître, and Warwick could not have done this: they were part of the Middle Ages themselves, and therefore as unconscious of its peculiarities as of the atomic formula of the air they breathed. But the play would be unintelligible if I had not endowed them with enough of this consciousness to enable them to explain their attitude to the twentieth century. All I claim is that by this inevitable sacrifice of verisimilitude I have secured in the only possible way sufficient veracity to justify me in claiming that as far as I can gather from the available documentation, and from such powers of divination as I possess, the things I represent these three exponents of the drama as saying are the things they actually would have said if they had known what they were really doing. And beyond this neither drama nor history can go in my hands.

Some Well-meant Proposals for the Improvement of the Play

I have to thank several critics on both sides of the Atlantic, including some whose admiration for my play is most generously enthusiastic, for their heartfelt instructions as to how it can be improved. They point out that by the excision of the epilogue and all the references to such undramatic and tedious matters as the Church, the feudal system, the Inquisition, the theory of heresy and so forth, all of which, they point out, would be ruthlessly blue pencilled by any experienced manager, the play could be considerably shortened. I think they are mistaken. The experienced knights of the blue pencil, having saved an hour and a half by disembowelling the play, would at once proceed to waste two hours in building elaborate scenery, having real water in the river Loire and a real bridge across it, and staging an obviously sham fight for possession of it, with the victorious French led by Joan on a real horse. The coronation would eclipse all previous theatrical displays, shewing, first, the procession through the streets of Rheims, and then the service in the cathedral, with special music written for both. Joan would be burnt on the stage, as Mr Matheson Lang[88] always is in The Wandering Jew, on the principle that it does not matter in the least why a woman is burnt provided she is burnt, and people can pay to see it done. The intervals between the acts whilst these splendors were being built up and then demolished by the stage carpenters would seem eternal, to the great profit of the refreshment bars. And the weary and demoralized audience would lose their last trains and curse me for writing such inordinately long and intolerably dreary and meaningless plays. But the applause of the press would be unanimous. Nobody who knows the stage history of Shakespear will doubt that this is what would happen if I knew my business so little as to listen to these well intentioned but disastrous counsellors: indeed it probably will happen when I am no longer in control of the performing rights. So perhaps it will be as well for the public to see the play while I am still alive.

The Epilogue

As to the epilogue, I could hardly be expected to stultify myself by implying that Joan's history in the world ended unhappily with her execution, instead of beginning there. It was necessary by hook or crook to shew the canonized Joan as well as the incinerated one; for many a woman has got herself burnt by carelessly whisking a muslin skirt into

88 Lang, who had also appeared in several of Shaw's plays, acted the title role in E. Temple Thurston's play The Wandering Jew, 1921, and in the silent film version which appeared in 1923.

the drawing room fireplace, but getting canonized is a different matter, and a more important one. So I am afraid the epilogue must stand.

To the Critics, Lest they should Feel Ignored

To a professional critic (I have been one myself) theatre-going is the curse of Adam. The play is the evil he is paid to endure in the sweat of his brow; and the sooner it is over, the better. This would seem to place him in irreconcilable opposition to the paying playgoer, from whose point of view the longer the play, the more entertainment he gets for his money. It does in fact so place him, especially in the provinces, where the playgoer goes to the theatre for the sake of the play solely, and insists so effectively on a certain number of hours' entertainment that touring managers are sometimes seriously embarrassed by the brevity of the London plays they have to deal in.

For in London the critics are reinforced by a considerable body of persons who go to the theatre as many others go to church, to display their best clothes and compare them with other people's; to be in the fashion, and have something to talk about at dinner parties; to adore a pet performer; to pass the evening anywhere rather than at home: in short, for any or every reason except interest in dramatic art as such. In fashionable centres the number of irreligious people who go to church, of unmusical people who go to concerts and operas, and of undramatic people who go to the theatre, is so prodigious that sermons have been cut down to ten minutes and plays to two hours; and, even at that, congregations sit longing for the benediction and audiences for the final curtain, so that they may get away to the lunch or supper they really crave for, after arriving as late as (or later than) the hour of beginning can possibly be made for them.

Thus from the stalls and in the Press an atmosphere of hypocrisy spreads. Nobody says straight out that genuine drama is a tedious nuisance, and that to ask people to endure more than two hours of it (with two long intervals of relief) is an intolerable imposition. Nobody says 'I hate classical tragedy and comedy as I hate sermons and symphonies; but I like police news and divorce news and any kind of dancing or decoration that has an aphrodisiac effect on me or on my wife or husband. And whatever superior people may pretend, I cannot associate pleasure with any sort of intellectual activity; and I dont believe anyone else can either.' Such things are not said; yet nine-tenths of what is offered as criticism of the drama in the metropolitan Press of Europe and America is nothing but a muddled paraphrase of it. If it does not mean that, it means nothing.

I do not complain of this, though it complains very unreasonably of me. But I can take no more notice of it than Einstein of the people who are incapable of mathematics. I write in the classical manner for those who pay for admission to a theatre because they like classical comedy or tragedy for its own sake, and like it so much when it is good of its kind and well done that they tear themselves away from it with reluctance to catch the very latest train or omnibus that will take them home. Far from arriving late from an eight or half-past eight o'clock dinner so as to escape at least the first half-hour of the performance, they stand in queues outside the theatre doors for hours beforehand in bitingly cold weather to secure a seat. In countries where a play lasts a week, they bring baskets of provisions and sit it out. These are the patrons on whom I depend for my bread. I do not give them performances twelve hours long, because circumstances do not at present make such entertainments feasible; though a performance beginning after breakfast and ending at sunset is as possible physically and artistically in Surrey or Middlesex as in Ober-Ammergau;[89] and an all-night sitting in a theatre would be at least as enjoyable as an all-night sitting in the House of Commons, and much more useful. But in St Joan I have done my best by going to the well-established classical limit of three and a half hours' practically continuous playing, barring the one interval imposed by considerations which have nothing to do with art. I know that this is hard on the pseudo-critics and on the fashionable people whose playgoing is a hypocrisy. I cannot help feeling some compassion for them when they assure me that my play, though a great play, must fail hopelessly, because it does not begin at a quarter to nine and end at eleven. The facts are overwhelmingly against them. They forget that all men are not as they are. Still, I am sorry for them; and though I cannot for their sakes undo my work and help the people who hate the theatre to drive out the people who love it, yet I may point out to them that they have several remedies in their own hands. They can escape the first part of the play by their usual practice of arriving late. They can escape the epilogue by not waiting for it. And if the irreducible minimum thus attained is still too painful, they can stay away altogether. But I deprecate this extreme course, because it is good neither for my pocket nor for their own souls. Already a few of them, noticing that what matters is not the absolute length of time occupied by a play, but the speed with which that time passes, are discovering that the theatre, though purgatorial in its Aristotelian moments, is not necessarily always the dull place they have so often found it. What do its discomforts matter when the play makes us forget them?

AYOT ST LAWRENCE   *May 1924*

89 All the villagers of Ober-Ammergau in Bavaria have participated since the seventeenth century in re-enacting the bible scenes of their famous Passion Play that lasts many hours.

APPENDIX

The Characters in History

JOAN The rise and fall of Jeanne D'Arc was meteoric. Born at Domrémy in 1412, inspired by voices, her conviction that she was sent by God to drive the English from France and see the king crowned won the support of Baudricourt and then the Dauphin in 1429. Her presence and white banner on the battlefield energised the French forces, gave their leaders new confidence, and struck fear into the English. The succession of victories in the English occupied territories that followed the relief of Orleans in May 1429 enabled the coronation in July. Her success was more erratic after her unsuccessful assault on Paris in September. She was captured by the Burgundians at Compiègne in May 1430 and sold on to the English, who oversaw her lengthy interrogation and the heresy trial which ended with her recantation on 24 May 1431. Her resumption of men's clothes and claim again to have heard her voices was charged as a relapse on 28 May and, following a hasty declaration of excommunication, she was handed to the English and burned on 30 May. The rehabilitation hearing, completed in 1456, declared the trial flawed and nullified the sentence. Beatified in 1909, she was declared a saint by the Roman Catholic church in 1920.

ROBERT DE BAUDRICOURT Governor of the garrison of Vaucouleurs, on the Meuse, Baudricourt finally agreed to see Jeanne, who first approached him the previous May, in February 1429. Her first powerful sponsor, he sent her to Chinon with six accompanying soldiers.

POULENGEY Bertrand de Poulengey, nicknamed Pollichon, one of Jeanne's escorts to Chinon, described her in his deposition for the re-trial as a good, devout young woman who had attended her father's cattle and horses.

LA TRÉMOUILLE Georges de la Trémoïlle, one of Charles' favourites, both profligate and ambitious, fiercely opposed Jeanne who disrupted his strategy of making peace with Burgundy. Never a duke, he was made a count on Charles' coronation day. He wielded significant power as Grand Chamberlain but Shaw incorporates with his responsibilities those of Arthur de Richemont, who was commander of the army and Constable of France. His interference in strategy contributed to the failure of the attack on Paris and Jeanne's eventual capture by the Burgundians at Compiègne. He fell from power in 1433.

ARCHBISHOP Regnault de Chartres (1380–1444), Archbishop of Rheims, crowned Charles VII in 1429. Initially supportive, he became hostile to Jeanne following the coronation, and sided with Trémoïlle.

BLUEBEARD Born in 1404, Gilles de Rais, one of the richest men in France and a cousin of Trémoïlle, had raised troops against the English occupation in 1426. Jeanne's chief protector, fighting with her at Orleans, he was made Marshal of France on coronation day. The first dramatisation of Jeanne's story, *Le Mystère du Siège d'Orléans*, 1435, was probably written under his direction. His sentence to death by hanging in 1440 for sorcery and child-torture informed the story of the monstrous Bluebeard, published by Charles Perrault in 1697.

LA HIRE Étienne de Vignolles, nicknamed La Hire, after fighting with Dunois at Montargis was made Captain of Vendôme in 1428. With Jeanne at Orleans and leader of the attack at Patay, he was one of her strongest supporters, famously abandoning his notorious swearing under her influence. A prisoner at Dourdan at the time of Jeanne's trial, he was later ransomed by Charles and, in 1438, made Captain General of Normandy.

THE DAUPHIN Charles (1403–61) proclaimed himself King of France in 1422 following the death of Charles VI, but remained uncrowned until Jeanne's military successes enabled the progress to Rheims and the strategic gesture of his coronation there. He did not attempt to ransom Jeanne after her capture. From c.1435, supported by Dunois, he became more active and, following reconciliation with Burgundy, oversaw the final expulsion of the English in the mid 1450s, gaining the soubriquet 'the Victorious'. In 1449, he petitioned the Pope for a new trial. Presided over by the papal legate, who was his cousin, this pronounced Jeanne's rehabilitation in 1456.

DUCHESS DE LA TRÉMOUILLE Jeanne, Countess of Boulogne and widow of the Duc de Berry, was wealthy in her own right. As the only other named female character in Shaw's play, her worldly triviality and disdain help characterise the Court but, as Trémouille's rather than Charles' wife, she provides a comic foil for Joan without impinging much on the action.

DUNOIS Jean of Orleans (1402–68), the acknowledged natural son of the Duke, and cousin and childhood friend of the Dauphin, dealt the first significant blow against the English at Montargis in 1427. He was with Jeanne at Orleans and, after her death, continued the rout of the English, becoming one of France's most renowned military leaders. Made Count of Dunois in 1435, he replaced La Trémoïlle as Grand Chamberlain.

THE CHAPLAIN John Bowyer Spencer Neville de Stogumber, a composite figure, is largely Shaw's invention, on the basis of the presence at the trial of the 'Keeper of the Private Seal of the Cardinal of England' who told Cauchon 'You favour her overmuch' (Murray, p. 187). Following the burning, various accounts tell of the penitence of an anonymous Englishman 'who hated her greatly'; of the royal secretary, Jean Tressart, crying 'we are all lost, we have burnt a saint'; and of Canon Loiselleur, one of the fiercest opponents of Jeanne, climbing weeping onto her execution cart (Murray, pp. 190, 192, 283).

The vicar of Stogumber in the Quantocks advised Shaw that the stress on his name came on the middle syllable, 'Stō-gúm-ber'. The vicar added that, as late as 1614, the name was still spelt 'Stockumber', but Shaw decided to retain his own spelling (corr. 13, 14 and 24 March 1924).

WARWICK Richard Beauchamp, 13th Earl of Warwick, had been on a pilgrimage to the Holy Land in 1408 and was subsequently prominent in Henry V's French campaigns, his ambassador to France, and his appointee as protector of the infant Henry VI. He commanded the army at Montargis in 1427 and was superintendent of Jeanne's imprisonment and trial in Rouen. Cauchon was his guest at a banquet held on 13 May 1431. He died at Rouen in 1439.

CAUCHON Pierre Cauchon, Bishop of Beauvais, had served as Chaplain to the Duke of Burgundy. Supported by the pro-English University of Paris, he claimed the right to try Jeanne on the legal technicality that although Rouen, under English control, was not in his diocese, Compiègne, where she was captured, was. Contrary to Shaw's assertions, as a partisan of English interests he evidently had a political agenda, appointing the assessors (some sixty, several in receipt of English payments) and, after the trial, gaining a guarantee of protection from Henry VI, whose coronation he attended. He was made Bishop of Lisieux and died in 1442, before the rehabilitation hearings, which, while largely hostile to him, especially in relation to the charges of relapse and the hasty execution, did record that, when berated for favouring Jeanne, he declared that he would act according to his conscience and seek the salvation of her body and soul.

THE INQUISITOR Brother Jean Lemaître, a Dominican monk, was the Inquisitor's Deputy in France. Instructed by the Chief Inquisitor, after avoiding the initial examinations as political not religious, he took part in the trial, 'much vexed at being compelled to attend' (Murray, p. 183). Ladvenu testified that a cleric who had refused to assist was imprisoned.

D'ESTIVET Jean d'Estivet, Canon of Bayeaux and Beauvais, a strong partisan of the English and closely connected to Cauchon, was Promoter for the Holy Inquisition. He, not Courcelles, put together the seventy (as opposed to Shaw's sixty-four) articles of the accusation.

COURCELLES Thomas de Courcelles was a theologian of the University of Paris, who had become Rector of the University in 1430. He read out D'Estivet's seventy articles at the sitting of 27 March, advocated the use of torture, and was subsequently responsible for translating the trial records into Latin. Although famed for his eloquence, he claimed failure of memory when called as a witness at the rehabilitation hearings. He became Dean of Notre Dame and delivered the funeral oration for Charles VII in 1461.

LADVENU Brother Martin Ladvenu, of the Dominican convent at Rouen, was appointed Jeanne's confessor, sought her enlightenment at the trial, and provided sympathetic testimony at the rehabilitation. Brother Isambard de la Pierre, not he, held up the cross at the burning but Isambard testified that Ladvenu, who was with him, was 'stricken and moved with a marvellous repentance and terrible contrition' (Murray, p. 165).

EXECUTIONER Geoffroy Thérage, Master Executioner of Rouen, reported to Warwick that Jeanne's heart and entrails would not burn and disposed of them in the river.

ENGLISH SOLDIER Although elaborated by legend, the story of the English soldier's two sticks was recounted at the rehabilitation hearings.

Sources for historical information are: *Enc. Brit.*; Murray; and Régine Pernoud and Marie-Véronique Clin, *Joan of Arc: Her Story*, translated and revised by Jeremy du Quesnay Adams, 2000.